To JOHN

With best wishes

Alan

HOVE,

SEPTEMBER,

2003

HEDLEY VERITY

HEDLEY VERITY

A Portrait of a
Cricketer

With a Foreword by Sir Donald Bradman, A.C.

ALAN HILL

KINGSWOOD PRESS

Kingswood Press
Kingswood, Tadworth, Surrey, KT20 6GT

First published 1986
© Alan Hill 1986

SBN 434 33560 6

Printed in Great Britain by
St. Edmundsbury Press Ltd, Bury St. Edmunds
and bound by WBC Ltd, Maesteg

CONTENTS

1 A BOY OF HEADINGLEY   1
2 WINNING APPROVAL IN LANCASHIRE   17
3 THE WEIGHT OF A LEGACY   28
4 AN "AVALANCHE FROM HEAVEN"   36
5 LETTERS FROM A FAMOUS SON   47
6 VERITY AND JARDINE – A RESOLUTE UNITY   63
7 THE GOOD COMPANIONS   70
8 MASTERY AT LORD'S   75
9 THE WHITE ROSES BLOOM   82
10 MISADVENTURE AT MELBOURNE   101
11 DOMINANT IN A BATTING ERA   110
12 FINALE AT HOVE   116
13 THE PATRIOT GOES TO WAR   121
14 VALOUR ON A SICILIAN PLAIN   130
15 APPRECIATION OF HIS CRAFT   143
   APPENDIX 1: Assessments of Captains and Others   150
   APPENDIX 2: Hedley Verity in First-Class Cricket   154
   (an analysis compiled by Roy D. Wilkinson and L. F.
   Hancock)
Index   173

To Grace and Douglas, my kindly allies, and Betty who knows the worth of a good Yorkshireman.

HEDLEY VERITY

A tribute by
SIR DONALD BRADMAN, A.C.

As I write these words it is hard to comprehend that over 40 years have passed since Hedley Verity lost his life in the service of his country in the Second World War.

In *Wisden's Almanack* 1944 there is a tribute to his career but I am pleased to learn that Mr Alan Hill has now produced, at much greater length than *Wisden's* space would allow, a biography worthy of the life and career of this great cricketer.

My first tour of England was in 1930 when I played against Yorkshire twice but Hedley Verity was not chosen in either match (that was his first year with the County 1st XI) probably because the legendary Wilfred Rhodes was still on deck.

But from then on, covering the next four Test series between England and Australia, we were great rivals and I grew more and more to respect him both as a gentleman and a player.

One of the great fascinations of cricket is that its statistics, if taken over a sufficiently long period, can give proof of a player's ability, not only as an individual but also in comparison with players of other eras. I don't intend to quote them here to any extent because they are adequately set out elsewhere, but would point out how consistently Hedley performed throughout the whole of his ten-year period in first-class cricket. In fact his county record was simply phenomenal.

After the first season (when he didn't play many matches) Hedley took over 100 wickets in the county championship in every year except 1934 at a cost of a mere 13.2 runs per wicket.

By a strange coincidence, that same year, 1934, saw his greatest performance when he took 14 wickets in one day at Lord's in a Test against Australia, the only cricketer ever to take 14 Test scalps in a day.

Another marvellous achievement was his 10 wickets for 10 runs off

19.4 overs against Nottinghamshire in 1932 – almost unbelievable under any conditions.

Yorkshiremen of bygone days may vote for Wilfred Rhodes as the greatest ever amongst the slow left-hand spinners. And they can produce impressive evidence thanks in part to the longevity of his career.

I played against Wilfred in his very last first-class match, when he was clearly past his prime, and even then one had to be very watchful against his lovely curving sinuous flight.

Verity was slightly faster than Wilfred – delivered the ball more over the top. In fact he was about mid-way in pace between Rhodes and Derek Underwood.

His ideal physique, his lovely economical, lazy run-up, were co-ordinated to put him in a perfect delivery position with a superb command of length and direction.

As a fieldsman he was extremely efficient and with the bat he achieved the role of opening for England, and did so with distinction in a style not unlike Herbert Sutcliffe.

But more than his cricketing skill was his sportsmanship and manly bearing under all circumstances. I never once heard him complain or offer a criticism and his acceptance of umpiring decisions was an example which many modern players could well emulate.

His whole career exemplified all that was best about cricket and I deem it an honour and privilege to have been on the stage with him in those golden days of the 1930s.

ACKNOWLEDGEMENTS

I am deeply grateful to the Verity family for their unstinting aid in producing this first full-length biography of a revered cricketer and patriot. It is largely because of the kindness and generosity of Miss Grace Verity, of Rawdon, Yorkshire, and Mr. Douglas Verity, of Pwllheli, Gwynedd, North Wales, that I have been able to retrace the climb to greatness of their illustrious brother and father. The wealth of material placed at my disposal included a revealing memoir written by the late Hedley Verity senior. From jottings of a proud father I was given many insights into the disciplines which were to serve England and Yorkshire so well.

The volume of correspondence from Verity's contemporaries – cricketers and supporters – at home and overseas has also provided heartening proof of the worthiness of the project. I must, especially, express my indebtedness to Bill Bowes, Verity's close friend and bowling partner in Yorkshire's years of triumph in the 1930s; Sir Leonard Hutton, Norman Yardley, Jim Kilburn, Hugh Bartlett and the late George Cox (Sussex); and Leslie Ames (Kent). In Gloucestershire Charles Barnett has recalled the benefits of his Test apprenticeship under Verity's guidance. Among Verity's England captains, R. E. S. Wyatt and G. O. Allen have made handsome contributions and indicated clearly how much they admired and respected their colleague.

From Australia my postbag has included the reminiscences of former Test rivals, W. J. O'Reilly, W. A. Brown, L. S. Darling, L. P. J. O'Brien and K. E. Rigg, all of whom remember the combative qualities of Verity and the skills of a cricketer who gained their enduring respect. Chris Harte, the Editor of "Cathedral End", the journal of the Adelaide branch of the Australian Cricket Society, and Rex Harcourt, the archivist of the Melbourne Cricket Club, were other most helpful correspondents.

John Kay, the former Lancashire cricket correspondent, with whose family Verity stayed during a crucial period as professional at Middleton, the Central Lancashire League club, has also rendered important assistance with a shrewd assessment of his old team-mate and friend. Tony Woodhouse, the Yorkshire cricket historian, has given valued help as have Mrs. Edith Winfield, Miss Mary Winfield and Mr. Jack Lees, of Rawdon.

I must also thank, most sincerely, Sir Donald Bradman, for contributing a foreword, and acknowledge the courteous assistance of the British Newspaper Library staff at Colindale, London. Other acknowledgements are due to the Yorkshire County Cricket Club and Lt. Col. D. J. Bottomley, the Curator of the Green Howards Regimental Museum at Richmond, North Yorkshire. He has provided much valuable material on Verity's wartime service and allowed me to quote from the book, "The Story of the Green Howards – 1939–1945" by Capt. W. A. T. Synge. Other contributors include Verity's hosts in Northern Ireland where the 1st Battalion of the Green Howards was stationed in 1941. Mr. J. W. Walsh and Mr. F. Walsh, now living in Zimbabwe and Newfoundland, and Mr. V. Craig, of Strabane, and Mrs. E. Wilson, of Omagh, have furnished telling observations on the character of their Yorkshire guest.

Contemporary newspaper reports in the Leeds Mercury, the Yorkshire Post and Yorkshire Evening Post and Manchester Guardian and various editions of Wisden Cricketers' Almanack have provided the nucleus of the printed sources in the book. Permission has been received to quote extracts from the following:

John Kay – Cricket in the Leagues, Eyre and Spottiswoode, 1970; Cricket Heroes, Phoenix House, 1959; W. E. Bowes – Express Deliveries, Stanley Paul, 1949; History of Yorkshire County Cricket – 1924–1949, Yorkshire CCC, 1950; D. R. Jardine – Ashes and Dust, Hutchinson, 1934; In Quest of the Ashes, Hutchinson, 1934; P. G. H. Fender – Kissing the Rod, Methuen and Co, 1934; Neville Cardus – Good Days, Hart-Davis, 1948; Australian Summer, Hart-Davis, 1949; Roses Matches – 1919–1939, Souvenir Press, 1982; Ralph Barker – Ten Great Bowlers, Chatto and Windus, 1967; N. W. D. Yardley – Cricket Campaigns, Stanley Paul, 1950. The quotation from "Visitations" by Louis MacNeice, published in Collected Poems, is reproduced by kind permission of Faber and Faber Ltd.

Other books consulted were: R. E. S. Wyatt – Three Straight Sticks, Stanley Paul, 1951; J. M. Kilburn – Yorkshire, Convoy Publications, 1950; Sam Davis – Hedley Verity – Prince with a Piece of Leather, Epworth Press, 1952; B. M. Wakley – Bradman the Great, N. Kaye, 1959; Hedley Verity – Bowling 'Em Out, Hutchinson, 1936; E. L.

Roberts – Hedley Verity – Yorkshire and England – 1930–1939, E. F. Hudson; Peter Thomas – Yorkshire Cricketers – 1839–1939, Derek Hodgson, Manchester, 1973; Dudley Carew – To the Wicket, Chapman and Hall, 1950; T. C. F. Prittie – Cricket North and South, SBC, 1955; S. Sanyal – 40 Years of Test Cricket – India v England, Thomson Press (India), 1974; Ken Dalby – White is the Rose, Leeds; Headingley Test Cricket – 1899–1975, Olicana Books, Otley, 1976; E. W. Swanton – Sort of Cricket Person, Collins, 1972; William Pollock – So this is Australia, A. Barker, 1937; Sir Leonard Hutton – Fifty Years in Cricket, Stanley Paul, 1984; J. H. Fingleton – Cricket Crisis, Cassell, 1947; R. C. Robertson-Glasgow – 46 Not Out, Hollis and Carter, 1948; Herbert Sutcliffe – For England and Yorkshire, E. Arnold, 1935.

Alan Hill
Lindfield, Sussex
September 1985

Live man and dead
Being each unique
(Their pain and glory),
Yet some will have left
By force or freak
To us the bereft
Some richer story;
Their say being said,
They still can speak
Words more unique,
More live, less dead.

– Louis MacNeice.

A BOY OF HEADINGLEY

"I have bred a better man than myself" – Hedley Verity senior.

"YOU'LL never rear him lass, it's a pity it is a lad," was the mournful cry at the birth of a great cricketer. There was quite a flutter in the family circle when Hedley Verity was born at Welton Grove, Headingley, little more than a long throw from the famous Leeds Test ground, on May 18, 1905. The despairing voice was that of the baby's maternal grandmother who was hugely upset because her own two sons had died in their infancy. Hedley was the only boy in his mother's family and the first since his father on the other side. It was hardly surprising that his arrival created such a fuss and jangled the nerves of a distraught grandmother.

Hedley, the eldest of the family, was joined two years later by a sister, Grace, with whom he enjoyed a happy and frolicsome childhood. Edith, always regarded as the 'kid' sister, was born nine years later and she was only 12 years old when she acted as bridesmaid at her brother's wedding in March, 1929. The bond between Hedley and his father was always strong and it blossomed into a comradeship of rare serenity. "Hedley could talk to his father in a way that many children find difficult," said one friend of the family.

Hedley Verity senior, a modest cricketer in the local sphere, was a coal merchant, a lay preacher and a chairman of the urban district council. He brought up his son with discipline, with tact, and with a great desire that one day his boy would make his mark in life. Hedley amply repaid his father's trust. How many fathers can say of their sons, with the sure knowledge that there can be no denial and no false pride, that "I have bred a better man than myself." That was the tribute Mr. Verity paid his son when Hedley was acclaimed an England cricketer.

Hedley Verity did survive, despite the fears of his grandmother, to reach a glorious if sadly curtailed manhood. Rhodes, as his exacting mentor, was won over by the boy's diligence. Yorkshire and even, implausibly, Lancashire where Verity honed his bowling craft in league cricket, had reason to be glad that he defied the birthday prophecy. The young Hedley flourished amid the zealous care and love of strict but devoted parents. The delightful comment of a Rawdon neighbour, soon after the family had moved from Headingley via the industrial suburb of Armley to the Airedale village, exemplifies their affection. He called at the Verity home, appraised the robust four-year-old looking on shyly behind his mother, and said: "My word, missis, it's good to tell that lad's been brought up in the country." Hedley's father, when told of the incident, replied: "My, that speaks well for the healthy properties of the air at Armley."

Yet, as always, there are pitfalls even for healthy children. A few days after the Rawdon man's compliment Hedley was close to suffering serious injuries. The boy next door had received money for running an errand. Hedley joined him as they raced to the nearest shop. The pennies were quickly spent on a bundle of fireworks. These were duly shared with Hedley with near disastrous consequences. By some mischance they burst into a blaze, severely burned his hand, and set fire to his clothes. Fortunately for Hedley a woman heard his screams and dashed to his aid to put out the flames. Another neighbour ran home for ointment and bandages. There were anxious discussions as to the identity of the boy among the villagers who quickly gathered round the shocked Hedley. The Veritys, as newcomers, were still unknown in Rawdon.

Meanwhile, at home, Mrs Verity glanced up from her household chores to discover that Hedley was missing. She set out to trace him and found the boy still screaming in a circle of sympathetic neighbours. He was taken home and, in his father's words, "for many days suffered painful reminders that it is dangerous to play with fire". The shock waves succeeding the accident very nearly cost Mrs Verity her life. She did not spare herself in nursing the boy back to health. So untiring was she in her ministrations that she collapsed one night. The doctor was hurriedly called and for a few days her life hung in the balance.

The distressing episode may have revived lingering memories of another more destructive fire for Hedley's parents.

The pioneering spirit of adventure, which was a marked characteristic of the Veritys and was to have tragic consequences, carried Verity senior's own father to North America in the 1880s. David Verity could not persuade his wife and their four young children to accompany him on a journey fraught with perils in the primitive travel conditions of that time. There were many enthusiastic letters, including overtures to

arrange a sea passage, and money from the exiled father to help soften the blow of separation. Then suddenly the correspondence ceased. The lack of news was worrying but it did not at first cause great concern, for it was known that David Verity had moved to a new area in either Canada or the United States. It was only gradually revealed that he had probably died along with many other unidentified men in a forest fire. Exhaustive inquiries failed to confirm his death, but these were days of rudimentary communications and elusive travellers and the bereaved family had finally to accept that their father was lost beyond recall.

It is a sad feature of the Verity saga that three generations of the family were left fatherless. David's son, Hedley was the first of the trio. Sixty years after his own father's death, Hedley senior witnessed the plight of his son's children, Wilfred and Douglas, after the death of their father in Italy in 1943, and there was yet another sickening blow for the family in 1975 when Wilfred himself was killed by a runaway cattle trailer while walking with his young son Hedley near their home at Otley. He was aged 43 and left a widow and one other child, Amy. The seven-year-old Hedley suffered a fractured skull in the accident, but he has recovered to become a quiet, thoughtful helpmate to his mother. The evidence today is of a charming, unembittered family. The shadows of their tragedies rest lightly upon them. Misfortune has brought strength and forged close ties.

Bravery in adversity has become almost a cliché of a storyteller; but it is especially true of the steadfast Veritys. Hedley Verity senior and his two sisters Mary and Elizabeth (the other girl Jessie was cared for by an aunt and uncle) were left to fend for themselves when their mother died. They set up home in a little house at Meanwood, not far from the later family address at Headingley.

The house at Meanwood was probably his first married home, too. In July, 1903, Hedley senior married Edith Elwick, a Sunday schoolteacher who as the eldest of the family had spent many of her teenage years looking after her two young sisters and caring for her father, a master plumber, when he became an invalid during the later years of his life. The newly married pair were in their late twenties and ideally matched after the responsibilities of their youth.

Mr. Verity must have been a tenacious, exceptional man, inching his way to prosperity through a mixture of jobs. His daughter, Grace, says he drove one of the first tramcars in Leeds before starting in the coal trade with the Armley and Wortley Coal company.

Edith Verity was as strong a character as her husband and members of the Verity family consider that Hedley junior inherited his resourcefulness and dedication from her just as much as his father. She was, to quote her surviving grandson, Douglas, "the steel of the family. She was only five feet nothing, but she had an inner core of determination."

Grace Verity relates: "Mother was fiercely loyal to the family and protective against all comers. No sacrifice was too great to make for us, or the grandchildren later. She'd go without things herself to see that we were all right. As long as she had something to give, Mother was happy."

Mrs. Verity was, however, reluctant to make the move away from her friends at Armley and Headingley to the rural isolation of Rawdon, seven miles west of Leeds. Mr. Verity had taken over one of his company's agencies at Rawdon. His company later provided him with coal supplies when he started his own business.

The little township on the road to the moors must have seemed awesomely distant in 1910, the year of the Coronation of King George V. The journey from Leeds to Rawdon involved a rib-shaking ride by tramcar, lasting over half an hour. There were no buses to the neighbouring towns of Harrogate, Ilkley, Otley and Bradford, and the nearest railway station was at Apperley Bridge, a mile and a half away from the Verity's new home at Sefton House situated at the now busy junction of the Leeds and Harrogate roads.

The Verity's friends at first considered the move a reckless venture. Then, as time went by and the exiles did not return, they came out from the smoke and grime of Leeds and reversed their verdict. They thought it was a splendid idea to spend a weekend in the country.

"Singularly beautiful for situation is Rawdon," wrote J.H. Palliser in his history of the village published in 1914. "It is backed by the wooded heights of the Billing, and commands a great stretch of country – eastwards in the direction of Leeds and westwards over the purple moorlands of Rombalds Moor.

"The old nobility may have gone," continued Palliser, "but in their stead has arisen a race of self–made nobles, born of trade and commerce, whose pretty villas or castellated towers stud the hillside or nestle in the wood, to the undoubted advantage of the landscape. The fortunate possessors of these abodes being almost exclusively Bradford traders, Rawdon is now but an aristocratic suburb of the 'metropolis of the worsted trade.'"

At the time of Verity's boyhood, Rawdon, on the northern slopes of the Aire Valley, had a population of just over 3,000 people. There were woollen mills, dyeworks, farms and printing works and a growing host of small traders – butchers, innkeepers, shoemakers, confectioners and small shopkeepers – and four schools. "Fifty years ago," wrote Palliser, "handloom weaving could be counted by the score; it would now be very difficult to find a loom in the township. There is not so much employment now for gentlemen's servants, gardeners, coachmen and labourers, the tendency being to run smaller estates with a reduced outdoor staff."

The mansions of the older gentry were falling into decline; but new, smaller houses were springing up, and cottages of all descriptions were in great demand by newcomers, like the Veritys, moving away from the industrial towns of the West Riding, into the peaceful fields of Rawdon. The exodus, said Palliser, had arisen through the opening of the Leeds to Guiseley electric tram route, and also the erection of new works in the township, which gave employment to a considerable number of additional hands.

Sefton House, the venerable stone-built dwelling where Hedley Verity senior, after his prodigious labours, established his coal business and talked cricket for many long hours with his inquisitive son, still stands with all the imperturbability of a trusted sentinel. It is now about 150 years old and a recent discovery of loom ends in a false roof of the house indicates that it was once used for home weaving and thus predates the building of mills in the area. Wool from Australia came to Rawdon to be woven in the houses of the village.

The guardian of Sefton House today is Grace Verity, a spry, neat and contented septuagenarian. She was the Standard One schoolmistress who drilled generations of children, including her own nephews, Wilfred and Douglas, and future Yorkshire cricketers, Brian Close and Bryan Stott, in their alphabets and tables. Any severity, one feels, must always have been lightened by her larkish humour. The chuckles ring out like a series of musical exclamation marks in her conversation. Brother Hedley, everyone says, shared this ready wit and appreciation of ridiculous quirks. "He had a happy knack of knowing exactly, almost intuitively, how to relieve any tension with just the correct humorous remark," says his younger sister, Edith.

It does not require a great leap of imagination to hear the childhood frolics of young Hedley and Grace among the nooks and crannies of the rambling, friendly house. Grace and Hedley were impish playmates, red-faced with indignation and accusing each other when they were sent to bed for misbehaviour. As children it was their joint task to scrub the living room floor on Friday nights. There were, inevitably, quarrels as to whether either had completed their section of the floor.

"When we were small," says Grace, "Hedley used to set his toy soldiers out on one side of the kitchen table, even then planning his manoeuvres, and Mother would put a line down the middle so that I could play tiddleywinks." Grace and Hedley would be rapidly incensed if there was any invasion of their territory. "We always stuck up for our rights," recalls Grace.

It was at their former home at Armley, in the network of boisterous streets, that Hedley was engaged in his first business transaction. He attempted to barter Grace for a rabbit. Grace still relishes the memory. "I was only very tiny and in my cradle. Hedley used to go regularly across the road to inspect the rabbit. One day the owner asked Hedley if he would like the rabbit and said he could have it if he brought along his baby sister."

Grace recalls being firmly grasped around the waist and heaved across to the neighbour's house. "Hedley said: 'I've brought the baby. Can I have the rabbit?'" Verity senior's version of the story suggested that it was rather more than a simple request. He said that his son dragged the rabbit in its hutch across the road and placed it safely in his own backyard. Then, fetching Grace's clothing, he gave it to the neighbour and returned home to instruct his mother firmly: "Give that woman that baby." "Oh, Grace", Hedley would say playfully in later years, "I do wish Mother had let me make the swop. I'd have been much better off with the rabbit."

The sobriety which distinguished Hedley Verity on the cricket field often collapsed into mischief especially within the family circle. The barrier of aloofness was lowered there and later with close cricket associates and friends, Bill Bowes, Charles Barnett and Leonard Hutton. Verity was cherished for his sincerity and his genuine concern for things that were important to others; but he could also play the droll and tease those who loved him. Best of all, he liked nothing better than to tell a joke against himself.

At Yeadon and Guiseley secondary school Verity was a conscientious and diligent pupil. He very quickly became a member of the school cricket eleven which was considered one of the strongest in the area. The batting was good, they had a capable wicket–keeper and, with the introduction of Hedley, at least two good bowlers. They were both left–handed. Stanley Shaw was fast and Hedley slow to medium and, as one contemporary related, "if one could not frighten opponents out, the other used to kid them out." Even then, at the age of 12, Hedley possessed a good sense of length and direction, tossing up a very slow ball that suggested a half–volley or a full toss but almost always confounded the expectations of the batsmen.

Verity was only eight years old when he was taken to see Yorkshire play at Headingley. Like all boys he had his heroes – George Hirst and

Wilfred Rhodes stood supremely at the pinnacle of his worship; and the batsman he idolised most was Jack Hobbs. Increasingly, cricket occupied his thoughts and aspirations. Hedley liked nothing better than to go by himself to watch county matches at Leeds or Bradford, and Scarborough and its cricket festival was the magnet for the family holidays. His mother and sisters built their sandcastles on the beach but Hedley, in company with his father, watched his adored Yorkshire at the North Marine Road ground.

His passion for Yorkshire cricket did, however, lead him astray on one occasion during his last summer at school. At the beginning of the season it was announced that the Yorkshire second eleven would play in a match at Horsforth Hall Park, a short tramcar journey from school. Hedley had looked forward eagerly to the event, but the distraction must have caused him to neglect his studies, for he was given a detention when the great day arrived. He decided, with only the smallest twinge of conscience, to go to the match and face the consequences. It was a thoroughly enjoyable day and he had no regrets about playing truant from school. Next morning he marched bravely into the classroom, as ready as any erring boy could be to take his punishment. He was even prepared to suffer the indignity of being sprawled across a chair and given a beating.

Any faint hopes that his absence had not been noticed were dispelled by an immediate summons from the headmaster. "At that time," the headmaster later commented, "I did not know how keen Hedley was on cricket, and he only escaped sound punishment by a small margin." He did, however, believe that the penalty had to be made to fit the crime. The selected discipline was even worse for Hedley than the searing strokes of the cane. Excessive love of sport, the headmaster decreed, had tempted the boy down a wayward path. Hedley was sternly told that he was barred from all school sport for the remainder of the term. The decision meant that he had played his last game for the school, for he went into his father's coal business at the end of the summer.

It was a penetrating shaft for a devout young cricketer, even one as philosophical as Hedley, and he smarted for many weeks as he watched the school eleven lose matches which they might have won but for his ban. He soon recovered his buoyancy and found consolation in weekend cricket, playing in the Rawdon club's second eleven. In one evening match at Rawdon he was called into the first team as a deputy for a senior player. He scored 47 and then took seven wickets at a modest cost. There was consternation in the visiting ranks at the news that they had been routed by a 14-year-old schoolboy.

After leaving school Verity worked at his father's coal depot at

Guiseley and was also placed under the supervision of a private tutor with a view to gaining secretarial and accountancy qualifications. He worked hard at the course throughout the winter, but as the days lengthened his interest waned and cricket practice took priority over his studies. One day Hedley ventured to broach a subject which was preying on his mind. He had decided what he had to say to his father, but he faltered at the hurdle. There was a moment of confusion before he stammeringly put his thoughts into words. "It's no use, Dad, you are wasting your money," he said. "I've made up my mind to some day play for Yorkshire. You've always told me that will mean sacrifice and great perseverance. I am prepared to meet these demands, but you are asking me to do something else which is just as difficult. I am afraid that if I try I may miss both."

Mr. Verity impressed upon his son the serious consequences if he failed in his objective, but he knew that his son had tussled hard with the problem before coming to the decision, and he knew too that the wisest course would be to allow the boy his head and do everything in his power to help him realise his ambition. It is a signal tribute to Verity's dedication, involving a spartan, lonely regime, that 10 years were to elapse before he brought home his Yorkshire cap.

Little did Mr. Verity realise the task he had undertaken in acceding to his son's appeal. Hedley came home regularly with cricket questions of increasing complexity. They were discussed with as much concentration as Verity senior gave to his own business problems. Hedley was spared many mistakes on the cricket field, but his father's knowledge of the game was limited and he later admitted that he became a learner as well as an adviser. "Any criticism, any faults", was the question asked when Hedley returned home from matches. His mother was not exempted from the post-mortems; she also listened and learned and became one of her son's fiercest critics.

One former local cricket colleague remembers the Veritys as spectators at a match at Horsforth Hall Park. "Hedley was bowling and his mother called me over from where I was fielding and said: 'Tell our Hedley he hasn't got a fielder (Mrs. Verity vigorously indicated with her finger the vacant position) over there on the legside.'" Hedley was speedily apprised of his mother's direction and just as promptly rectified the error. He was aware from experience that she was a stern taskmaster. Many were the tongue-lashings he received from her if he missed a catch or foolishly lost his wicket. Throughout his career Hedley despised flattery, but he delighted in constructive criticism. He regarded such critics as his best friends. He revelled especially in the cricket squabbles with his mother. He knew she was only trying to help.

The idealist, who stunningly announced his class to an intrigued cricket world in the early 1930s, laboured long in the sporting shallows before reaching his appointed goal. Only a few privileged confidantes in local sporting circles, and much later on the fields of the Lancashire League, knew the extent of his endeavours, the setbacks and disappointments and the strength of character which propelled him to glory. The diffidence which stayed with Verity all his life made his later achievements even more remarkable. But it also had the beneficial effect of leaving him impervious to triumph or defeat. He never indulged in self-pity. Verity senior said: "This shy disposition can be very good and useful to a point. It saved him from many snares, but it must have been a heavy handicap for such an ambitious boy as Hedley. It required considerable moral courage and will power for him to force himself to do the things he wanted to do or he felt were important."

One of Verity's confidantes was Frank Whitaker, a student at the Rawdon Baptist Theological College. Hedley, as a boy without any influential patrons to prize open cricketing doors, was conscious of the scepticism, even derision, with which his ambition was regarded. One evening he sat on a five-bar gate with Frank and explained to him his feeling of frustration. "Do *you* believe I can ever play for Yorkshire?" he asked. "No one but my father does."

Hedley Verity senior had pledged his help in the quest, but he has since related that his boy was never pampered, even though moral support was, of course, always at hand. There was the security of the family business which undoubtedly played a part in his progress, but the young Hedley never took advantage of his good fortune. The spirit of independence was evident at an early age. He had set his heart on a collection of childrens' encyclopaedias, an expensive present. His father told him that he would buy the books if Hedley paid him back in weekly instalments. The boy's slender pocket money allowance put this out of the question. Father and son then solemnly agreed that the purchase was possible if Hedley cleaned Mr. Verity's boots every day. A sum of money was allocated for the task and Hedley made his weekly payments. The contract extended over a long period and Verity senior had almost forgotten the agreement when one morning he found his boots uncleaned. He expressed his surprise to Hedley and asked the reason for the negligence. Mr. Verity was promptly told: "I have paid my last instalment."

At his father's coal depot at the neighbouring Guiseley railway station

Hedley interspersed his duties with regular cricket practice. In the corner of the office was a makeshift bat fashioned from a wooden railing with one end whittled down. On the desk was a bundle of rags which had been rolled into a ball and tied tightly together with string. Hedley used his improvised bat and ball for practice during his lunch hour. They were later replaced by an ancient but proper bat and a composition ball. One day a window was discovered broken in the office. Hedley was questioned about the breakage and emphatically denied that he was the culprit. "I didn't do it and I wasn't bowling either," he replied under interrogation. Hedley was advised to take a "collection" for the over-enthusiastic batsman and it was suggested that a new pane of glass should be the first charge on the fund.

In the winter months when he was driven indoors by rain and snow Hedley spurned all other relaxations as he adopted rigorous tactics to build up his physique and improve his fitness. As a future Yorkshire player he had to be able to withstand gruelling tests of endurance. At the Guiseley railway depot he developed his stamina by joining the workmen in shovelling coal into their carts. It was, by any standards, tiring work, but he was undismayed. He called it "physical culture". There was a glow of pride as he watched his arm muscles grow strong and harden.

The powerful legs, which were to sustain him through marathon bowling spells for Yorkshire and England, were the legacy of skipping exercises in the house and garden or training runs along the quiet footpaths of Cragg Wood near his Rawdon home. Grace Verity remembers: "Hedley used to go down to the wood with a skipping rope in his pocket. When it was quiet he would run and skip. Jogging was unheard of in those days. People would have given you a strange look. If anyone came along he would put the rope away until they had gone." The evening runs covered a distance of around three miles and took Hedley to Apperley Bridge station, on to Calverley and back home through the wood. Hedley wore his heavy working boots for these exercises and he was not satisfied unless he returned home in a state of near exhaustion.

On a less physical scale he addressed himself to the refinements of his batting technique. This activity was conducted in the privacy of his bedroom. Back and forward stamped his feet. He practised his shots with a not altogether steady pendulum of his bat in front of the wardrobe mirror. His parents gazed at each other with horror as they listened to the bangs resounding through the house. Learning how to play straight was one thing, but there was the possibility that Hedley might become too adventurous as he aped his heroes. The mirror remained unbroken but the furniture did not escape unscathed. The brilliance of Hedley's imagined boundary hits did produce the occasional splinter. Sister Edith today feels that her parents' displeasure probably turned to pride in the bruised furniture when Hedley achieved fame as a cricketer.

In 1921, the English cricketers also trembled before the might of Warwick Armstrong's all-powerful Australians. It was a sun-blessed summer and the 16-year-old Verity made the most of this precious time, as a rapt spectator at the Headingley Test match and spending every available minute at the local cricket field where, as one observer remembered, "he was the first to get there and the last to leave." The summer also coincided with a coal strike and the Veritys, father and son, had even more time in which to practise cricket. Verity senior, anxiously viewing the prospects of his business, doubtless had mixed feelings about his enforced idleness; but it left Hedley free to concentrate on what was for him the real business.

Hedley Verity junior was selected to play in his first league match for Rawdon at Calverley that summer. He returned home in a pensive mood. His parents gently coaxed a subdued Hedley to describe the events of the afternoon. "Well, how have you got on?" he was asked. "We've lost," was the terse reply. "How did *you* go on?" was the next question. Hedley shuffled unhappily and said: "They didn't put me on to bowl." Amid reassuring smiles there followed a polite inquiry as to the total of his runs. Back came the glum response: "None." The Veritys were now in a torment of uncertainty. "What happened then?" Hedley was close to tears. He covered his shame with a grimace. "I only had one ball and it hit the middle stump and smashed it to bits." The clouds of despondency did not lift at all that evening. "They will never pick me again," said Hedley as he trooped forlornly to bed.

The gloom persisted through the following days until the team sheet was pinned up for the next match. Hedley eagerly scanned the list to spot his name. He had been given another chance. The delighted boy ran all the way home to announce proudly: "They've picked me again." He was able to unfold a happier tale after that match. The opposition scored massively on a perfect wicket, but Hedley emerged from the batting spree with figures of three wickets for 39 runs, a foretaste of the bowling thrift which was to become one of the hallmarks of his craft.

A week later he received his first press commendation. The *Leeds Mercury* reported: "A feature of the match between Horsforth and Rawdon was the bowling feat by Hedley Verity, junior, a very promising youngster of only 16 years of age. He took five Horsforth wickets for 33 runs. He is one of the youngest players in the Yorkshire Council this season, and he is a regular member of the Rawdon team." In June there was another note of praise in the *Yorkshire Post*. "The clever bowling of Hedley Verity, the youthful Rawdon bowler, who took five wickets for 15 runs against Yeadon Green Lane, was largely responsible for the ultimate victory of his side by five wickets." By the end of this perfect summer, with the odds stacked against the bowler, the studious young Hedley had given notice of his burgeoning talents. He had taken 29 wickets at a cost of 13.8 runs each to demonstrate his accuracy even in unfavourable bowling conditions.

In 1922, the newly retired George Hirst, later to become one of Hedley's revered teachers as Yorkshire coach, joined another England and Yorkshire stalwart, Bobby Peel, on a talent scouting mission sponsored by a local newspaper. This was a season of bowling experiment for the 17-year-old Verity, then a medium pace bowler, and he failed to observe the tenet of Rhodes – the model, upright delivery – in his first attempts to spin the ball. Like many an embryonic spinner, he began to stoop badly and consequently lost length and direction. He quickly regained control, reverting to his normal faster style to the relief of his Rawdon colleagues.

His later associates at Accrington, the Lancashire League club, said he had a good command of swing, both into and away from the batsman. One of his Lancashire hosts thought his outswinger was copied from Abe Waddington, who played for Yorkshire in the 1920s, and that his inswinger was prompted by George Hirst. The observer remembered how a prominent Haslingden batsman, a punishing forward player, had been very severe on Verity's inswinger in one match. In the return game at Accrington Verity's first ball was an outswinger which hit the off-stump to the batsman's considerable surprise.

At the Headingley nets in 1922 Peel supervised the trial and said of Hedley: "His pitch is excellent and he uses his head well." Bobby did, however, believe that Verity's bowling would improve with a little extra pace. Verity himself later remembered Peel's assessment as an example that few men are equipped by nature to be fast bowlers. At the trial session, he recalled, Peel had said: "Can't you bowl faster than that?" "I tried," said Hedley, "but only earned the compassionate remark: 'It's a pity; you're a good fast bowler wasted.'"

Peel was clearly puzzled that a boy of Verity's height and physique could not summon up the extra pace of a fast bowler. He perhaps remembered his incomprehension when Verity followed in his footsteps as a master slow left-arm bowler.

Other good judges in Yorkshire were similarly at a loss in categorising the Rawdon boy. One man offered the verdict: "He will make a good bowler, but he will be an even better batter." Verity's batting aggregate for Rawdon in 1923 seemed to support that opinion, for he totalled nearly 500 runs and recorded his highest score, 83 not out against Tong Park.

The second Monday in August was a great day for cricketers and other folk at Rawdon. It was the day of the annual feast – a raucous assembly of giddy carousels, bizarre sideshows, pedlars of baubles and brandy-snap, and the music of the hurdy-gurdy men. The moors of Rawdon and other Yorkshire villages and towns became enticing places for those with a few pennies to squander on a midsummer night. Rawdon's feast celebration also marked the time when their cricketers tussled with neighbouring rivals, Yeadon. Grace Verity remembers one such match in Hedley's early years. Rawdon were bowled out for 48 and Yeadon looked set for victory as they reached 32 for two wickets.

"We've got 'em beat this time," chorused the Yeadon fans. Grace Verity retained her optimism. "I shouted back: 'A game is never won until it is lost.'" Hedley, by some oversight, had not been given a bowl. He then entered the attack with devastating results. Yeadon's last eight wickets added only nine more runs and they were all out for 41. The *Wharfedale and Airedale Observer* reported: "This was the first time since 1914 that Rawdon have defeated Yeadon in a Yorkshire Council match. They owed their victory to the excellent bowling of H. Verity and S. Pratt. Verity was especially good, as he went on as a change bowler and only bowled four overs, securing five wickets for eight runs."

At the end of the 1923 season the *Yorkshire Evening Post* enthused in prophetic terms: "One of the most promising cricketers in the Leeds district is H. Verity, of Rawdon. This season has been his most successful one. He bids fair to become one of the best cricketers Wharfedale has produced."

Rawdon, the village and its people, always remained a cosy retreat for Hedley Verity throughout his career. It was a place of good fellowship where he could be at ease after his cricket toils. He enjoyed the camaraderie of Sefton House, likened by one member of the family to a "station waiting room" where the Veritys' customers were given a cup of tea before stepping out of the parlour into the coal office to pay their bills.

The lessons of courtesy and gallant behaviour, the simple, old-fashioned values, taught by upright but not intolerant parents, helped to fashion Hedley's resolute lifestyle. One of his great joys, as a baritone singer of local repute, was to take part with his sisters Grace (contralto) and Edith (soprano) in the annual oratorios at the nearby Benton Congregational Church. After church, on Sunday evenings, there were merry sing-songs at Sefton House. Friends in the youth fellowship choir, often as many as 20 or more, sang their rousing tunes across the crowded room. Outside the house other neighbours perched on the railings and joined in the singing.

More than likely there would be a dog barking in unison with the happy company. It was called "Prince", a fiercely protective mongrel who was rescued and adopted by Hedley when it failed to find a buyer at a Bradford market. "I'll have him," said Hedley, and Prince became his inseparable companion. Prince was quite a character, responding easily to Hedley's training. He learned many new tricks. He always accompanied his master to cricket practice at the Rawdon ground. Hedley would toss his coat on the ground and instruct the dog to mount guard over it. There was no question of compromise; when Prince was told to look after anything he did so against all odds. After practice Hedley, knowing well the consequences, would nonchalantly ask anyone going in the direction of the coat (and its guardian) to bring it back to him. Prince growled with anger at their impertinence and would not permit anyone other than Hedley to touch the coat. Hedley often laughed at their unsuccessful efforts to retrieve the coat.

Hedley Verity's cricket apprenticeship at Rawdon ended in 1923 and, on the advice of friends, he moved to Horsforth Hall Park. His start with his new club was less than propitious; he had started the season with high hopes, but he was still struggling to find his true form by Whitsuntide. On Whit Monday his fortunes took an upward turn when he took eight wickets for 23 runs to rout his old adversaries, Yeadon. On the following day, at Horsforth, he scored 53 runs.

In another match at Horsforth he batted steadily through the innings on a difficult wicket. It was a slow and dour effort, not at all to the liking of one spectator. His mother, not at that time well-known on the Horsforth ground, chanced to sit next to the unimpressed onlooker. She listened, inwardly fuming at his grumbling asides on her son's merits. At the close of the innings she turned round to the man and said: "He's still there, mister." "Yes", replied the man in a tone of exasperation, "I see he is." Mrs. Verity was determined to make her point. "He would have got a lot more runs if there had been anyone to stay with him," she said. The man pondered deeply, his face relaxing as he realised he had been a little uncharitable. "You're reight there, missis," he answered as he walked away.

Batting, and there were many grafting displays like the one which had disenchanted the Horsforth critic, did seem to have taken precedence over Verity's bowling in the early 1920s. In his first season at Horsforth he scored 482 runs at an average of 20.8, while his bowling, although still economical, yielded only 25 wickets.

Practice continued to dominate Verity's leisure hours, both on the cricket field and also on the school playground at other times. His friends were enlisted to field for him when he bowled and bowl to him when he batted. "He even got the kiddies in the village to run and fetch the ball," recalls Grace Verity. "I used to tremble for the safety of the windows in some of the streets and alley-ways he discovered as suitable for practice," said his father.

In his years at Horsforth, Verity marshalled his batting resources to such a degree that in one season he scored almost 1,000 runs in all matches. He was, indisputably, an all-rounder of immense promise. In 1926, his last season at Horsforth Hall Park, Verity scored 488 runs and took 62 wickets for nine runs apiece to win the Yorkshire Council League junior bowling prize and very nearly carry off the senior award as well.

Verity now came under the stewardship of George Hirst and Yorkshire invited him, along with other aspiring youngsters, to their summer trials at Headingley. He played in several matches for the county colts and, interestingly, his colleagues included future Yorkshire seniors, Arthur Mitchell, Wilf Barber, Cyril Turner and Arthur Wood. Verity's inclusion in these games seemed largely due to the strength of his batting performances in club cricket. As a bowler he was permitted only 63 overs and took only five wickets at, by his future standards, an exorbitant cost of 29.20 runs each. His bowling average left him next to the last in the Yorkshire Colts' list.

There is one question which has never been satisfactorily explained except in terms of Yorkshire canniness and the long apprenticeships of those days. Hedley Verity, incongruous as it may seem, had to cross the Pennines to learn his trade and further his claims in Lancashire League cricket. Some might say that Yorkshire were being unduly cautious and remiss in not allocating Verity to a club within the county. George Hirst had earmarked him for special attention at the nets and gave the boy a glowing recommendation in introducing him to Accrington where Verity held his first professional appointment. Why, bearing in mind Hirst's enthusiasm, was he not given work to do in one of Yorkshire's vast nursery of league clubs?

It is true that Verity was a late developer as a bowler; he did not play for Yorkshire until he was 25; and he first had to convince Wilfred

Rhodes that he was a worthy successor. There were also many other ambitious young men waiting hopefully for the call in this time of cricket plenty. Rhodes was still resplendently in charge, showing no sign of a decline as Verity moved, perhaps reluctantly, across the border. Yet Yorkshire so nearly lost a great cricketer to Warwickshire, where in one of life's little ironies, he was rejected like Rhodes before him after trials.

Yorkshire might so easily have had cause to rue their caution. Fortunately for them there were benefactors in the Lancashire mill town of Middleton who helped to sharpen Verity's skills in three fulfilling years. One of those hosts was Edwin Kay, the former Lancashire president. "Hedley was very proud of being a Yorkshireman," says Kay. "Playing for Yorkshire was his ambition and everything he did was with this aim in view. It was not easy for him but he used to say that the best things in life rarely were and he was prepared to fight for success."

Inspiring Verity in his quest was a little plaque that hung over his bed at his Rawdon home. The plaque bore a simple quotation which became his creed for life. It read: "They told him it couldn't be done. He made up his mind that it could – and he did it."

2

WINNING APPROVAL IN LANCASHIRE

"To be a Middleton player when Hedley was professional was not just to play cricket, but to live it." – John Kay.

THOSE friends in Lancashire who championed Hedley Verity in the late 1920s believe that the turning point in his career came when he accepted the responsibilities of professionalism at an early age. They say that it was this added challenge which brought the cutting edge to his cricket and transformed him into a great player.

Verity moved to Accrington in the summer of 1927 and thus followed in the footsteps of Bobby Peel, another famed Yorkshire and England left-arm bowler who had played for the Lancashire League club nearly 30 years earlier. Peel, a strong-minded and unrepentant man, moved to Lancashire after an indiscreet exchange with Lord Hawke, Yorkshire's imperious ruler. He was a victim of the winds of change sweeping through Yorkshire cricket at the turn of the century.

By contrast Verity was a novice and was labelled as such by the veterans at Accrington who lacked either the vision or the will to aid Verity in his immaturity. They were palpably not interested in being coached by an unproven youngster; they were more concerned with winning trophies in common with other clubs in the Lancashire League. Accrington was not a place for beginners as the shy young Yorkshireman very quickly discovered. It must have been a hurtful experience and a blow to his pride after his swoops of success in the little ponds of club cricket back home in Yorkshire.

Before Verity's departure for Accrington an intriguing playlet was enacted on an entertaining day during the Scarborough Festival of 1926. Accrington were seeking a professional for the following season and Tom Lancaster, a Yorkshire cricket veteran, was a member of a deputation which travelled to Scarborough with the intention of securing the services of a famous Australian bowler. A series of events both on the journey and in Scarborough plunged them on to an entirely different trail. By accident or design they met another old professional at one of the stations at which the train stopped on the way.

The man entered the compartment and, with a gesture of surprise, expressed his curiosity about their journey. "What are you lot after?" he asked. Lancaster and his colleagues explained their errand and the hopes of signing the Australian. "I wish you success," said the man, "but I think you will be unlucky." There was dismay among the deputation at the prospect of a wasted trip. "Do you know of anyone else?" queried the Accrington travellers. "Well", said the man after some considerable thought, "if that's what tha'rt after, ah can put thi' on't reight lad. He's only a young 'un; he's never been out pro-ing, but he's a good 'un and he's a coming man." "Ah," said Lancaster, "and who is he?" "Hedley Verity", was the confident reply.

At the Scarborough ground the deputation, now alert and determined to hunt down their new quarry, met George Hirst. They again told their story to Hirst and asked him if he could arrange an interview with Verity. "I think I can get him for you," said George with a touch of impatience. "But I'm not sure he will be interested."

The cat and mouse interlude continued as the Accrington officials asked Hirst if he could suggest another candidate if Verity should prove unavailable. "No", said George, "I don't know of an experienced pro' such as you want. I do know this lad, Verity. I can recommend him but he has no professional experience, except that he played for Yorkshire seconds last season. He's a good left-arm bowler and a useful bat, but you want an *experienced* man."

The piquant little drama now dipped into a frantic chase as the Accrington deputation became convinced that Verity was their man. Further inquiries elicited the response that he was staying in Scarborough. Another guide, Billy Fletcher, endorsed Hirst's recommendation and said he thought Verity was on the ground. But Verity could not be traced and it was finally revealed that he had returned home to play in a local club match.

Fletcher promised the Accrington representatives that he would get in touch with Verity and ask him to contact them. He then caught the next bus to Leeds and headed straight for Verity's home to break the news to an astonished young cricketer.

On the following Saturday afternoon, during a game at Yeadon, Tom Lancaster arrived to cast an eye on the elusive Verity in what was to prove his last game with Horsforth Hall Park. Players and spectators murmured in puzzlement as Lancaster and Verity's father talked earnestly on the boundary edge. The sequel to this discussion was a successful trial at Accrington and the contract was signed which was to speed Verity into the challenging arena of Lancashire League cricket. It was quite an upheaval for the 21-year-old Yorkshireman; he was leaving home for the first time; and he could not then remark philosophically, as he did in his Yorkshire and England days, "I don't mind if I have to climb a different pair of stairs every night." This was the declaration of a mature man who was attuned to the nomadic life of a cricketer.

The recruitment of Verity as professional was a new departure in the policies of the Accrington club. On September 18, 1926 the *Accrington Observer* commented: "Instead of engaging a player with an established reputation, Accrington have secured the services of a young cricketer who is new to the professional ranks ... it is satisfactory to know, however, that his abilities are highly spoken of by leading Yorkshire cricketers."

Alec Jackson, one of a small coterie of encouraging men at Accrington, said later: "Hedley was introduced to us at a friendly gathering by that good, old left-handed Yorkshireman, Tom Lancaster. He told us that we had secured a find, a left-hander, who could swing the ball both ways." Jackson said that Verity, who had been used to bowling on a small ground at Horsforth Hall Park (the sightscreen was only 30 or 40 yards behind the bowling crease), had a natural tendency to push the ball through a little faster, on a good length but on the short side. This policy, he said, with his ability to swing the ball both ways made him a diffcult bowler to hit.

"Unfortunately for Hedley," said the Accrington man, "he followed C. B. Llewellyn at the club. Charlie could swing the ball but he relied on spin. 'Toss 'em up and they won't hit them all', was his maxim. Llewellyn also had an uncanny instinct of being able to assess, almost at a glance, the strengths and weaknesses of opposing batsmen. He was ideally equipped for the soft wickets in Lancashire and Verity was expected to follow his example." Future events were to show that Verity had digested the formula, but he had to move to more congenial surround-ings before he could achieve the right mix in accord with his own methods.

Jackson added: "This was a very valuable experience for Hedley. But spinning the ball wants a lot of practice. To attempt to bowl in his usual style with a field more or less set for spinners was not possible."

As a batsman at Accrington, Verity was advanced in theory and Jackson said: "He had the correct 'county' style of moving his feet and using his pads as the second line of defence; but he so often forgot to use his bat to a straight ball. It remained suspended in mid-air. Then as now [the comments were penned at the height of Verity's career] lbw with Hedley was a common verdict."

In his early days at Accrington Verity fully measured up to the recommendation of George Hirst. He was welcomed into the home of an elderly Lancashire couple whose daughter had recently married and left them feeling lonely. He was, according to his father, "happy in the comforts and affection showered upon him." "In fact," said Verity senior, "I felt afraid they would spoil him; they nearly made him a man of Lancashire, so closely did he approximate to the habits and customs of his new home in Burnley Road."

In his first game for Accrington at Bacup, watched by a contingent of curious supporters, Verity took five wickets for 48 runs; but it was not quite enough to avert defeat in a keenly contested game. Against Rawtenstall, the reigning league champions, Verity had a match-winning return of 3 for 21 in 18 overs, and he gathered another four wickets, again at negligible cost, to overwhelm Ramsbottom.

Before the rains descended in a miserable summer Verity produced an analysis of 6 for 40 against Towerhouse. The visitors were dismissed for 83, but the Accrington batsmen did not reach double figures in their reply. They were all out for nine, a total which had the statisticians reaching for the record books. It remains one of the lowest scores in the history of the Lancashire League.

The memory of a disastrous batting display was supplanted by the wavering form of Accrington's new professional in the succeeding weeks. Verity struck the worst bowling spell of his career. It was not just a loss of form; he had also pulled a muscle in his bowling arm and he was afraid to say anything about the injury. In June he faltered uneasily and took only 14 wickets in the month. He rallied pluckily to emerge with credit in the bright intervals of the remaining games when the rains relented.

At the end of the season, with the finances throughout the league in disarray, the Accrington secretary commented: "Our choice of professional, so very bright at the opening, did not turn out to be quite the success we had thought. It was very discouraging to the players and undoubtedly had an effect on their play. The committee felt the position very keenly and their burden was not lightened by the attitude taken up by a section of the spectators and, I am sorry to say, by some of our own members."

Hedley Verity must have inwardly groaned after his daunting experiences in his first season as a professional. He had a batting average of 5.25, and even the atrocious weather conditions could not excuse such a disturbing lapse in form. Verity senior was also seriously concerned about his son's cricket future. He recalled sitting with Tom Lancaster and watching Hedley bat in one match at Accrington. He asked Lancaster if he could offer any explanation. "There's nowt wrong with him," said Tom. "It's just a phase every cricketer goes through." At that precise moment Hedley reached forward to a ball pitched on the middle and leg stumps and was bowled as it turned to the off and beat him.

Angered by the ease of the dismissal, Mr. Verity was just setting off to the pavilion to vent his wrath when he was stopped. "Tha'll say nowt to him," said Lancaster. "But," Verity protested, "he was bowled by the same ball which he uses to get his opponents out. He knows better than to play like that." "He's all right and tha'll let him alone," insisted Tom, and that was the end of the matter.

Verity's bowling also came in for censure by an angry and disappointed father. However, in this case and from his own account, there were mitigating circumstances. "Any bowler of Hedley's type depends very largely for success on good fielding," said Mr. Verity. "I am not saying the Accrington players were bad or even poor fieldsmen, but they were seldom in the right place at the right time." The mild critique seems to hide a private fury at the injustices of an unhappy summer.

The fielding misdemeanours did not escape young Hedley's notice. In one match his father took him to task for placing a man on the square-leg boundary. "He's no use to you there. Why don't you bring him in?" asked Mr. Verity. Hedley replied heatedly: "I've brought him up many times, but he always drifts back again. They all do, they wander all over the place. It's no use. I've given over bothering with them."

Verity was able to maintain his close field placings in another match despite the fears of an Accrington critic that it was tantamount to committing suicide in those helmetless days. The short-leg fieldsman took one simple catch, then another, but the dissenter remained adamant that the tactic was wrong. When the next batsman, locally renowned as a powerful hitter, came to the wicket the spectator exclaimed: "Remove that fieldsman; he's going to be killed." Verity senior responded with the soothing reply: "Don't worry. He's perfectly safe." From Hedley's second ball the feared smiter surrendered meekly, putting up a sitter of a catch. The critic gasped in astonishment. He could not believe this testimony to Verity's accuracy. The unharmed short-leg was the recipient of five catches that afternoon and Verity took seven wickets for 23 runs.

Verity senior always declared that Hedley bowled as well as ever at Accrington, but said that his son was handicapped by his youthfulness. "The other players were mostly older than himself and he failed to impress them. They thought for themselves and would not respond to his intention and purpose," he said.

The Accrington club were still prepared to keep faith with Verity and he was offered an improved contract for the 1928 season. However, in the meantime, Verity had discovered something that shocked and unsettled him. Accrington had, on one occasion, refused to release their professional when he was invited to play for Lancashire. This was, in Verity's view, a heresy. It did not fit in at all with his deep-rooted ambition to wear Yorkshire's colours. He felt that to sign another contract with Accrington would jeopardise his chances. He declined the offer and moved to Middleton in the Central Lancashire League. He accepted a reduction in pay in return for a promise by Middleton that they would release him if Yorkshire required his services. His new employers were as good as their word and never once failed to honour the bond.

"He's good and he's *cheap*," was the verdict of the Middleton officials after they had watched Hedley Verity in action at Accrington. Middleton could not afford the luxuries of big-name players and at five pounds a week Verity was a bargain. The club committee had been urged to inspect the Yorkshireman by Lionel Cranfield, one of the shrewdest of Lancashire League professionals and the inspirational guide for many youngsters at Middleton. Cranfield had announced his impending departure in July, 1927, and he told the club: "Verity is a better player than you would think from his results."

Middleton little knew that the signing would prove a momentous event in the club's history and subsequently lead to an association of great significance for English cricket. In later years they proudly boasted that they had had much to do with the grooming of a great cricketer. Verity did not dispute that claim. He never lost an opportunity of returning to the scene of his early triumphs that gave him the confidence he so badly needed to bridge the gap between the good player he always was and the revered one he eventually became.

John Kay, the former Lancashire cricket correspondent with whose family Verity stayed during his years at Middleton, says: "The older players, who had been brought up under Cranfield, did not fancy playing under a youngster. They retired or moved on and this let in a new generation of players. This was the ideal situation for Hedley. It was exactly what he wanted."

Verity was fortunate in that he was in at the beginning of a new era at Middleton. The Lancashire club took the gamble of recruiting him, as they later did in welcoming two other future England stars, Frank Tyson and Basil D'Oliveira. At Middleton Verity joined players in his own age group and, even more importantly, he struck up a fine relationship with the club captain, Ernest McDougall.

It was a happy combination and yet, in his first season, there was little hint of the glories ahead. Verity was tall and angular, a left-arm bowler who swung the ball into the right-handed batsmen and away from the left. He sometimes straightened the ball on pitching and usually managed to find an economical length. With the bat he was correct and not without scoring strokes and he was a serviceable fieldsman either close to the wicket or in the outfield. It was a modest beginning and very few people in Middleton or elsewhere in the Central Lancashire League rated Verity more than a useful all-round cricketer.

"We who were in the side knew him better," says John Kay. "At the nets and in the dressing-room Hedley set a fine example." Verity, prematurely grey in his early twenties, was a man of authority at Middleton, commanding the respect of the unruliest player. There was an instant recognition that you could not trifle with him. Kay recalls that Verity was astute enough to know at the age of 22 that he could not go about his job of coaching and fostering team spirit in the manner of a more experienced cricketer. "He never once suggested things should be done his way. Yet he got us all to do what he wanted without question and without much argument."

Verity could, as his son, Douglas, has said, be "frivolous and impish in many ways," but he did not deviate from a serious attitude to matters that counted. The severity rarely toppled over into outright anger. When it did he could be fierce, especially in the nets where he expected disciplined behaviour.

In one isolated burst of temper at Middleton Verity rounded on a player who had, without thinking, lit a cigarette during a practice session. His reprimand carried more impact precisely because it was unexpected and out of character. At other times Verity, if he was angry, counted to ten. He was never hasty as a professional. But he made it clear that cricket was an important business – "you are going back to school," he would say – and he would not countenance any distractions on the Towncroft cricket field.

"To be a Middleton player when Hedley Verity was professional was not just to play cricket, but to live it," says John Kay. "Every night in the week we practised in the nets. From six o'clock until dusk we were apprentices learning our craft. If it rained we played indoors, or talked about this, that, or the other of cricket."

Quite often, after four hours of net practice, Verity and his fellow players would push and pull the heavy roller up and down the pitch being prepared for the next match. The chore was lightened by one of the players, a ukulele entertainer and George Formby fan, who strummed along as they rolled and rolled. Afterwards they would relax in the pavilion and enjoy another musical round with Hedley's fine voice prominent in the impromptu choir. Then they would all return to the Kay's home for a fish-and-chip supper and a debate on a current cricket topic. The discussions often lasted until midnight and even later.

John Kay recalls: "It did not need Hedley to open the debate. It could be anybody – and particularly one who had failed in the previous match. He would ask what we all thought about the manner of his dismissal and then would come a searching cricketing analysis of a major or minor problem. There would be differences of opinion. Quite often there was no degree of unanimity about how the unlucky batsman got out. He would perhaps lean to the view that the ball came in quickly from the off.

"If the batsman at the other end at the time was one of the party he would almost certainly disagree and even those who saw it only from a distance, either the dressing-room window or the vantage point behind the bowler's arm where the late batsmen were prone to gather before it came to their turn to bat, would advance their personal theories."

John Kay's twin brother, Edwin, also played for Middleton. Edwin played for the club for 25 years, scored well over 10,000 runs, and, on Verity's recommendation, was offered but declined a trial with Worcestershire. Middleton also had a jovial wicket-keeper called Freddie Pearson whom Verity regarded as one of the best who ever kept to him – and said so after years in first-class cricket.

Keeping a watchful eye on the Kay household was father Teddy, who was a member of the Middleton club committee and had promised Verity's father that his son would come to no harm in Lancashire. Shepherding the flock was a mother, who, like her counterpart back at Rawdon, patiently understood the importance of cricket to her menfolk. There were also a couple of daughters, Marian and Bessie, who often wondered what it was all about but never questioned the rightness of the family mania. Hedley Verity was, from the start, captivated by the cricket camaraderie and fanaticism of his hosts.

In the late 1920s the subtleties of left-arm bowling were the preoccupation of the disciples of Wilfred Rhodes. Verity, in the fields of Central Lancashire League cricket, quietly committed himself to a plan which would banish his rivals and bring him enduring fame with Yorkshire and England. At the Yorkshire nets it had been intimated to him that the goal was in his grasp if he changed direction. George Hirst and Wilfred

Rhodes had taken him aside to suggest that as a seamer (or medium pace bowler in the parlance of that time) he was only one of many available to the county. As a spinner, if he concentrated on the job, he would have a better chance because Rhodes was contemplating retirement.

Verity seized his opportunity. He never doubted his ability to produce what was required but it meant starting all over again, and to do this he needed the co-operation of all with whom he played. He told the Middleton skipper about Hirst's advice and was not only given the go-ahead but also a promise that everybody at the club was behind him. John Kay remembers his friend's return to Middleton after the urgent discussions at Headingley of the previous winter. Before the start of the new season Verity told the assembled players: "Look lads, it has got to be different this year. I am going to bowl spinners. I am going to start straightaway in the nets." One of the Middleton players, in the early, trying weeks of the experiment, quipped: "Tha'd be better off bowling quick, Hedley."

The decision to turn from seam to spin was a success thanks to the team spirit prevailing at Middleton and the patience and encouragement of the club committee. But Verity did have his moments of despair and in one of these periods of gloom he accepted an invitation from Warwickshire to go to Edgbaston for a trial. He was recommended by Ted Leyland, formerly head groundsman at Headingley (and the father of Maurice). Leyland shared George Hirst's opinion of Verity and he passed on his endorsement to Syd Santall, the Warwickshire coach. Verity appeared in the nets at Edgbaston during the summer of 1928.

Ralph Barker, in his book, *Ten Great Bowlers*, wrote: "The man who had to bat against Verity was a young player who had moved from the staff at Lord's. His name was H. T. Roll. He padded up under Santall's instructions and went to the nets with Santall, Leyland, and several members of the Warwickshire committee.

"The net wicket at Edgbaston was perfect, and absolutely bone hard. The studious-looking young bowler from the Lancashire League pushed them through somewhat faster than was traditional with his type. His bowling presented no problems, the wicket was plumb, and the ball did not bend an inch. Roll, in fact, was a very fine player, one who at the time certainly looked like reaching the top. After about 10 minutes the Warwickshire committee decided that they had seen enough. The trialist was not asked to bat." Verity was saved for Yorkshire cricket by a wicket beyond his powers and a stubborn young batsman who treated him without respect.

The peremptory dismissal by Warwickshire had the effect of reinforcing

Verity's determination to play for Yorkshire. The visit to Edgbaston must surely have been an aberration. However, the transition from league to county cricket was not made without some misgivings. Verity could have signed a three-year contract, worth between £15 and £20 a week and more than three times his Middleton salary, with East Lancashire, the Blackburn town club. East Lancashire, in common with other Lancashire League clubs, had made tentative offers to Verity in 1930. He did not discourage them, but he was not really interested in returning to the Lancashire League. He had set his sights on playing for Yorkshire who, however, offered him no advice nor any security until he made the grade. Yorkshire did not then offer contracts and there was no guarantee of regular money or a place in the team until a player was awarded his county cap.

John Kay recalls one occasion when Yorkshire asked Middleton to release Verity for a game with the county. Permission was duly granted, but the question was raised: "What are your intentions regarding Verity?" John Nash, the Yorkshire secretary, responded with a guarded expression and said: "Oh, we think a lot about Hedley."

A letter containing the East Lancashire offer arrived from Blackburn. It stayed unanswered, if not forgotten, in Verity's pocket for over two weeks. It was followed by a telegram containing the curt message that he had 48 hours in which to make up his mind. Verity was at the crossroads. He had recently married Kathleen Metcalfe, the girl with whom he had toddled along the streets of Headingley and had later been reunited at the youth club social at Rawdon. Security was in his grasp. John Kay believes that Verity must have privately anguished over the decision more than any other in his life.

As his own father was away from home and had not then replied to a letter asking for advice, Hedley turned to Teddy Kay for guidance. "What do *you* want to do?" Kay asked. Hedley replied that he only had one thought in his mind – to take his chance with Yorkshire. "Then do so, but give it all you've got," said Kay.

Hedley Verity made up his mind. He wired East Lancashire rejecting their offer and 10 minutes later received a letter from his father proferring almost identical advice to that given by Kay senior. It included another rallying statement. "You are a married man now and life will be harder. Make your decision, work hard and never be satisfied with anything but the best. I hope you choose Yorkshire," wrote Mr. Verity.

Middleton tore up Verity's uncompleted contract. They let him go and play for Yorkshire, saw him succeed brilliantly and shared his happiness. John Kay, as a cricket writer, later covered the fortunes of Lancashire, but today he says that his allegiance and that of his family were inextricably tied to a Yorkshireman who had flourished and prospered in their company. They had played and learned together. Edwin Kay says: "Hedley left a remarkable legacy behind him at Middleton. He provided the nucleus of young players who played a major part in the success of the club in the 1930s when Middleton were one of the strongest sides in the league.

"These were great years and nobody took a greater pride in our accomplishments than Hedley Verity." Equally, it can be said, Verity never failed to acknowledge how his Middleton friends had helped him at the most critical juncture in his cricketing life.

3

THE WEIGHT OF A LEGACY

*"Tha'll get more bounce than Wilfred, so work it out for thissen
how to tackle them as fancies hittin' and them as doesn't."* –
George Hirst.

WHEN Hedley Verity was very young George Hirst said of his pupil: "I
know it is in him, one day he will break out and there will be no holding
him." Verity was always preparing himself for the Yorkshire call. He
had never idled as a cricketer; he played or tried to play as a county
player should even as a boy, and he was criticised for it. Others said later
that it must have been a hard time for him.

His day was not far off in the summer of 1929 when he made a trip to
Rawdon to play for his old club in the village feast game. On the
following day Verity travelled to Headingley to meet old friends and
watch his county favourites in action. By chance Yorkshire required a
substitute for a Colts' match later in the week and Hedley was asked if he
would fill the breach. Verity had fretted over Yorkshire's tardiness,
questioning friends on the claims of other spinning contenders. He did
not hesitate and was duly catapulted into a decisive trial match between
the county's second eleven and a team of young Yorkshire amateurs.

The colts scored 420 before the declaration and the amateurs followed
on 229 runs behind. Their second innings was a tale of utter woe. They
were dismissed for 56 and Verity took five wickets for seven runs.
Returning to Middleton, Verity maintained his dominating form and
reached 100 wickets for the club to finish at the head of the Central
Lancashire League averages. He also achieved one other objective, his
first century for Middleton in an evening benefit match. John Kay recalls
Verity's determination to reach three figures before he left the club.
"Hedley said I must get a hundred; I might as well get it tonight, and he
did."

At the start of the 1930 season Hedley Verity was unknown outside a
small circle in Lancashire and Yorkshire. By the end of the summer his
name was on everybody's lips. In 12 games he took 64 wickets at a cost of

12.42 runs each to head not only the Yorkshire averages but the national bowling list as well.

The *Yorkshire Post* commented: "The extraordinary rise of Hedley Verity, the young Rawdon slow bowler, has been one of the major topics of Yorkshire cricket conversation during the past season, and for a colt to finish at the top of the list is a feat few, if any, other players have accomplished in their first season." Percy Fender, the former Surrey captain and a judicious cricket observer, wrote: "I have only seen him once but I was much impressed by his command of length and flight. He is a fine, upstanding fellow, who delivers the ball from a great height and with a delightfully easy action. There seems every reasonable hope that there will not again in the next 10 years be any need for England to go through on her own wickets without the assistance of an orthodox slow left-arm bowler played simply and solely for his ability as such."

The profits of this and other tributes was the result of the "10 years of hard work" predicted by his father when the young Verity had first rejected parental doubts. The deeds of 1930 sealed a gruelling and singleminded apprenticeship. But it was only a beginning and the fulsome praises – "the new Rhodes", "another Wilfred" and "Wilfred II" – must have echoed disquietingly in Verity's mind. He was being called upon to shoulder an awesome responsibility.

From Isaac Hodgson, who played for Yorkshire from the start of the county club in 1863, through the brilliant but wayward talents of Ted Peate and Bobby Peel to the supreme artistry of Wilfred Rhodes, "one of our national possessions", as Neville Cardus called him, Yorkshire's chain of slow left-arm bowlers was one of the wonders of cricket, appreciated both inside and outside the county.

An onlooker, commenting on Verity's eight wickets for 60 runs against Leicestershire in his first championship appearance at Hull, remarked: "For some time folks have been wondering whether the greatest succession of left-handed bowlers any county ever knew has run dry at last. But Verity is destined to supply an emphatic negative unless shrewd and discerning critics are at fault in their judgement."

Reflecting on such an exalted succession, Verity must at times have felt uneasy about the task which lay ahead of him. Adding to his concern were the voices of the sceptics who alleged that his successes in 1930 flattered him and were the result of weak opposition.

George Hirst did, as always, offer solace in an unenviable situation. He quietly and wisely told Verity that he could not hope to match

Rhodes in terms of action and tactics. "Tha's a lot taller," said George, "tha'll get more bounce than Wilfred, so work it out for thissen how to tackle them as fancies hittin' and them as doesn't."

Verity made his debut for Yorkshire in a friendly match against Sussex at Huddersfield on May 21, 1930, just three days after his 25th birthday. Wilfred Rhodes, then aged 52, looked on rapt in contemplation and trained his binoculars upon Verity from time to time. He had just announced his retirement and he was well aware that his verdict could make or break his prospective successor. Verity bowled for over an hour in his first spell. He only once erred in length and was hit for six by Cook.

Another towering six, vigorously struck by Maurice Tate, greeted Verity when he returned to the Yorkshire attack. Tate had obviously enjoyed the ringing sound of his bat and he tried to repeat the shot off the next delivery. The ball again soared skywards, but it failed to carry the field. Waiting out in the deep was Arthur Mitchell. He raced forward and then dived, hands outstretched, to take the catch. Mitchell was to make similar plunging catches in his more accustomed position, perilously close to the bat in the gully. The scorebook entry at Huddersfield: "c Mitchell b Verity" marked the start of a brilliant alliance which was to astound numerous opponents over the years.

Verity emerged from the match with figures of three wickets for 96 runs in 46 overs, hardly a startling return, but as two stumping chances had gone astray, he could look back on his county debut with satisfaction. "There was one period when Verity was the only Yorkshire bowler who could keep the Sussex batsmen quiet," commented one writer. "This was during his first spell, and although he suffered later through a typical Tate onslaught, his rhythmical and easy action at the end of a run of seven paces, together with the skilful manner in which he varied his flight and pace, suggested that we shall see more of this tall, young professional."

"Old Ebor" (A. W. Pullin, the Yorkshire cricket correspondent) wrote: "Verity bowled exceedingly well, keeping an immaculate length and constantly having the Sussex batsmen in trouble . . . I should like to see this young man bowling on a wicket which gives him a little help . . . ."

Bill Bowes, one of Verity's closest friends and a superb ally of the left-hander during Yorkshire's great years in the 1930s, has noted that his partner did receive the necessary help in the first, crucial weeks of his first-class career. "From the moment that Hedley joined the Yorkshire side for his next trial match against Glamorgan at Swansea it rained almost incessantly for weeks. The sticky wickets that were my misfortune were just the initial slice of luck that Hedley needed."

Bowes tells the droll story of his own dismay and Verity's delighted response to stormy weather in another match at Edgbaston. Yorkshire had scored 468 for the loss of eight wickets at the end of the first day's play. "It was a lovely evening, and I suggested to Hedley that we should walk back to the hotel. We had scarcely gone 400 yards from the ground when there was a sudden rainstorm. We sheltered most inadequately under a tree and we were both half-drenched. I looked at Hedley and said: 'Ever since you came into the side it's done nothing else but rain. Can't you fall downstairs and break your neck or something – and let somebody else have a chance!'"

"The depth of feeling I put into those words seemed tremendously funny to Hedley and he afterwards repeated the story many times. I was no less amused by his reply. 'Bill', he said, 'I'm so pleased to see this rain. I feel like getting wet through – and then I might oblige you by catching my death of cold.'"

Arthur Booth, Horace Fisher and Stan Douglas were others competing for Wilfred Rhodes' bowling position in 1930. Booth, a wily little man from Featherstone, was Verity's main rival. He had to wait until 1946 before he achieved a place in the Yorkshire team. By then he was 43 and almost as old as senior county players, Wilf Barber and Maurice Leyland, who had returned to the side after war service. Yet in his first full season of first-class cricket he headed the national bowling averages with 111 wickets at a cost of 11.61 runs each. "Arthur was built like Wilfred," says John Kay. "He was small and he tossed the ball well up; but he didn't spin it as much as Hedley." Most of Verity's early games for Yorkshire were on bad wickets and he did not squander his opportunity. "This is the secret," says Kay. "Good players can only get into county teams when the conditions are right." Wherever Verity played in his first weeks with Yorkshire he was presented with ideal conditions. Booth was less fortunate in his occasional appearances for the county.

The rains poured down from implacable skies during this bleak summer, but they did relent sufficiently for Verity to display his command. At Swansea, in only his fourth match for the county, he was almost unplayable before a deluge caused play to be abandoned. He took nine wickets for 60 runs to rout Glamorgan. His off-spinning partner, George Macaulay, broke the sequence of wickets in contrast to two other memorable days when he failed to disrupt Verity's glory after he had pledged himself to do so.

The question of Rhodes' successor was earnestly debated during the rain stoppages. Some people supported another left-hander, Maurice Leyland, whose own bowling abilities were not as negligible as he self-disparagingly claimed. Maurice used to say in typical understatement: "I would love to bat against myself." Leyland was a better bowler than he admitted and there were many observers who wondered whether he could fill the double role of leading batsman and slow bowler as another Yorkshire and England man, the ebullient Roy Kilner, had done before him.

At Bristol where spinners like Gloucestershire's own renowned craftsman, Charlie Parker, rejoiced in the devilry of the wicket, Verity further advanced his claims. Rhodes, in the Yorkshire manner, tied up the batsmen at the other end. Verity was left free to take five wickets for 18 runs in the course of nine overs and five balls. Dipper and Sinfield, the Gloucestershire openers, were not parted until the score had reached 52, but the innings then collapsed. Gloucestershire were dismissed for 125 and such were the problems set by Verity's waspish spin that the rest of the innings lasted less than two hours. Parker's figures in the match, admittedly in less favourable conditions, were 3 for 100. It must also be said that the Yorkshire batting was rather better.

Hedley Verity struck a golden vein on the heaven-sent pitches of 1930, but his successes did not mean as much as the methods which produced them to one of his Yorkshire mentors, the redoubtable Emmott Robinson. Bill Bowes says that Robinson was a fine judge of cricket and, most important of all, no detail was too small for him. "I remember that when I was married Emmott arrived at our house just before tea. He had a brown paper parcel under his arm, and when he put the parcel on the table, he said: 'Ah've brought summat to help thee wi' thi cricket. Ah've had one like this for a long time, and it hasn't let me down yet.'" It was a barometer – a good one – and Bowes wondered how often the weather glass at Robinson's home had been responsible for Yorkshire putting their opponents in to bat.

Verity's nine for 60 feat against Glamorgan elicited one of Emmott's formidable lectures. "Now look here," he said, "you have what we call a stock delivery – that is your natural ball bowled straightish and on a good length. Well, sometimes you bowl a slower ball and sometimes you bowl a faster ball and, because of that, the place we call good length alters for each ball.

"You've taken nine wickets for 60 runs today. You ought to have had 'em for 20 runs. You are pitching about the same place."

Emmott added: "Now think on – for your bowling you should have three different lengths. Your faster ball wants to pitch a yard shorter than your stock delivery, and your slower ball wants to go a couple of feet farther up." Fine art in bowling, according to Robinson's credo, meant that the length should vary according to speed and it should be combined with direction.

Bowes recalls how his teacher used to say: "For 10 years you learn something new about cricket every day. After that you remember what you've forgotten." Bowes himself encapsulates the philosophy in the neat phrase: "You have a library full of knowledge, but you can only use one book at a time."

In time Hedley Verity was to accumulate his own special wisdom. It was of such profusion that another old friend and England colleague, Charles Barnett, speaks of his debt to Verity's computer-like capacity for storing facts and then spilling them out as preparations for big games. At the beginning of an exciting decade Verity was content to listen and learn. His father remembered the thrill and pleasure of watching Hedley and Wilfred Rhodes deep in conversation and his pride at the interest taken in his son by a supreme bowler.

Rhodes taught Verity all he knew about the game mainly because the two men shared a similar temperament. Both master and pupil were, in Verity senior's words, "silent, impenetrable, persistent and patient." Persistence was one of Verity's leading and occasionally taxing qualities. He so harried George Hirst with his questions that the Yorkshire coach once turned to him and said: "Go on, I've told you all I know. You know as much as I do. It's up to you now to find out for yourself." Hirst later remarked to Verity's father: "He takes it in just like a sponge takes water."

The wicket at Dean Park, Bournemouth on the penultimate stage of Yorkshire's southern tour of 1930 was of the sporting variety. A. T. Barber, the Yorkshire captain, put Hampshire in to bat after winning the toss. There had been a lot of rain in the early morning and for most of the day a powerful sun enabled the bowlers to obtain just the kind of assistance they needed. Verity followed up his feats at Swansea, Hull and Bristol by taking seven wickets for less than four runs each. His figures were: 24.4–11–26–7.

"It was between lunch and tea," wrote one correspondent, "that the full effect of the drying wicket was seen, and it was Verity who made the most of it. Bowling a splendid length and using finger spin to great purpose, he had the Hampshire batsmen in difficulties from the time he took the ball after lunch until he was relieved an hour-and-three-quarters later. His work was truly impressive, and even when he was not taking wickets he deceived the batsmen again and again by his variation of delivery. They did not know whether the ball would spin away or swing in from the off. The suppleness of his action imparted nip to the ball after pitching."

Phil Mead, Hampshire's champion and the lynchpin of the county's batting for 30 years, was one of Verity's prized victims at Bournemouth. Mead was dismissed for nought in the first innings, caught by Mitchell at slip. Verity took his first three wickets for five runs and was on a hat-trick in the second innings. Mead came out to face the challenge and, by Verity's own account, the great man should have departed scoreless again. Verity set his field, ignoring or more probably neglecting Rhodes' advice to place a fieldsman a yard nearer the bat. Mead pushed forward defensively to try and deny the Yorkshire bowler. The ball glanced off his bat and fell precisely, as Wilfred had indicated, a yard short of Mitchell at short square-leg, and the chance was lost. Verity told this story against himself and ruefully said: "Wilfred *knew*."

Verity took another six wickets in the match against Hampshire to achieve notable match figures of 13 wickets for 83 runs. However, before the match was over he had again been taken to task by Emmott Robinson. Robinson and Wilfred Rhodes, too, were not easy men to please. Bill Bowes has related how these Yorkshire elders would sternly point Hedley and himself upstairs for their nightly tactical discussions. "Off we went to the hotel bedroom and there the shaving stick, toothbrush, hairbrush and contents of a dressing-case would be pushed around the eiderdown to represent the fieldsmen as our mistakes of the day were discussed in detail.

"They were hard and demanding taskmasters, but they were right, always right. On the night after Hedley took his seven wickets against Hampshire we found Emmott and Wilfred awaiting us in the lounge when we returned from the cinema. 'We've been waiting a long time – we'd better go, else it'll take till midnight,' Wilfred growled."

What, Bowes wondered, had he done wrong? But there was no comment as they left the lounge and moved upstairs. "We entered Emmott's room, and with a skill born of practice and a thorough appreciation of the job in hand, the masters placed their fieldsmen – the customary toilet articles – in position on the eiderdown. I was convinced I must be the culprit. My bowling figures for that day had shown 20 overs, four maidens, 43 runs and only one wicket."

Verity did not seem in any danger of a reprimand; but Bowes noted that the positions of the toilet articles did not represent the field that he had used that day. "Now then, Hedley," said Emmott, "what did you do today?" Verity smiled complacently and replied: "Seven for 26, Emmott." Robinson struck the woodwork at the foot of the bed in his disgust. "Aye, seven for 26, an'it owt to 'a bin seven for 22. Ah nivver saw such bowlin'. Whativver wa' t'doin to gie Judd that fower?" he asked. In the opinion of Robinson and Rhodes, the batsmen would have had more fours, too, if they had given the thought to their batting that they expected Verity to give to his bowling.

"How could any young man, coming into such an atmosphere, get a swollen head?" asks Bowes. "Yet they were not ogres, and they believed the best time to tell a lad of his failings was when he was riding on top of the world, not when he was down."

Hedley Verity, despite these strictures, was giddily cresting the cricket waves in 1930. *Wisden* thought he was the natural successor to Rhodes and commented: "A notable event in Yorkshire's season – possibly one fraught with great importance to the future of the county – was the appearance of Verity." Lord Hawke, the Yorkshire president, in his review of the season, wrote: "All I hope is that Verity will keep his head and not lose his length, and then he, with Bowes, are the bright hopes of the future for Yorkshire and England."

Wilfred Rhodes, departing the Yorkshire scene amid the unease of his admirers, had made his decision. He had watched and guided Verity through his trial season. To Arthur Booth, Verity's closest rival for the privileged position, he said: "I'm afraid that you've missed the boat. I'm retiring. Hedley's got the job now and I reckon he'll keep it."

Two final words, issued to the Yorkshire committee with all the solemnity of a royal proclamation, sealed Verity's future. "He'll do," said Wilfred, "he'll do."

4

AN "AVALANCHE FROM HEAVEN"

"It was one of those rare days when everything is set right for the bowler at one end, but not for the man at the other end." – Hedley Verity.

HEDLEY Verity did not betray the trust of his master counsellor. In 1931 he began his march to greatness which was to establish him as a conqueror in his own right. It was by any standards a remarkable first season. He took 188 wickets at a cost of 13.52 runs each to head the Yorkshire bowling averages; he was second to Larwood in the national list, but only by 1.30; and he became only the third bowler in the county's history to take all 10 wickets in an innings.

At the start of the season the intense interest displayed in Rhodes' successor promised a searching ordeal. That Verity was able to pass his test with flying colours says much for a stout heart which did not flinch under pressure. One writer commented: "It is no exaggeration to say that not only Yorkshire but all England is watching Verity. Let us hope he emerges triumphantly." Charlie Parker, the Gloucestershire and England bowler, was another of the assembly of cricket jurors. "I watched him carefully," related this wise practitioner, "because he has been called the Rhodes of the future. As a left-arm bowler myself, I can see a great future for Verity. He has not yet the guile of Rhodes, but the promise is there."

At Lord's, in the opening match of the 1931 season, Verity and the newly-capped Bill Bowes, who was playing for the MCC in opposition to Yorkshire, came under keen scrutiny. Both players quickly showed that they had profited from their toils in the nets. While Bowes took the wicket of one of his teachers, Emmott Robinson, Verity finished with five wickets for 42 runs and Yorkshire were denied victory by rain. "Verity kept such a good length on a wicket that was lifeless that he had the batsmen playing all the time and when the wicket changed in the afternoon – and definitely gave the bowlers assistance – he showed his power," commented the *Yorkshire Post*.

Neville Cardus looked on admiringly as Verity moved into action at Lord's and he reacted thus: "He is gifted unmistakably. His left-hand spin was quick and occasionally waspish on a turf that never really got sticky. He has nothing in common with Rhodes, except that they are both left-handers. Even when he has developed into a master – as in time I fancy he will – his style will be entirely different.

"Verity is not a slow bowler in the absolute sense; he varies his pace so much that he can be described as slow medium as truthfully as he can be called slow. He runs to the wicket with free and easy trots; his arm comes well over and his best ball is the classical left-hander's."

Cardus related how Verity dismissed Hendren with his "diploma ball" at Lord's. "It went through the air alluringly, drew Hendren forward, pitched between the middle and leg stumps and then whipped across to the off, finding the edge of Hendren's groping bat and spinning from it to the hands of Holmes at slip. The ancient dodge of the slow left-arm bowler. I can see Peel at it now, with memory's eye, and Briggs, and the incomparable Blythe."

Verity walked, with scarcely a pause in his stride, into the ranks of an illustrious procession. In the opening five matches he took 35 wickets and the proudest moment of all in an eventful season came at Headingley. As the only uncapped member of the Yorkshire side, he claimed 10 wickets for 36 runs against Warwickshire on his 26th birthday.

The 10 wickets' triumph was recorded in Verity's 14th first-class match and 17 years had elapsed since Alonzo Drake had taken all 10 wickets for Yorkshire against Somerset at Weston-super-Mare. There was, perhaps, a fleeting moment of avenging pleasure after his rejection by Warwickshire three years earlier. The sour thought, if it did occur, would have been just as quickly expelled as it flashed across his mind. Of greater significance was the fact that the tumble of wickets had given Yorkshire another victory. "Hedley was impervious to figures," remembers John Kay. "The circumstances of the game and the needs of the team always took priority." Verity, it should also be said, would never admit that he had bowled badly. He would invariably say: "I've bowled better."

The question did not need to be asked on that May day at Headingley. It was emphatically one time when he had "bowled better". Even so, the congratulations did yield the dignified, self-effacing reply. "It was one of those rare days," said Verity, "when everything is set right for the bowler at one end, but not for the man at the other end." He preferred to acknowledge the contribution of his colleagues in the field and the bowling of his partner, George Macaulay, who had sent down 18 overs for 20 runs. Back home at Rawdon the joy was unconcealed. "It's *real*, lad. It's 'istory," they told the modest hero.

Verity's exploit provided a crushing riposte to those critics who had derided the Leeds wicket. "It's as unnatural as ever and it doesn't give the bowlers a chance," they said. Other dismissive observers described it as a "sponge" or "hearth rug" following the opening day of the match when the fast bowlers had failed to extract any response from the wicket.

There were only 4,000 spectators present on this historic day to see the colt Verity accomplish a feat which had eluded his predecessors, Peate, Peel and Rhodes. It was a raw, dull day at Headingley; the spectators were overcoated and others carried rugs as a protection from the breeze which had more than a lingering touch of winter to it. In the early hours of play there was nothing to suggest that a crowning achievement was in the offing. Holmes and Sutcliffe completed their 59th three-figure partnership to help give Yorkshire a lead of 97 runs on the first innings.

The sun was just beginning to push its way through the clouds when the Warwickshire second innings began at a quarter to four. By six o'clock the match was over and Yorkshire had won by an innings and 25 runs. The previously benign wicket was imbued with mischief; the roller had brought moisture to the surface; and a ball from Bowes rose wickedly to strike the shoulder of Warwickshire opener Croom's bat. The omens were good for Yorkshire – and Verity – and Greenwood was swift to recognise the gifts at his disposal. The Yorkshire captain introduced Verity and Macaulay into the attack with the total at 16 and he straightaway took a running catch at mid-on off Verity to dismiss Croom. In Verity's third over Wyatt moved forward purposefully to lift the ball with a tremendous swing of the bat over the rails and almost on the members' stand for six.

"Verity was not worried," reported the *Yorkshire Post* correspondent. "He calmly and cannily went his way, giving the ball the spin the state of the wicket demanded. Now and then he slipped in a faster ball, and all the time he used his command of flight to keep the batsmen wondering.

"Wyatt stepped out twice as though he intended to repeat his earlier stroke, but each time he changed his mind and played safe." Verity's fourth over produced two runs, the fifth was a maiden, and the seventh brought the wickets of Wyatt and Norman Kilner.

The Warwickshire total was 33 when Wyatt struck out viciously again at Verity and Holmes held the catch in the covers. Mitchell had now been moved from the onside to a backward point position not more than four yards from the bat, a position in which he had fielded for Sydney Barnes at the Bradford League club of Saltaire. It was a favourite trap set by Rhodes and now Verity was the beneficiary of Mitchell's athleticism. His new ally pounced to take a catch offered by Kilner. At the tea interval Bates and Parsons were struggling hard against the increasingly confident Verity.

The Warwickshire camp was pitched in gloom, but no-one imagined, least of all one spectator who left at tea to attend to business matters, that the innings would subside so quickly. In the six overs bowled by Verity after the resumption he conceded 13 runs and took two wickets.

At half-past five there was the usual move towards the exit of the members' enclosure. But when Bates' wicket fell, some stopped to watch the next over. This 16th over brought four wickets, all to Verity.

Any thoughts of going home were abandoned. Trains and buses were forgotten. All that mattered was the precious 10th wicket. After Verity had dealt the final blow to crown his own and the crowd's joy, one man summed up the general rejoicing with these words: "I've two hours to wait for my train, but I'm happy. I've waited a lifetime to see this done," he said.

Hedley Verity himself described the 16th over and the crash of wickets which settled the match as an "avalanche from heaven". He was twice denied a hat-trick and the zeal of his execution meant that one wicket remained for him to complete the achievement. The last three overs of the innings plunged him into a lather of anxiety. There was a buzzing noise all round the fringe of the field and Verity realised that a great wave of excitement was surging backwards and forwards across the ground. "It was the greatest test I could have had," he said. "When I caught and bowled the last man, Paine, the walk back to the pavilion seemed to take hours."

Before the astonishing 16th over Verity had almost thrown away the chance of taking all 10 wickets. It showed how much he was immersed in the team effort. His own figures were secondary to the cause. Verity dived at short-leg in an attempt to take a catch off Macaulay. He went to the ground with his right arm stretched out, severely tore the skin, and bowled for the remainder of the innings with the arm bound below the elbow.

Kathleen Verity had intended to watch the match before lunch, but she was deterred by a headache. She found a seat in the afternoon among people who did not know her, and it was not long before the ripple of compliments made her blush with pride. "It is very nice to be a cricketer's wife among a crowd when he is in form," she said. "But then matters might have been the opposite, and the comments would have made me blush just the same."

Grace Verity heard the news of her brother's success at her Rawdon school. She remembers the delight of her headmaster, normally a strict and unemotional man. "He came into the classroom and said: 'Do you know what's happened? Your brother has taken 10 for 36. It's been on the wireless.'"

Typically, the triumph did not interfere with Verity's plans to return home to Rawdon for a birthday party. Amid the congratulations of team-mates and opponents all he had to say was: "It's been a right grand birthday." Typically too, his father tempered his praise with stern words of advice. "You're a famous man now," said Verity senior as his son's praises were sung throughout the country. "You'll have hundreds of new friends all at once. They'll be offering you advice. Well, listen to what they say and thank them kindly. Then come to me and I'll tell you if it's right or not." Later on, when Verity had been selected to play for England, he reminded him of his earlier words, but added: "You'll have more friends than ever, now. Well, do as I said, and please yourself. You know better than I."

At Bradford, one week after his historic feat against Warwickshire, Verity was brought rapidly down to earth by Kent's peerless left-hander, Frank Woolley. Woolley hit 188 out of 270 in two hours and three-quarters. His score included four sixes off Verity and three more off Robinson and Bowes. The hero of Headingley trooped off the field at Park Avenue with a less appealing set of figures – 0 -70.

Les Ames, the former Kent and England wicket-keeper, recalls the ferocity of the Woolley innings on a sticky wicket. "Frank had never seen Verity before and when I came into bat he said: 'I don't know who this left-hander is, but he's a good bowler. You'd better stay down at the other end and I'll try and look after this fellow.'" Ames says Woolley did stay at Verity's end for most of the Kent innings. "Frank kept on hitting Hedley with the tide all the time. He was that kind of player, he would always take a chance. If a bowler was bowling well, he would have a go. But for Frank we wouldn't have got a hundred against Hedley on that wicket."

Woolley rode his luck – he was twice missed in the deep by Mitchell and Oldroyd – but this was a superb piece of batsmanship. He was as merciless as he was brilliant and Verity's first 10 overs cost about six runs each. At least four of Woolley's mighty sixes rattled the ball on the tiles of the football stand roof. Arthur Wood, the Yorkshire wicket-keeper, said they reminded him of the drumbeats of a boy scouts' band – rat-a-tat-tat, rat-a-tat-tat! Two other of Woolley's six-hits had they been straighter would have landed on the adjoining football field itself. The last of the sixes, struck from the pavilion end, sent the ball careering against the ridge of ornamental tiles on the point of the stand roof. The secret of all the towering shots – and at least six of the Kent batsman's 16 fours only just failed to clear the boundary by a yard or two – was perfect timing.

Hedley Verity was subdued by a batting master at Bradford, but there was no shame in this lesson. In maturer days he also suffered at the hands of other fine stroke-players, Eddie Paynter, South Africa's Herbie Cameron and Hugh Bartlett. Bartlett, a tall-scoring Sussex batsman and a protégé of Woolley, hit Verity for six 6's in two overs at Headingley in his peak year, 1938. He scored 94 in 75 minutes before being caught by Maurice Leyland on the long-off boundary. Bartlett, a London stock-broker, today remembers being "drained with emotion" as he was roared back to the pavilion by an appreciative Yorkshire crowd. The sequel to the innings was the award of his Sussex county cap. The award sealed the promise made to him by the county captain, A. J. Holmes during the journey up to Yorkshire. "If you score 50 I will give you your cap," said Holmes. "A 50 against them is worth 100 against any other county."

Verity recognised that these batting thrusts were the inescapable lot of the slow bowler and even relished them as a counterpoise to other days when he perhaps sighed at the ease of his conquests. The judgement over the years is that he was happier when he won his battles in less favourable conditions and against the major players of his time. He revelled in the sheer joy of bowling for bowling's sake. "It is a joy that grows and intensifies to an amazing extent when you are given the ball and the role of the matchwinner is yours," he once said.

Verity's stirring performances in 1931 were rewarded with England caps against New Zealand at the Oval and Manchester. He also represented the Players against the Gentlemen in matches at the Oval, Lord's and Scarborough. By the end of the season he had bowled well over 1,000 overs and had four times taken 10 or more wickets in a match and 18 times five or more in an innings.

He was watched in the Warwickshire match at Headingley by a member of the Test selection committee. The presence of the Test selector was noted by the *Leeds Mercury* and provoked the querulous comment: "Although Verity is now looked upon as a regular member of the Yorkshire eleven, so far he has not been awarded his colours. Are we going to have him bowling for England before he has been granted recognition by his county?"

Verity's merits were acknowledged by the award of his county cap on

June 13, just about a year after he had begun to play in the aggressively competitive Yorkshire team. A month later a letter arrived from Pelham Warner, the chairman of the Test selectors, inviting him to play against New Zealand at the Oval. His fee for the match was £20 plus a third class railway fare.

At the beginning of July Verity took 11 wickets for Yorkshire against the tourists at Harrogate. The match was left drawn with Yorkshire 46 short of victory after being set a challenging target of 238 runs in two and a half hours. Before his Test debut Verity had taken over 100 wickets at a cost of 13 runs each. He was one of four changes in the England team at the Oval after Tom Lowry's New Zealanders had shared the honours at Lord's. The quality of their play in the only scheduled Test match brought an extension of the series to include two other Tests.

Sutcliffe, Duleepsinhji and Hammond scored centuries at the Oval before England declared at 416 for four. New Zealand were dismissed for 193 and 197 and lost by an innings and 26 runs. The decisive bowling thrust was made by Gubby Allen who took five wickets for 14 runs, including four for four in one spell, in the first innings. Verity had match figures of four wickets for 75 runs in 35 overs.

"Verity," said the *Cricketer*, in its comments on the match, "will be even better when he puts his right foot further towards cover point when delivering the ball. At present he bowls too full-fronted, but his run-up to the crease is beautiful. He bowls off his toes – and he can spin the ball." Verity was again selected for the third Test at Manchester where he did not bowl in a rain-affected match.

Wisden selected Verity, along with his Yorkshire colleague, Bill Bowes, as one of its "Five Cricketers of the Year." In making the award, the following verdict was expressed: "There is no doubt that in once again carrying off the championship, Yorkshire owed a great deal to the fine work accomplished by their left-arm bowler. It is greatly in his favour that, unspoilt by success, he realises that he still has a good deal to learn, particularly in the subtle variation of his pace and flight, which can only come by continuous practice."

Cricket, for Hedley Verity, glittered with the heroics of fiction in 1932. For the second time in consecutive seasons, he took all 10 wickets in an innings against Nottinghamshire at Headingley on July 12. His figures of 10 wickets for 10 runs are still a world record. They surpassed George Geary's 10 for 18 for Leicester against Glamorgan at Pontypridd three years earlier. That evening a Yorkshire newspaper declared: "Verity of Verities, all is Verity" and the *Sphere* produced the classic line: "*Magnus est Verity et preavalebit.*"

The seeds of the Notts' debacle lay in the thunderstorm which had raged over Leeds on the previous afternoon. Pace had devastated Yorkshire in their first innings and one writer commented: "It will be bad luck for Notts if the rain continues to prevent any more play in this match in which the bowling of Larwood and Voce has given them such a big advantage."

Hedley Verity senior recalled: "When I reached the ground on the Tuesday morning people were standing around discussing the prospects. All were agreed that if play was possible, we should have some interesting, if not sensational cricket." Play did begin at 12.30 and Brian Sellers, the Yorkshire captain, immediately declared with his team's total at 163 for 9 to concede a deficit of 71 runs.

The absurdity of the gamble caught the breath as did similar daring by a man close to Sellers in temperament, Stuart Surridge during Surrey's great years in the 1950s. Sellers, like Surridge, had two spinning aces at his command. And in Hedley Verity he had a bowler, who perhaps more than any other of his time summoned every ounce of energy in a crisis. "If you wanted the best out of Hedley," says Bill Bowes, "you told him it all depended upon him." Verity never failed to respond to this trick. It stung his vanity as an artist.

Yorkshire looked set for a wearying and unprofitable afternoon as Keeton and Shipston doggedly took root. Notts had clearly declined the challenge. Verity bowled nine successive maiden overs before conceding a run and the game seemed to be wending its way quietly to a draw.

Verity senior watched the gentle flow of the match in company with a group of Rawdon friends. He remained confident that the stalemate would be broken. His son said later that all he could hope for before lunch was to keep the batsmen quiet while the wicket was drying out. "Afterwards," he said, "it was a different matter. The sun came to my aid just long enough to make things difficult and, well, I took advantage of it. I was able to get sufficient spin on the ball to prevent the batsmen settling down."

On the boundary the Rawdon clan fretted with impatience. Verity senior listened to their grumbles and said: "You need not bother at all until Hedley brings up a second slip. Then you can sit up and take notice." Another man, more intent on the game than the others, suddenly exclaimed excitedly: "My, that one one turned." Immediately the eyes of the Rawdon spectators turned eagerly to the play. The conversation stopped and the attentive men leaned forward on their seats. Mitchell had been brought up to reinforce the slips.

Verity's first two overs after lunch were maidens and off the third ball of the third Shipston took two runs. Another maiden followed and then the first wicket fell to the first ball of Verity's fifth over. The total was 44 and Keeton was caught by Macaulay at slip. He had scored 21 and so had Shipston when three runs later he was caught at the wicket off the second ball of the left-hander's seventh over. The next victim was Arthur Carr, the visiting captain and one of three Notts batsmen to be dismissed twice without scoring in the match. He was caught, as in the first innings, by Barber in front of the sightscreen after attempting a six-hit.

According to Bill Bowes, Carr stormed back to the dressing-room, collected his bag and all his equipment and threw them into the professionals' room. "Here, take the lot," he said. "It's a hell of a lot of good to me when I get a pair!" It was the second time that season that he had disposed of his kit in anger. On the first occasion he had returned the next day to rescue his equipment. "This time he didn't get a chance," says Bowes. "It went irretrievably."

Carr's wicket fell at 51 but Arthur Staples and Walker took the score to 63. Verity started his 10th over with a full toss which Staples hit for three runs and off the fourth ball of that over Walker collected another run. The second, third and fourth balls of the 11th over produced Verity's first hat-trick. Walker was brilliantly caught at slip by Macaulay; Harris fell to a catch at backward point by Holmes; and Gunn was lbw to a straight ball which was flighted to deceive him. In Macaulay's next over Arthur Staples took a single and Verity ended his 12th over by having Staples taken at slip and persuading Larwood to loft a catch to Sutcliffe at extra cover. The stage was set for another hat-trick in Verity's next over, but Lilley edged the ball clear of his stumps to score three runs. Voce actually played the next ball comfortably in the middle of the bat, which was quite a feat in the prevailing panic, before he was caught by Holmes. All that now remained was for Wood to provide a triumphant flourish and scatter the bails to stump Sam Staples.

Verity bowled 113 balls without a run being scored off him on this thrilling day at Headingley. He conceded the 10 runs in four overs; the other seven he bowled after lunch were all maidens. The analysis shows that 15 deliveries gave him seven wickets for three runs, including the hat-trick. The 10 victims, all but one of whom had made a first-class century, went down for 23 runs in 65 minutes. "Verity, using the priceless gift that is the slow left-hand bowler's, made the ball turn quickly after lunch," reported the *Yorkshire Post*. "He made it spring sharply out of the cup its spin created when the ball pitched and the Notts batsmen, playing back defensively, did the rest. He was the master with the control of spin and flight and a responsive pitch." Holmes and Sutcliffe needed only 95 minutes to score the 139 runs for a 10-wicket victory. "There could be no miraculous change in the wicket to account for, much less to excuse, the vast difference between the batting performances," was the gloating verdict of another Yorkshire observer. At the end of the day scorecards were bought as souvenirs by spectators as fast as they could be printed. Hedley Verity, as the hero of the hour, was besieged in the pavilion. Hundreds of people clamoured for his autograph. He signed as many as possible until he finally said they would have to wait for another day.

"The achievement proves", the *Yorkshire Post* enthused the following morning, "not so much the possession of technical skill and artifice as the gift of that natural skill which is the indispensable foundation for artifice and for great bowling. Verity does one thing supremely well; he bowls the left-hander's 'going away' ball irresistibly, as none has since the great Rhodes.

"He is also mastering those subtleties which make slow bowlers independent of the weather; perhaps that is of more importance to Verity, as the England bowler in Australia we hope to see him, than even such a resounding feat as yesterday's. There is another aspect of the matter: to take an opportunity with both hands, to make the utmost of it, demands those qualities of resolution and self-certainty on which greatness must be founded."

It is interesting to reflect that in neither of Verity's 10-wicket feats against Warwickshire and Nottinghamshire did he once hit the stumps. He obtained his wickets each time with the ball pitched on the leg stump or leg and middle stumps which spun away in rising flight. Others would later comment on the part that Verity's height as well as his finger spin played in his major successes. Curiously, the performances against the two teams were identical; eight of the batsmen were caught; one was stumped and the other leg-before-wicket.

As a postscript to the Notts match, it should be noted that George Macaulay, the bowler at the other end, refused to bowl wide of the stumps as Verity approached his record. "If he's good enough to get nine, let him earn the 10th. I shall get it if I can," said Macaulay.

Hedley Verity's associates had bluntly told him at the outset of the 1932 season that he would need to produce an outstanding qualification, something really special, if he was to achieve his next ambition – a trip to Australia. After his performance against Nottinghamshire, there was little doubt that his ambition would be fulfilled, beginning an era of prized and challenging contests against the magnificent Australian batsman, Don Bradman.

The steel of Verity's temperament was subjected to its sternest trial in the Test arena and his rivalry with Bradman became the talk of the cricketing world. Jim Kilburn said the honours between the two men were not so much divided as added together, bowling enhanced by the power in the batting and batting elevated by the skill and persistence of the bowling.

"I could never claim," wrote Bradman, "to have completely fathomed Hedley's strategy, for it was never static or mechanical." It was no idle tribute. Don Bradman did not fumble about after courtesies with either the pen or the bat.

5

LETTERS FROM A
FAMOUS SON

IN the winter of 1932–3, after only two full seasons in first-class cricket, Verity was chosen to tour Australia under the leadership of Douglas Jardine. Though this was his first tour, Verity was 27 and thoughtful enough to appreciate how much the honour meant not just to himself, but to his family and friends. He therefore decided before his departure to record his impressions of the tour in a diary.

Verity's selection, along with three other Yorkshiremen, Herbert Sutcliffe, Maurice Leyland and Bill Bowes, meant a lot to the people of Yorkshire too. A surging throng of around 5,000 people gathered at Leeds Central Station to voice their pride in a grand farewell to England's Yorkshire contingent. Shortly before the departure day, Verity had been greatly honoured to receive a visit from his boyhood idol and former tutor, Wilfred Rhodes, who offered encouragement and advice. At the station itself, another of the great Yorkshire left-arm bowlers, Bobby Peel, a bright-eyed 70-year-old, presented each of the Yorkshire tourists with a white rose. Like his colleagues, Verity much appreciated this gesture of goodwill.

Entries in the diary start on board *RMS Orontes* on September 17, 1932, when Hedley records with a note of surprise that "the ship is perfectly steady, just like an hotel", and continues to bubble with the wide-eyed naivety and enthusiasm of a schoolboy on his first trip down the river.

"This is a truly wonderful experience for anyone," he records after two days. "It will be a wonderful holiday and education apart from the cricket." A day later he gleefully notes after a slightly rough crossing of the Bay of Biscay: "We have three in bed, Larwood, Paynter and Mitchell."

On the morning of September 21, they sight Africa: "A glance through my porthole on the starboard side on waking up at 6.30 a.m., and there in the early sunlight is Africa. Up and on deck straightaway."

Occasionally Verity reveals a touch of the "Englishman abroad". His first impression of Toulon, for example, is "how like Plymouth". From Gibraltar and Toulon, the *Orontes* steams on to Naples, where the party spent a day sightseeing in Pompeii, through the narrow straits between Italy and Sicily and on into the Red Sea.

"The doctor was at my table," Verity records cheerfully, "and he tells me that three stewards died on this trip last year from the heat." On October 8, the *Orontes* arrived at Colombo where the custom was for the touring team to play a game against the national team.

"The setting for the match was, to me, the most remarkable thing," Verity relates. "A decent-sized crowd, about 7,000, mostly native, although nearly all the English population turned up. A background of vivid green trees, coconut and palm, planted along the roads which run round the ground, every tree full of natives who have climbed up to see the match. A crowd which makes a great noise on the slightest provocation . . . ."

After nearly a month on board, Verity is still intrigued despite the monotony of the voyage. "Same uneventful round," he writes on October 12, "yet always interesting. That sounds funny, but I find endless interest in watching weather, fish, cloud, angles of sun, all strange to me."

Exactly a month after the day of departure, the *Orontes* docked in Fremantle. The serious business was about to begin. "It seems a pity to finish the voyage," writes Verity.

As they crowded the quayside to greet the MCC party, the Australian cricket public remembered the successes of another left-arm bowler, Jack White, of Somerset, on the previous England tour in 1928-9. But they were sceptical about the prospects of the untried Hedley Verity after only two seasons in first-class cricket. He was a Test novice despite the spurring rattle of English wickets in conditions more sympathetic to his craft.

Verity himself knew how much he would need to learn before he could even hope to be successful where so many slow bowlers had failed. Years later he said: "To a bowler, cricket in Australia means hard work and plenty of it. The wickets there are a batsman's paradise." John Kay says that Verity acknowledged that he would be a workhorse on overseas tours. "He knew that was why he was picked; but he never shirked the task and he was never happy out of the side."

The widely held opinion in Australia was that Verity would pose few problems because of the readiness of their batsmen, following Bradman's example, to go out and slaughter slow bowling. Bradman felt that Verity might prove useful on a "suitable wicket", but he could not envisage a place for him in the Test eleven. On arrival in Australia Verity instantly quelled the criticism not only by bowling so tightly as to keep his opponents wary of him, but by the splendid stamina he showed himself to possess in long spells.

As his diaries show, Verity had difficulty in coming to terms with Perth where the tourists drew their opening match against Western Australia. "Perth appears to be a new city," he writes, "with modern streets and banks and businesses . . . but the bush starts straight outside. One sees men riding into town on horseback, and saddlers' shops are plentiful. The town is the capital of Western Australia, yet trains leave here only twice a week."

After trips into the bush and to York races, Verity's tour began in earnest in the match against a strong Combined Australian XI. He took seven wickets for 37 runs, the first six in succession after the MCC had merrily totalled 583. Bradman was one of his victims and one of the marvels of the day was that the great Australian was twice dismissed, the second time by Allen, for a combined total of 13 runs. Bradman's failures, astounding to his countrymen, were not revealed until the evening because gales had caused a complete breakdown in telegraphic communications. Gubby Allen recalls that this curtain-raiser match was used by Australia to, in theory, allow their batsmen to obtain some practice. Fingleton, Richardson and McCabe as well as Bradman played in the match at Perth and they must have been highly displeased to have their practice so rudely interrupted.

Allen says that the MCC were keeping their fast bowlers "hidden from Bradman". In the event, they were not missed as Verity dug deep into his bowling repertoire. Overnight, the Australians had scored 59 without loss, but the wickets tumbled as soon as play was resumed on a rain-damaged wicket. After taking Fingleton's wicket in his first over, Verity shocked the spectators by dismissing Bradman in his second over. "Fifteen thousand people stood up to cheer the small, compact and blue-capped Bradman as he walked to the crease," related one writer. "They gasped with disbelief as Hammond, in the slips, was seen to dive forward with the ball in his hand. Bradman was out for three. The crowd uttered a big sigh as Bradman returned to the pavilion at a jog-trot instead of his usual crawl."

The Australian eleven were bowled out for 159 and lost another four wickets in the follow-on. "We caught them on a turner," says Allen.

"Bradman was beautifully caught, one-handed, by Wally off Hedley at first slip. He made it look so easy." Jack Hobbs, who was reporting on the game, said it would have been no catch at all to anyone else in the side.

October 29: I am writing this on the train bound for Adelaide, after a full day's cricket. We got a sticky wicket and I had an excellent return of 7 for 37. The match was drawn. Visited the trotting races at night, leaving Perth at 10.30 p.m. These trains are very primitive. There are two trains per week on this 2,000-miles run (the journey to Adelaide involved three nights on the trans-Australian express). The track is unballasted for long stretches. The dining car only holds about 40 persons. The train goes jolting and rolling along, so much so that one is apt to get jumped out of bed in the night.

October 30: When we awoke this morning we were well into the bush. Hour after hour the same landscape. You cannot imagine the extent of it. All ideas of distance must be revised. Even the trees are getting more stunted and scarce, low scrub and undergrowth taking their place. Now everything is sandy and dry, barren and sun-parched.

A pipeline runs alongside the railway, which conveys water to Kalgoorlie, which place we reached this afternoon. Kalgoorlie was once one of the most prosperous gold-mining towns in the world. We passed several large mines in the district and very many small shafts – mere holes in the ground – some of them no longer in use. The mayor greeted us, and a large crowd of people was on the platform. We only stayed 10 minutes but had a peep out of the station; what we saw was the usual backwoods town: corrugated iron buildings, verandahs with tethering rails for horses, wide but unpaved streets. The mayor of Kalgoorlie told me that he walked to this place 40 years ago – 400 miles through the bush with the gold rush. A big, bearded man, he looks the part.

October 31: During the day we saw several mirages, and they certainly look like the real thing. On foot here a man would never have a chance. It is hot during the day and cold at night; no water, nothing but what appears to be an endless stretch of sand and scrub – saltbush is the name given to it.

Adelaide, November 2: There was a civic reception in the Town Hall today. The building is large, the room where the reception took place was larger and as imposing as Leeds Town Hall, and was packed to the doors. Good speeches were made by everybody. In the afternoon we had some practice. The cricket ground here is good, a green outfield as good as any in England, the wicket, as usual, the bare, black shining one of Australia. The practice wickets are very good, and a large crowd of barrackers were even there for practice, and kept up a running commentary. Adelaide is a very nice town. Big buildings, wide streets, everything a modern city desires. Plenty of parks and open spaces, most of them lined with palm or other sub-tropical trees. There is a line of hills to the north and east, too, which add to the beauty of pleasant surroundings.

November 3: Practice morning and afternoon. Pictures at night by invitation. The cricket ground is set in beautiful surroundings, and is much better appointed than any in England except Lord's, and will hold large crowds comfortably. They have one of the famous Australian scoreboards here, one that records everything.

At Adelaide the tourists again showed excellent batting form, and after declaring at 634 for 9, they secured an easy victory by an innings and 128 runs. Verity mystified his opponents once again to claim five wickets for 42 runs in 25 overs. More than half his overs were maidens which indicated the extent of his dominance. His figures on the final day were even more impressive than the full analysis. They read: 0–13.6; M–7; R–19; W–4. The Australian cricket devotees were by this time taking serious notice of him. "The South Australian innings," reported one newspaper, "crumbled before the steady assurance of the Yorkshire left-hander."

Douglas Jardine said that Verity, as White had done before him, quickly discovered and was able to exploit the extra margin of error which a slow bowler is given in Australia. Both players responded to the different concept of length bowling brought about by the pace of the pitches. "Instead of a patch of approximately five feet in length they are afforded nearly double that distance," commented the England captain.

November 7: I bowled unchanged until lunch and kept everybody quiet. I put the brake on, and in the innings got three for 45, bowling 28 eight-ball overs. Brown bowled very well and the Australians were out for 290. Following on, we got two of their second innings wickets for 103 before stumps were drawn.

November 8: Continued our attack and got them all out for 218, winning by an innings. Again I was in good form, and by accurate length and flighting, an occasional ball turning as well, I managed to return: 25 overs, 5 for 42. Bill Bowes bowled well. The weather is very hot.

November 9: Today it was so hot (97 degrees in the shade) that we spent all the morning and afternoon bathing at Glenelg; we stayed until train time for Melbourne, and the water was very welcome.

November 10: Our train was running into Melbourne as I awoke this morning. After breakfast we attended three receptions and a lunch, cricket practice in the afternoon, followed by official attendance at the Opera House at night, to see a performance of "The Gondoliers" by the D'Oyly Carte Opera Company. The cricket ground here is not beautiful but very efficient. Double-decker stands, Australian score-boards and accommodation for 70,000 people.

November 17: Melbourne is a well-planned town. All streets are straight and cross each other at right angles. Buildings are not put down anywhere, anyhow, but all in proper order. Many of the new ones are like American skyscrapers. As I was returning from the ground through the park, I saw some birds catching and eating beetles alive. They are not like English beetles, but much larger, about 1½ to 2 inches in the body, and can fly. Some of our chaps have been bitten by mosquitoes this last day or two.

November 18–19: I am not playing in the match against an Australian XI. Allen played a good, forcing knock, and our total reached 282. Our battery of fast bowlers then started, but were very unlucky for a long time. Bowes got Woodfull lbw at 72, however, and Don Bradman arrived. He was soon making some brilliant but rash shots, eventually being lbw to Larwood's good length one. He sat back expecting the bouncer. It looked to me as if he was rattled, a state of mind that may be a big help to us in the Test matches.

November 23: The weather is unsettled. Lightning during the morning. We left for Sydney at 5.30 p.m., our journey taking us through sheep farms and wheat country. My first impression of Sydney is that of a big city, modern and Americanised. From the window of our hotel we can see the famous bridge, and part of the equally famous harbour. It is easily the largest and best city we have so far visited. I had a look at the bridge at night. It is a fine sight and a great piece of engineering. From the top of it you get a good view of the harbour, a magnificent natural harbour. It is over a mile to walk across the bridge.

November 25: The match with New South Wales begins today. Our skipper lost the toss. McCabe and Fingleton made a good stand, but our fast stuff upset everybody else and they were all out for 273. A great day for us on that wicket. I bowled six overs for 30, McCabe getting 18 off one over. I am afraid I hardly fulfilled my job of quietening them while the fast bowlers rested.

November 26: Sutcliffe and Wyatt carried their score to over 100 for the first wicket this morning. Wyatt lbw 72. At close of play Sutcliffe was still not out for 155. A great and chanceless innings. O'Reilly was the best bowler; medium pace and keeps a good length, leg-break action, but the ball never or rarely turned, often running into the batsman.

November 27: Went for a motor trip round the coast, both north and south, during the day. The coastline is a succession of lovely bays and inlets, golden sands and great 'bush' to the edge of it. We had a dip at Palm Beach, 14 miles away from Sydney. Everybody bathes out here at the weekends, it is so hot. The beaches are full of people in swimming costumes, no-one thinks of being dressed.

The view that there would be no place for Verity in the England team proved to be a mistaken one. He was chosen, in recognition of his splendid bowling at Perth and Adelaide, for the first Test at Sydney. He bowled 17 overs in Australia's two innings but his perseverance brought no reward. The Yorkshire bowler should, however, have obtained his first Test wicket in Australia on the fourth day. Ames made a rare blunder and failed to stump Nagel off Verity's bowling. The next ball yielded one run and robbed England of an innings victory. The formalities had to wait until the following morning when England required only nine balls to take the last Australian wicket and one other ball to win by 10 wickets.

December 2: The morning of the Test match opened fine and warm amid considerable excitement. Our team was only announced at 11 o'clock. I just got last place in preference to Brown and Tate (three of us for it). Jardine lost the toss and we went out to field on a beautiful Sydney wicket of easy pace. Voce and Larwood bowled magnificently, Allen fast. All I had to do was to bowl a few overs occasionally – to rest the others – for as few runs as possible.

December 3: The crowd made more noise than I have ever heard outside an F.A. Cup final. The Australian score of 360 was better than appeared likely at one time, but not a formidable one by any means on this wicket. McCabe, not out, played a really great innings, one to be classed among the greatest in these encounters. Sutcliffe and Hammond are still together at the close of play, with the total at 252 for 1. The match looks to be ours. . . . O'Reilly, whom we thought might be our main source of trouble, has been punished and subdued by Sutcliffe.

December 6: Our last four wickets fell before lunch, O'Reilly doing the damage. Our total: 524. Larwood again bowled finely and very fast, and got five wickets for 29 runs, making 10 wickets for the match. We could not break the last-wicket partnership. I gave away 15 runs trying to get the wicket. Rather a bad match for me. The wicket was still good at the end of the day. The Australians don't shape at all at the quick stuff bowled at leg and middle to a leg trap.

Hobart, Tasmania, December 21: Bill Bowes and I set off by tramcar to the outskirts of the town, and then climbed Mount Wellington on foot. About half-an-hour's walking brings us to a gully by a stream. We follow this for three or four miles, climbing steeply all the time; our track, crossing and recrossing the stream, reveals one cascade after another, tumbling noisily from the rocks below. The whole stream and our path is dark, the sun being excluded by dense sub-tropical vegetation and tremendous overhanging trees. . . . As the timber thins out in the last two miles an amazing panorama greets us. Below – ever so far below – can be seen Hobart; slightly to the left, beyond the harbour, from left to right of the picture, we can see three ranges of hills, all virgin forest, merging into the open sea, on the right.

December 23: Cricket! We lost the toss against Tasmania and went out to field on a beautiful wicket. I was first change and got a wicket first ball, heavy and persistent rain ending play for the day in the same over. A real Manchester day.

December 24: The ground was literally under water and unfit for play, but the umpires said it was. It was impossible to stand, and the ball splashed water and mud every time it dropped. No regular bowlers were put on. Tasmania declared their innings at 5 p.m., having scored 103 for five wickets. We got 56 for no wickets by the close. A Christmas Eve to be remembered.

December 25: We are invited to go for a picnic and drive to Port Arthur – the old convict settlement – by some people staying at our hotel. We started off at 8 a.m., having breakfast in the bush 20 miles away from any human habitation. We cleared a likely spot on the mountain-side, put up blankets to break the cold wind which was blowing; lit a fire, and cooked bacon and eggs, steak, etc – a novel Christmas breakfast.

December 26: The wicket had dried out over the weekend. Wyatt was out for 51, total 90. Everybody got a few except the skipper and Paynter: Ames, 56, Leyland, 67, while I played for 54 not out. The skipper declared with the score at 330 at the tea interval, and Bill Bowes got four wickets. I only bowled four overs. There was a dance at night to close our Christmas celebrations. The weather is like an English July day, hot sun tempered by a breeze from the sea.

December 27: Left Hobart at 9 a.m. for Launceston, returning by the same route as we came, boarding the S.S. Mariana at 2.30 for the mainland. A freshening breeze and squalls of rain at about 3 p.m., as we went down the river, gave promise of a rough night, a promise soon fulfilled. As soon as we left the river we got the full force of the gale and heavy seas. Dinner over, I went on deck and stayed there in spite of everything until 9.30, being one of the last to go below. We pitched and rolled; shipped seas over the front; and spray continually swept the boat deck and went right over the top of the funnels. I became sick on going to bed. Down below all night: pitch and toss; groans from every timber and plate; a sudden jerk and splash; followed by rumbles overhead as we hit and shipped a heavy sea, which went the length of the deck. The gale was still blowing strong when we entered the Heads of Melbourne at 6 a.m., and quietly steamed up the bay to the harbour, arriving 9.10 a.m. – an hour late.

December 28: A quiet morning on reaching the hotel.

Bill Bowes replaced Verity in the second Test at Melbourne and achieved the signal feat of bowling Bradman with his first ball in Test cricket. But there was an ironic outcome to the substitution. England needed only 251 runs to win but lost by 111 and O'Reilly and Iron-monger, two spinners, were Australia's matchwinners. O'Reilly had match figures of 10 for 129 and Ironmonger, making the ball lift and turn abruptly, took four wickets for 26 runs in England's second innings. Verity, in his account of the match, declared that O'Reilly should be classed in the best of company. "He varies his pace between medium and slow and bowls a fast one. As he can make the ball turn either way on a wicket giving him any assistance, it would appear that he is a godsend to Australia at the moment. On good wickets his leg-break does not turn, but he is very accurate and runs the ball into the batsman. Today he was never mastered; held in check at times, but he always persisted and ultimately triumphed."

The belief persists that Verity's figures on this Australian tour, though good, might have been even better had he not been omitted from the Melbourne Test. His record of 11 Test wickets for just over 24 runs each was impressive considering the circumstances of the tour. Verity bowled 135 eight-ball overs, including 54 maidens, for 271 runs to concede only 2.01 runs per over in the series and he was second to Larwood in the averages. In all first-class matches Verity headed the MCC averages with 44 wickets at an average of less than 16 runs each. Larwood, with 49 wickets (average: 16.67); Allen, with 39 wickets (23.05) and Voce, with 32 wickets (27.06) were all placed behind him on this fast bowlers' tour.

Verity was restored to the side for the remaining Tests, but his bowling was eclipsed by his batting until he routed a demoralised Australia in the final Test at Sydney. He scored 45 and 40 in crucial stands of 96 and 98 with Paynter and Ames at Adelaide. He also had the fillip of Bradman's wicket when he caught and bowled the Australian in the second innings. It was interestingly, as with Bowes, his first wicket against Australia. "Bradman could not master Larwood," commented one writer, "but he had a liking for Verity's slows. One ball which he slammed to the boundary bounced into a group of screaming girls." Bradman completed his 50 in 63 minutes and, at this point, had scored eight boundaries. Another big hit off Verity resulted in a glorious six over long-on.

"Verity had, however, lured Bradman into a false sense of security," continued the report. "Bradman tried another big hit off the next ball, failed to connect properly and only succeeded in returning the ball to the bowler, who made a fine catch."

Bob Wyatt tells the story of another duel with Bradman on the 1932–3 tour in a match against New South Wales at Sydney. "I was captaining the side and after rain overnight Verity and I went out to inspect the wicket. Hedley pressed his thumb into the turf and said: 'Poor Don'. "'Poor Don' came in," says Wyatt, "and proceeded to make a very rapid 70. Hedley was never allowed to forget that incident."

Wyatt praises Bradman as the greatest run-getter of all time. "Don, unlike others, including Jack Hobbs, never gave his wicket away. He would be taking fresh guard at 200." He was less impressed by the Australian in difficult conditions. "I only saw him get runs on two wet wickets, at Sydney against Verity and against Wilfred Rhodes at Scarborough. Each time he did not play like Hobbs or Hammond but had a go and rode his luck." Wyatt adds the rider: "Mind you, he hadn't had a lot of experience on wet wickets and he might (Bowes and Verity thought he did) have developed into a good player on such wickets."

Larwood's magnificent effort on the second day of the fourth Test at Brisbane in which he took four wickets for 31 runs brought about the collapse of Australia. It was a day of gruelling heat and Jardine said that Larwood was indebted to "Verity's extraordinary accurate bowling" at the other end. "Verity bowled 27 overs for 39 runs, and though he did not get a wicket, no batsman played him with confidence," said Jardine.

Brisbane, February 11: I awoke this morning, bedclothes and pyjamas wet through the heat. Paynter was taken ill last night. Fever from mosquito bite and effects of the sun. The doctor suspects tonsillitis, too. The hot night has not improved his condition, and I am afraid he is definitely out of it for a few days. Larwood and Allen opened our attack. Larwood, in his third over, bowled Bradman. With a legside field he was backing away to cut the ball. Ponsford followed next over, bowled behind his legs. I am now doing my quietening stuff again, after Hammond had bowled two overs at the left-handers, Darling and

Bromley. Allen relieved Larwood when he tired and had Darling caught straightaway by Ames. 292 for 6 was a great and badly-needed recovery. We are now trying hard to follow it up. After lunch the Australian innings soon closed, although Bromley hit a few flashy shots. They were all out for 340 – a good, but not a winning score. I had none for 39, in 27 overs, and did my quietening job adequately.

Verity had another reason to remember the Brisbane Test with pleasure, for he took part in another vital batting partnership with Eddie Paynter. "At the close of play on the Saturday, Paynter had retired to hospital with a severe attack of tonsillitis, and I was informed that there was not the least chance of his being able to play on the Monday," wrote Jardine.

"Good sometimes comes out of ill, and though Paynter should certainly have reported to me that he was not fit – for he was feeling far from well before the commencement of play – it is hard to blame over-keenness at any time, and quite impossible on this occasion in view of his subsequent memorable performance."

Jardine added: "When I called at the hospital to see him on the Sunday he was looking much better, and was the first to agree with me that if he had to 'break bounds' and bat on crutches he would do so, were it humanly possible, and without a thought for the consequences."

Bob Wyatt is on record as saying that Jardine angrily commanded Voce, who was not playing in the match, to fetch Paynter from his sickbed to the ground. That Jardine should have issued such an instruction without a further check with the hospital on his colleague's condition seems unpardonable, but perhaps the England captain was distracted by his team's health in the Test. Another account relates that Paynter began to "betray symptoms of ominous restlessness", as he listened to the radio commentary intoning the news of the decline of the England innings.

Paynter himself remembered the unpleasantness of running a temperature in stifling bake-oven heat; his swollen glands and the pain of trying to swallow; and his agony in lying in bed and being told at far too frequent intervals of England's batting reverses.

"Wickets were falling at such short intervals that I felt the smallest contribution would be acceptable to my team to make a respectable reply to Australia's first innings total of 340," said Paynter. He told the hospital matron that he was going to the ground. "All right," she said, "but you do it on your own responsibility. And, remember, come straight back at the finish."

At the ground Paynter hardly had time to buckle on his pads when a roar from the crowd announced that another wicket – Allen's and England's sixth – had fallen. Ames, England's last recognised batsman, was briskly swept aside, but Larwood and Paynter added 55 for the eighth wicket before Verity joined the Lancastrian.

February 13: Larwood was sent in to hit while the bowling was tired, getting 23 before being bowled by McCabe. Paynter, in the meantime, had blocked up one end for some time. I joined him, staying until the close of play. 271 for 8 – a bad day for us. Our hopes of a winning lead not only gone, but in grave danger of defeat. There is nothing in the wicket to account for the collapse. O'Reilly had, of course, bowled wonderfully well; his three for 91 at the moment does not flatter him, as we never got on top of him all day. He is proving a thorn in the flesh in every Test, even when large scores are made he always makes us fight all the way. As at Melbourne, our batting proved irresolute in the face of a determined attack, particularly the middle portion. A golden opportunity has gone and we must now again pull it out of the fire.

"I scarcely know how I survived the ordeal," later recalled Eddie Paynter. "My head was splitting, perspiration streamed off me, but at the close of play I was still unbeaten, with Hedley as my gallant partner." Overnight the Australian media stretched taut the drama and excitement of the contest. The tenor of the news and radio bulletins was that England still required 69 runs to equal the Australian score and had only a sick man as their chief hope in the task. On the following morning Paynter resumed to a sympathetic reception and he and Verity added 92 for the ninth wicket, taking the score from 264 for 8 to 356. England thus unexpectedly gained a lead of 16 runs.

February 14: Again we were greeted by a very hot sun in a cloudless sky, when the game was resumed this morning. One is always going to remember this match for the great heat in which it was played. The Australian attack was entrusted to Ironmonger and O'Reilly. I gave a very difficult chance of a legside stumping early on, otherwise despite all the bowlers being called on, we both settled down and were still together at lunch. Paynter did most of the scoring, while I played 'doggo' for him. A rare struggle we both had with O'Reilly, too. As a side we must find some means of attacking him. Personally, I should say hit him over the top and compel him to open out his field. The other bowlers were accurate all the time, giving nothing away, but O'Reilly was the most dangerous, with his variations of flight and pace with a close-set field, No praise is too high for Paynter. A sick man, he has played magnificent cricket in a blazing sun and a temperature of about 100 degrees; a torrid heat, too. I was left with 23 not out, after batting 2½ hours. In that time I think I can claim to have been on top of the bowlers, and mastered everything they attempted.

Twice during his innings of 83, which lasted nearly four hours and included 10 boundaries, Paynter eased his throat with gargles and tablets. There were other hiccups along the way. Verity was missed by Wall at short-leg off O'Reilly and a misunderstanding between Bromley and Ponsford brought another escape when the Yorkshireman lofted the ball into the long field, again off the unlucky O'Reilly. But Verity, defiant and circumspect for the most part, deserved his luck. England's morale was lifted by the Lancashire-Yorkshire alliance and they went on to win by six wickets.

Paynter was fortunate in his partner: there was no more reliable tailender than Verity who, as one writer related, was a watchful and temperate batsman with few of the airs and graces, but a great measure of solidity and shrewdness. In later years Paynter recalled the contribution of Verity in one of the pluckiest of Test rallies. "Hedley was wonderful. His patience was inexhaustible. That day he played with the same resolution and courage as he displayed fighting and dying for his country."

Bill O'Reilly, whose bowling might so easily have squared the series at Brisbane, also remembers the fearlessness of his old rival. "He was the very essence of a team man. Everyone knew that without doubt he was giving the game all he had – in fact, 'boots and all' as our Australian cliché goes."

O'Reilly recalls: "Hedley and I used to regard each other as special competitors in the fray. We were eager to find personal confrontation in the thick of the fight. I took wonderful value out of whacking him out of the ground during rushes of blood to my head at Sydney, Lord's and Leeds."

He adds: "Hedley's revenge was sweet when he 'kept me out' with ease on three compensating occasions at Brisbane, Adelaide and Manchester. All Australians admired Verity immensely as a fully involved opponent demanding careful attention at all times."

Australia were inattentive and caught off guard in the final Test of a controversial series at Sydney. Verity, released from the constraints of his holding operations in earlier matches, took eight wickets for 95 runs, five of them in the second innings for less than seven runs each. Woodfull and Bradman put on 115 runs for the second wicket, initially against the leg-theory bowling of Larwood, but Australia's last eight wickets fell for 67 runs. Voce, in fact, began the collapse with the dismissal of McCabe after Larwood had retired with a foot injury.

February 27: Richardson and Woodfull again opened the innings for Australia and off Larwood's second ball Richardson was brilliantly caught at short-leg by Allen; Richardson thus "bagging a pair". With Bradman in, the huge crowd of over 40,000 was all excitement, while our bowlers, especially Larwood, went all out for another quick wicket. . . .

Jardine had used Larwood in short spells with the object of unsettling Bradman who, according to one writer, "jumped out to the slow bowling with almost reckless abandon." Bradman paid the price of his aggression, for "in making a fierce lunge at a ball from Verity (the left-hander's quick ball), he missed and turned round to see his stumps spreadeagled." Leo O'Brien, the Victoria batsman, remembers the unexpectedness of Verity's faster ball which deceived him in a State match against the MCC. "At Sydney," says O'Brien, "Verity bowled Bradman with that faster ball when Don was well set and stroking the ball fluently to all parts of the ground."

Verity's narrative continued with his description of the dismissal of Bradman:

Woodfull was as safe as can be at one end, making brilliant forcing shots. Bradman's shots were, however, unorthodox. He ducked almost at everything, in fact, but he managed to stay and make his 50. Voce had a try and I came on when Bradman was in his 40's and bowled over the wicket, my object being the spot made by Alexander (the Australian fast bowler) on or just outside the leg stump. Bradman tried to knock me off it after I had bowled two maiden overs to Woodfull. He positioned quickly, hitting me for two 4's from off the leg stump square through the covers. Next ball he tried it again, hit over the ball and was bowled. His slashing hitting had paid to the tune of 71 runs.

Verity proceeded to wreck the Australian batting with a superb spell of spin bowling. "Flighting the ball into the breeze and getting plenty of turn on it, despite negligible assistance from the wicket, he kept all the batsmen tied up," commented one writer. Australia's last three wickets fell for five runs. England, even allowing for the fatalism of a team already beaten in the series, had performed marvellously to dismiss Australia in less than a day.

Verity describes the closing stages of the match:

I continued to worry Woodfull. Twice I nearly bowled him with balls which turned off the worn patch. After tea, taken with the fall of the fourth wicket, Voce and myself resumed bowling, Darling partnering Woodfull. In my second over Darling hooked a ball rather riskily and attempting to repeat it gave an easy catch to mid-on. The game had definitely turned in our favour now. Still it was a grim and exciting struggle. Woodfull only needed a partner to spoil our growing hopes. Oldfield started confidently against Voce, but was uncomfortable at my end, and in trying to drive he hit the ball up to extra cover.

Lee now joined Woodfull and, although a natural hitter, he tried to play the other game. Woodfull, playing a great innings, now tried to force the pace and with Lee snicking Voce and then Allen, who relieved him, for fours, the scoring quickened momentarily. Allen, bowling with plenty of fire in an attempt to clinch our advantage, succeeded, Woodfull playing on (177 for seven). Australia's doom looks sealed unless our batting also collapses. In my next over I bowled O'Reilly and had Alexander lbw next ball. Lee had a crack at Allen but was bowled by the fifth ball, and the innings closed for 182.

With 25 minutes' batting to conclude this amazing day (the wicket is still good) Jardine took Wyatt in with him. Alexander and O'Reilly were the bowlers. Our skipper caused tremendous booing, hooting and general uproar by objecting to Alexander running on the wicket. The crowd was indeed really nasty. Alexander went round the wicket next over (which probably made his offence worse) and bowled bouncers.

In the last over of the day he hit Jardine, and the howl of delight and the cheers which went up would be a revelation to the people at home. The pair survived the day, however, both being not out, the score at the close being 14 for none. A good day for England; the game appears ours now unless it rains overnight, which seems unlikely.

February 28: The victory is ours. The end came at 3.45, Hammond fittingly hitting a six after a great innings. Our total of four wins represents a splendid tour.

Verity's late but notable haul of wickets demonstrated the perception of the selectors in pitching him into the cauldron of Anglo-Australian cricket. As Bob Wyatt says, in an appraisal of Verity's potential at that time, "I don't think his critics realised how good Hedley was compared with what he became."

Hedley Verity arrived home in Rawdon from Australia in the early hours of a Sunday morning in May, 1933. He had travelled by road along with his father and a family friend from Scotland after the MCC party had docked at Glasgow. He had been expected to arrive about 10 o'clock but the journey had been prolonged by a violent thunderstorm. It was approaching one in the morning before his car turned into the village. Most of the people of Rawdon had gone to bed but not quite all the village slept. There was a cluster of lighted windows on the little housing estate where Verity lived and when the Yorkshire bowler stepped from his car he found himself surrounded by a group of friends and neighbours.

Verity explained that he would have been home hours earlier but for the storm which had caused them to drive cautiously for many miles. His father offered another explanation for the belated return. At several points on the journey home calls had been made by Verity with greetings from people in Australia who had entrusted him with messages to relatives and friends in the north of England.

In the following days Verity tasted the full fruits of his cricket enthusiasm and the laurels were probably all the more acceptable because they came from people whose friendship he cherished most of all. His father, in his official role as chairman of the Rawdon council, welcomed Hedley at a civic reception organised by the council and the local cricket club. A silver salver was presented to the England tourist by Thomas Rigg, the captain of the school cricket team. In another expression of thanksgiving, over 2,000 people stood in torrential rain at Micklefield Park, Rawdon to cheer their honoured townsman.

The happy homecoming was sealed by an appreciative letter from Douglas Jardine to Verity senior, stressing that although slow left-arm bowling by Rhodes had not proved effective on the 1911–12 tour of Australia, it was Hedley – following Jack White – who had put it back as a trump card. "Hedley has come through his first tour triumphantly, no mean feat to start with the stiffest tour, but particularly for a slow left-hander," wrote Jardine. "On and off the field Hedley has been a real friend and a grand help to me – you must be a very proud father and with very good reason."

6

VERITY AND JARDINE

A resolute unity

"Jardine's fighting power was a wonderful source of inspiration to us all." – Herbert Sutcliffe.

JARDINE'S tribute to Verity reflected an intriguing friendship which had grown up between the two men during this historic tour. It was a friendship brimming with mutual respect and Verity never deviated from his view that Jardine was unequalled as a captain.

The England captain was a "powerful friend but a relentless enemy," in the words of Bill Bowes, and he pulled no punches during the heat and stress of the "bodyline" tour. Bowes says that Jardine had so much courage he would have tackled lions bare-handed. "Players used to say: 'If it ever comes to fighting for my life I hope I have the skipper on my side.'" Verity paid his captain the signal tribute of naming his second son after him. "D.R.J. was a man any father could accept as a model for his son," says Bowes.

Jardine was later to repay this compliment with an eulogy which must have thrilled the earnest young Test recruit. "Verity is at the moment perhaps the only modern exponent of the slow left-hander's art," wrote Jardine. "He has been perpetually compared with the past masters, Peate, Peel and Rhodes. Without being in a position to speak from personal experience of two of these three bowlers, I should require a lot of convincing before awarding the palm to any of them in preference to Verity. I venture to doubt whether any other bowler of his type has proved such a master on all kinds of wickets.

"The oldest head on young shoulders playing in England today is his. He can teach, nor is he above learning. It is a pleasure to see him set or vary his field, and having set it, bowl to it. No captain could have a greater asset on his side than Verity. He would make a great captain himself." Bob Wyatt remembers Jardine's keen appreciation of Verity's skills as a bowler and the "Yorkshire grit which impelled him always to give of his best." Wyatt believes that Jardine and Verity were of a similar temperament and had a mutual understanding in their outlook on cricket.

The tribunal of history, among them scandalmongers or writers unqualified to make judgements, has vilified Jardine to a degree almost unprecedented in cricket post-mortems. It is clear that he was a maligned man and more knowledgeable critics have said that Jardine had a warmth and charm that in the long run survived a forbidding austerity.

In the view of one impartial observer the controversy surrounding the "bodyline" tour became a *cause célèbre* because a section of the Press built upon one emotive incident (involving Pelham Warner and the Australian captain Bill Woodfull) and sustained the antagonism as a sales winner. Jardine did, however, flaunt his colours as a ruler and it was this posture, probably more than anything else, which resulted in him being reviled by the Australians for his tactics. But the criticism only served to stiffen his resolve to bring back the Ashes. His personal popularity came second to that ambition.

Bob Wyatt, as acting captain, first used the leg theory style of attack on the 1932–3 tour in a match against an Australian XI at Melbourne. He dismisses the idea of it being a pre–determined policy before the team went out to Australia as "absolute nonsense". "It was a very hard, fast wicket at Melbourne," says Wyatt, "and after Larwood had bowled a few overs with the new ball the shine had gone and the ball wasn't leaving the bat. It tended to come in a bit and the Australians, as mainly bottom–handed batsmen, played the ball on the onside.

"There was little chance of catches in the slips so I gradually moved the fielders over to the legside, not with a view to bowling bouncers, but simply to stop runs. Of course, every now and then the fast bowlers dropped one short. But this was perfectly legitimate as a shock tactic." Wyatt says he afterwards mentioned his use of leg theory to Jardine. The England captain replied: "That's interesting. We must pursue the matter." Jardine was impressed by the discovery of a "totally unsuspected weakness" on the leg stump by leading Australian batsmen who would be meeting England in the subsequent Test matches.

As the cricket world knows, Jardine employed leg theory to England's advantage; but on his return home he strongly maintained that the bowling on the tour was not a direct attack on the batsmen. Larwood, as his chief collaborator, was equally adamant that he had never intentionally bowled at any man.

In his Australian journal Hedley Verity described the bitter atmosphere prevailing during the third Test at Adelaide. The anger of the crowd rose to fever pitch when Oldfield tried to hook Larwood, missed and was struck on the head and knocked out. "Larwood, and indeed, all of us, were subjected to the worst demonstrations I have ever seen. We were repeatedly counted out. Larwood walked back to repeated boos and hoots from the crowd, and running up and bowling while it was still continuing. . . . Feelings are running high and everything short is attributed to leg-theory."

Verity maintained that Larwood rationed his bouncers – "not 10 in 25 overs" – and felt that the Australians had no real cause for complaint. "Both Oldfield and Woodfull were hit by good length balls which reared, Oldfield's pitching on the off-stump to an offside field." Bob Wyatt says that the dangerous ball was not the bouncer. The greater concern lay in the uneven bounce "when you did not know whether you were going to play the ball up by your armpit or down by your waist."

Jardine's personal courage was acknowledged by even his fiercest critics. Wyatt illustrates his captain's pluck and resolution in recalling an incident in the fifth Test at Sydney. "Australia had brought in Alexander (the Victoria fast bowler) to bowl 'bodyline' at us. He hit Douglas on the hip and the crowd roared its approval. Jardine started to rub his hip but stopped when the cheers started up. When we got back to the pavilion to change there was blood running down his leg." Wyatt adds: "Douglas was full of guts."

On the next day England lost two wickets in scoring 153 runs needed for victory on a crumbling wicket. Wyatt, who opened with Jardine, remembers that Bert Ironmonger, the Australian left–arm spinner, was quickly brought into the attack. "I got hit on the glove and I went down to tap the wicket. Douglas came charging down the wicket and said: 'What the hell are you doing? You don't want to make it *look* difficult.'" Wyatt replied: "Well, it's not very easy, is it?" Soon afterwards Jardine lunged forward to a ball from Ironmonger and edged a catch to Richardson at slip. Wyatt was unable to reiterate his views on the state of the wicket until the end of the game. "If Douglas had been at the other end and passed me, I should have said: 'You don't want to make it *look* difficult.'"

Jardine, as an Oxford undergraduate, scored 94 against the visiting Australians in 1921. He went to Australia in the winter of 1928–9 with the MCC team under the leadership of Percy Chapman, taking part in all five Test matches. He made a major contribution to England's success by 12 runs in the fourth Test, scoring 98 and sharing with Wally Hammond in a third wicket partnership of 262. He also scored three centuries in successive innings, against Western Australia, Victoria and New South Wales.

R. C. Robertson-Glasgow said that Jardine, at 19, was the completest young batsman he had seen, both in method and temperament. It was related that while Jardine was still a preparatory schoolboy, he had politely but firmly corrected his master on a point of technique and supported his view by a quotation from C. B. Fry's book on batsmanship.

In later years Herbert Sutcliffe, the Yorkshire and England opening batsman, considered Jardine the best tactician he had known as a captain. "His method of studying the game," said Sutcliffe, "set every member of the team working on similar lines and his fighting power was a wonderful source of inspiration to us all."

One of Jardine's Australian rivals in the 1932–3 series, Jack Fingleton, described his opponent as "aloof and discerning with a cold, judicial mind in gauging people and events before committing himself." Fingleton said: "Jardine did not want to be rushed into friendship and gusto – he preferred to do his own picking and choosing. . . ."

Sutcliffe thought Jardine was a "queer devil" – "he takes a lot of 'knowing'" – when he toured with him in Australia in 1928–9, but he revised his opinion on the next tour four years later. "Then I learned that Jardine was one of the greatest men I have ever met. He was a stern master, as straight as they make 'em, and he had the courage of his convictions. It was unfortunate for him that they did not meet with general approval, but that did not alter his outlook. He planned for us, cared for us, and fought for us on that tour. He was so faithful in everything he did that we were prepared on our part to do anything we could for him."

Others remembered Jardine's preparations and his study of individual methods and how he took immense pains to weigh the abilities and inclinations of his own team. When relaxed Jardine displayed a droll wit befitting his Scottish origins. After batting in a wearisome fashion in a Test in Australia he once apologised to an Australian for playing like an "old spinster defending her honour."

Jardine was, in the view of others, an elitist as a leader and he admired Hedley Verity in the same manner that he responded to other great players, including Sutcliffe, Voce and Larwood. Another contemporary, Ian Peebles, said Jardine was not a bully but he despised weakness. "Dealing with him, one had to stand firm at all points within reason, an attitude which he appreciated and which made for good relations."

Arthur Mitchell, who accompanied Verity on the 1933–34 tour of India, was less than enthusiastic about Jardine's abilities as a captain. "He had little time for the lesser fry," said the Yorkshire batsman. "He would set fields for the second string bowlers and say: 'Bowl to that.' He did not take them quietly on one side, talk tactics with them, and make the most of their talents. He expected them to be like Hedley and the other big star players and, of course, they could not deliver the goods. He was quite intolerant of the second best." Jardine's Surrey team-mates took a similar view to Mitchell; but his excellence as a captain was unquestioned when he had proven players under his command.

But even the greatest players were not immune from criticism or allowed to relax their efforts. Hugh Bartlett tells the story of Jardine's disquiet during a moment of indiscipline by Bill Voce at a practice session on tour. It was a revealing episode and an insight into Jardine's exacting standards which matched those of Verity. "Jardine had set his players around the field and was hitting catches to them," says Bartlett. "One hit went miles in the air and he shouted: 'Voce'. Bill, who was fielding on the boundary, saw the ball, then turned his back and caught the ball behind him." Jardine was furious at what he considered a folly by a bowler whom he admired and he said, more in sorrow than anger: "Imagine, Bill, if you'd done that in a Test match in front of 80,000 people." He did not need to say any more. The catching practice was not designed for pranks. It was a dress rehearsal for Test cricket.

Bill Bowes believes that Verity shared some of the relentless traits of Jardine. However, the granite in the Yorkshireman's personality was softened by a more compassionate view of his subordinates as was to be proved by his military leadership. The overthrow of Jardine resulting from the events of the 1932–3 tour of Australia severely shocked Verity. He did not particularly like the "bodyline" tactics; but he stood absolutely and with conviction behind his captain. Verity was especially upset by the treatment that Jardine received from the English cricket establishment and thought that his friend's early retirement was a great loss to the game.

Bowes says that until the Australian tour Verity did not know Jardine other than as a determined and able cricketer and opponent. "We had been on board ship for about 10 days," recalls Bowes. "I remember Hedley coming to our cabin one night and saying that he had been having a long chat with Jardine and how enjoyable it had been." The England captain, pursuing his objective of wresting back the Ashes, was intent on finding a role for the Yorkshire left-hander in his master plan. Jardine told Verity that unless the pitches in Australia had changed during the four years since the previous tour he did not think the Yorkshireman's type of bowling had much in its favour except as a tightly restrictive means of containing the Australian batsmen while the fast bowlers rested. "The skipper wanted to know if I had any ideas of bowling to Bradman with this in mind," said Verity.

Bowes remembers Verity's enthusiasm after his talk with Jardine. "Hedley was most impressed with the skipper; he said he had splendid theories and was obviously a keen student of the game." Jardine had expressed his confidence in England's batting but, said Verity, "he is concerned about our ability to get the Aussies out, or at least contain them." Verity added: "He kept tossing in a very apt quotation. He is a well read and intelligent man."

Edwin Kay, another confidant of Verity, says that his friend had voiced some doubts about going on the tour because of a disagreement with Jardine with regard to placing fields for left-hand batsmen. Subsequently, during the voyage to Australia, Jardine had asked Verity to meet him for a tactical discussion in his cabin. The door was locked behind them and, according to Kay, Jardine said the conversation would continue until they either agreed or agreed to disagree. As Verity did not funk issues at any time, one can be sure that he responded briskly in the argument before weighing up the evidence in his captain's favour. The outcome of the conversation, in the light of Bowes' comments, points to the fact that Verity cast aside his doubts and resolved the bowling dilemma.

Certainly, the "enjoyable chat" had one lasting effect in Verity's unswerving support for his captain. "Hedley was not 100 per cent behind the tour tactics," says Kay, "but he admired the courage and tenacity that Jardine showed in pursuing what he was sure was the only way to beat the Aussies."

The mask of arrogance worn by Jardine and which appeared to denote an unemotional and unyielding man was lowered when he appeared in a match against Yorkshire at Sheffield soon after the 1932–3 series in Australia. Jardine was thrilled by the reception he received when he went out to bat for Surrey. One writer said: "I remember him doffing his Harlequin cap to all four sides of the ground to acknowledge one of the finest receptions I have seen any cricketer given on any ground."

Jardine was deeply moved by the applause at Sheffield and the expression of loyalty and admiration which told him that Yorkshiremen recognised his contribution to England's cause. One of his regrets, he said on that occasion, was that he had not been born in Yorkshire. The fearless rival would have been an acquisition. Jardine's respect for Yorkshire cricket was confirmed at another time when he said that one of his criteria in selecting England players was to establish how well they had played in the north. "A batsman's record against Yorkshire, if good, is no mean passport," he said.

Jardine retired from cricket at the age of 33, at the peak of his talents.

He was lost to the English game when very much needed. He was present as a journalist at the Leeds Test against Australia in 1934. One spectator looked up at the Press box, as Bradman moved inexorably on to his triple century, and called out: "We want you out there, Jardine."

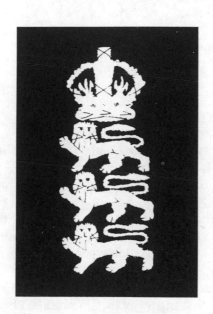

7

THE GOOD COMPANIONS

*"I know of no other cricketer upon whom one could rely
whatever the state of the match. He really was a 'rock'. Nothing
seemed to flurry him." – Charles Barnett.*

GIVEN the mutual respect and friendship between the two men, it was not
surprising that Verity was the first name to be pencilled in on Jardine's
selection list when he was appointed captain of the MCC tour to India
1933–34. "I need you to come on this tour very much," Jardine told
Verity.

It was on the tour of India that Verity formed another lasting friendship, with a young Gloucestershire batsman, making his first overseas
tour, Charles Barnett. At Jardine's suggestion, Barnett came under
Verity's guidance.

"I well remember the day we sailed from Tilbury to India," says
Barnett. "It was my first trip away from home and I had just parted from
my mother. I felt a bit under the weather. Hedley was so understanding.
He turned to me and said: 'I think a walk along the deck is indicated.'"

Barnett has never forgotten this gesture of solidarity. The two men, as
England cabin-mates on two overseas tours, became known as the
"David and Jonathan" of MCC teams. William Pollock, ranging over
the leisure interests of cricket friends, said theirs was a literary affair, and
that they would generally be found with their noses buried in books. On
one voyage Pollock remarked: "Yesterday we had a slight list to port
which I could not account for till I discovered Verity reading Lawrence's
Seven Pillars of Wisdom."

Barnett's gloom quickly turned to pleasure on the voyage to India. Of
Jardine's team he says: "They were a lovely mixture of gentlemen and
players. Some of the players were gentlemen and some of the gentlemen
were players." Barnett and Verity shared a cabin for the first time on this
trip. "We were early risers," says the Gloucestershire man, "and we
always enjoyed a swim before breakfast. It was a very relaxing start to
the day, splashing about in the water and drying off in the morning

sunshine and soft breezes." In the afternoons they would laze in their deckchairs, with Verity perhaps reading one of his favourite Kipling stories. "Hedley was a wonderful companion," says Barnett. "Living with him on tour you didn't have to make plans. It was simply: 'Right ho! Time to get up, and off we would go down to the pool or out for a game of golf." Their evenings did not fall into the riotous category. They were generally spent talking about cricket and working out strategies. Barnett explains: "Both of us were a bit tired. We were hardly worked as cricketers."

"Through Verity's influence," wrote Sam Davis, "Barnett soon came to see cricket not merely as a game, but as an ideal which demanded preparation of the mind, constant observation and the exercise of the player's highest intellect." Barnett remembers the tutorials before a Test match. "We had two hours of solid slog assessing and analysing the problems of the following day. I was schooled by Hedley as to exactly what I could expect in the match."

Barnett was also deeply impressed by the distinctive calm that Verity showed both on and off the field, and by the conspicuous absence in him of elation when a game was won or of disappointment when it was lost. "I know of no other cricketer upon whom one could rely whatever the state of the match. He really was a 'rock' when the chips were down. Nothing seemed to flurry him."

India had only just been elevated to Test status and this was the first official tour of the sub-continent by an England team. It was a happy excursion for Verity, who was charmed by a country of rich and variable beauty. Throughout the heat and strain of an exhausting tour, lasting from mid-October until early March, Verity showed his finest form. He took 72 wickets at a cost of just over 15 runs each; he headed the Test averages with 23 wickets at only slightly higher cost; twice took 10 or more wickets in a match; and five times five or more wickets.

In the third and decisive Test at Madras in February Verity over-whelmed India with a devastating piece of bowling. He took seven wickets for 49 runs in the first innings and 11 wickets in the match. India included in their ranks two sets of brothers – C. K. and C. S. Nayudu and Wazir and Nazir Ali – a unique event in Test cricket. Colonel C. K. Nayudu was India's first Test captain and their finest all-rounder of that time. Jack Hobbs said of him: "You have only to see him pick up a ball to know that he is a born cricketer."

In the Madras Test the England openers, Bakewell and Walters, unfurled their strokes against an Indian attack weakened by the with-drawal of Nissar, who was taken ill on the eve of the match. They shared a century partnership and at lunch England were 125 for 1. Afterwards they were jolted out of their complacency by Amar Singh, who took four wickets for 48 runs in 21 overs. Between lunch and tea, England lost six wickets for 97 runs. Verity once again demonstrated his staying powers as a batsman, scoring 42 valuable runs and helping Jardine to stem the decline. The pair added 97 for the eighth wicket and England recovered to reach a total of 335.

India suffered an early blow when the tiny Jeoomal Naoomal tried to hook a rising ball from the Northamptonshire fast bowler, Clark. He was struck in the face and had to retire. C. K. Nayudu was also dismissed, this time without physical discomfort but in an unfortunte fashion. A ball from Verity struck him on the pads and the bowler scarcely had time to appeal before the ball slipped through to break his wicket.

Verity built upon his good fortune as the Indian batsmen struggled uneasily against him. Mushtaq Ali, then a slow left-arm bowler but who was later promoted to open the batting with Vijay Merchant, remembered the perils of batting against Verity and his partner, Jim Langridge.

It was one of the few occasions that the Sussex bowler was able to show his worth at England level. "They had to be played with extreme caution," recalled Mushtaq Ali. "I was most impressed with the rhythmical run and action of Verity. While he maintained an immaculate length and unbelievable accuracy, his face maintained a graceful charm."

India were bowled out for 145 but Jardine did not enforce the follow-on. Walters hit a sparkling century and England set their opponents a target of 452 runs. India lost two wickets (effectively three in the absence of the injured Naoomal) for 65. On a crumbling wicket Verity and Langridge warmed to their task. They shared nine wickets but India fought gallantly until the end. Amar Singh, following his bowling success, raced to 48 in 40 minutes, and the Yuvaraj of Patiala and Merchant added 84 runs for the sixth wicket. Once they were separated victory was assured and England won by 202 runs to clinch the rubber.

At the end of the Madras Test Verity joined a party at which his host was Lt-Col Shaw (his future Green Howards' commanding officer) and was congratulated on his performance. He was asked what he would like to drink to celebrate the occasion. He responded with a shrug of his shoulders and said that all he wanted just then was a biscuit or two.

Verity and Langridge bowled 80 overs, sharing eight wickets between them, in India's first innings in the first Test at the Bombay Gymkhana ground. The estimated attendance over the four days of the match was 250,000. The vast, gleeful crowds found abundant delight, even in the nine-wicket defeat, in a century by the 21-year-old Lala Amarnath on his Test debut. Brian Valentine, making his first appearance for England, also topped three figures. He plundered 136 runs in a hectic innings lasting less than three hours. Valentine was the dominant partner in a fifth wicket stand of 145 with Jardine and the rally enabled England to total 438.

India trailed by 219 on the first innings and lost two wickets for 21 runs in a dispiriting start to their second innings. Their pride was salvaged by Nayudu, despite the handicap of a bruised hand, and the exciting Amarnath. "Amarnath played an attacking innings hitting all round the wicket," wrote one observer. "At one end the batting was governed by thought and experience; at the other it was marked by the dash and exuberance of youth."

The partnership between Amarnath and Nayudu at Bombay yielded 186 runs. Amarnath enjoyed the double honour of being the first Indian to score a Test century and the first among his countrymen to obtain a hundred on his Test debut. "The huge crowd of 50,000, little caring about the position of the match, cheered as the young Punjab player scored with leg glides, cuts and drives that left the fielders standing. Every bowler, even the great Verity, was treated with scant respect as Amarnath scored 84 out of 118 in boundaries," wrote Saradindu Sanyal. It was to be Amarnath's only Test 100 in a career extending over 20 years.

England again dominated the second Test at Calcutta, effectively resolving the match with a first innings total of 403, and India were fortunate to escape with a draw. Langridge, the top scorer with 70, and Jardine were the partners in a stand worth 81 runs. Verity, following his eight wickets in the match, rode his luck (he was missed twice in the covers) to emerge unbeaten with 55 runs. The innings completed a profitable batting time in Calcutta, for the Yorkshireman had been undefeated on 91 in the previous drawn match against an All-India eleven. Verity and Townsend, as a formidable ninth wicket pair, had twice excelled themselves with stands of 70 and 142 in the two games in the city.

"Verity wears a composed air," reported the *Calcutta Statesman*, "he has a flair for turning up at the right time. Memories are fresh of his stand with Paynter in Australia which went far towards winning the Ashes for England – and the position in the second Test did not impose any hardship on him. His batting average following his stay in Calcutta will go up with a deserving jump."

Jardine, the "high priest of English cricket", as one writer described him, returned home a triumphant captain, and at the peak of his powers as a batsman as well. The tour of India was his international swan song. His exit from the Test arena was the price the MCC had to pay to cement the bond of Empire and restore relations between the two countries before the visit of the Australians in 1934.

"Jardine, with great dignity and magnificent disdain, informed the MCC that he not only would not be available as a candidate for the captaincy of the England side, but also that he had no desire even for a place in the team," wrote Percy Fender.

8

MASTERY AT LORD'S

"The crowd and the Pavilion were treated to an exhibition of bowling which, whether judged by standards of accuracy or general ability, may possibly have been equalled, but certainly has never been surpassed." – Douglas Jardine.

THE violent, agitated mis-hit which lifted the ball high and straight over the wicket in Hedley Verity's Test at Lord's in 1934 was a disaster for Don Bradman and Australia. The scandalous stroke appeared to represent the torment of a great batsman averting his eyes at looming defeat. Verity was the bowler who had tempted Bradman into this rash stroke and England's close fieldsmen wavered dizzily beneath the skied catch. They all had plenty of time to get under the ball even before it stopped going up. Neville Cardus recalled that as wicket-keeper Les Ames came forward to take the catch "Bradman stood aside, exposed in momentary embarrassment, like a dejected schoolboy."

Ames remembers his palpitations as the ball flew from the top edge of Bradman's bat. "Everyone was petrified to go for it. Hammond could have caught it easily as could Sutcliffe or Verity, moving into position from the bowler's end. The shout went up: 'Yours, Les.' I would have been quite happy if someone else had taken it. It was up there so long that there was time to think about it. If we hadn't taken the catch there could have been trouble. But I did take it at silly point, very silly point."

Wally Hammond described the dismissal in the following words: "Verity knew Don's weakness. He left the long field wide open for a whole quarter of an hour. It looked like an oversight; but no one with Bradman's experience would dream that Verity was guilty of an oversight.

"Out on the classic turf of Thomas Lord, in the clear sunless air, with thousands breathlessly watching, every one of us knew what was coming; the only thing we did not know was *where* it was coming from. . . . Verity came tirelessly up to the wicket, his long arm came through. Bradman, grim-faced, slashed whip-like against the spin with his face set towards the far outfield – but the ball did not go there. It went spinning heaven-high. . . . I watched it come down with a whirr into Les Ames' big gloves. Verity, standing at the wicket, showed not the slightest expression on his face, though he knew, as we all did, that that ball had won the match. Probably he was already weaving a spell for the next victim?"

Sir Pelham Warner remembered the stern countenance of Woodfull, the Australian captain, as Ames took the catch. "I can see now the look that Woodfull gave Bradman as he walked past him to the pavilion," he said.

Bob Wyatt, England's captain in the match, describes Bradman's blunder as a "desperation shot." "There he was on a wicket upon which he did not fancy his chance. So he tried to hit his way out." *Wisden* commented that at one period during the 1934 season Bradman created the impression, to some extent, that he had lost control of himself and went into bat with an almost complete disregard for anything in the way of a defensive shot. Douglas Jardine said: "Bradman seemed to have made up his mind that a rate of scoring of anything less than eight runs an over was beneath his dignity." Other observers thought that Bradman was affected by his experiences in the "bodyline" tour of 1932–33, but the Australian moved back on to his pedestal with another 300 against England at Leeds and a double century at the Oval.

Bill Bowes promptly expunges the blot and counters allegations of indiscreet batsmanship which have perplexed many people who witnessed the aberration at Lord's. The barbaric nature of Australian wickets where the ball in turn reared wickedly and crept perversely, provides the essential clue. "They were diabolical, impossible," says Bowes. "Sometimes the ball would fly and hit the batsman on the neck or shoulders and then it would scuttle along the ground. If you tried to play disciplined cricket on such pitches you would be lucky to average 12. The vigorous, adventurous approach, edges and all, would give you seven or eight runs more."

Bowes says that all the Australians, not just Bradman, would go on to the attack on this type of pitch. George Hirst used to say: "It's either you or me for it," and the Australians took a similar line in bravado. "Get banging," was their response, "we will get more runs having a whoof than we will playing doggo." Bowes stresses that Bradman, at the time of the Lord's imbroglio, was on only his second tour of England. "He was playing according to the Australian method then but in later years when he was more experienced in English conditions it was a very different matter. I never saw him bat on a 'sticky dog' but I did see him on a pitch where the ball was turning and you couldn't get the ball past his bat." Verity also rejected the oft-expressed view that Bradman was less than a master on damaged pitches. He once referred to his rival's two innings of 59 and 42 in 1938 against Yorkshire at Sheffield. "It was a pig of a pitch," he said, "and he played me in the middle of the bat right through."

Hedley Verity twice dismissed Bradman at Lord's in June, 1934, to mastermind England's first victory over Australia at the headquarters since 1896. He captured 15 wickets for 104 runs to equal the record of his mentor, Wilfred Rhodes, at Melbourne 30 years earlier. Verity was irresistible after rain on the Monday when he took 14 wickets for 80 runs, six of them in the last hour of a momentous day. Herbert Sutcliffe said that if Arthur Mitchell, Verity's Yorkshire ally, had been in the England team the amazing return would have been more amazing still.

Over 50 years on, Sir Donald Bradman adds a rueful footnote to Verity's achievement. The following extract is from a recent letter in which he says "this was a piece of fate which might so easily never have occurred." Sir Donald writes: "England batted first and made 440 on the Friday and part of the Saturday. When we batted the pitch was firm and dry. At the fall of the first wicket I went in and just happened to be in very good form. I had made 36, including seven 4's and three in succession off Verity, and I was anxious to go on the attack.

"It so happened that my captain, Woodfull, begged me to be less aggressive because, apparently, he feared I was going to throw my wicket away. In endeavouring to carry out his wishes I did restrain myself and in so doing, 'held' a shot against my better judgement and was caught and bowled by Hedley.

"Over the weekend it rained and Australia had to continue batting on a rain-affected pitch. Had I been allowed to continue batting on the Saturday in my own way I am in no doubt that we would have easily saved the follow-on. If we had saved the follow-on, England would have had to bat on that sticky on the Monday. The course of the match would have been changed and Hedley would never have got the chance to bowl at us in our second innings, which enabled him to put up such a wonderful performance."

Criticism was, however, heaped upon Bradman for his spectacular tactics in Australia's first innings at Lord's although Neville Cardus was thrilled by the "terrible power and splendour" of his batting. Percy Fender said: "Bradman gave himself no time in which to accustom himself to the pace of the wicket, and went for all the bowlers, except Bowes, as if he had been there an hour." Verity was hit for three fours in succession in his first over and Geary conceded 14 runs in another over. Bradman and Brown scored 50 runs in half-an-hour, but it was too good to last."

"Bradman's innings came to an end with, for me, a sickening suddenness; mischance brought down the young eagle," wrote Cardus. "This is not to detract from the cleverness of Verity; he sent down an over which contained subtle problems of flight and pace variations. The third ball almost saw Bradman caught and bowled; he hit too soon, and Verity fell on the ground far down the wicket in his effort to hold a prize worth having indeed. The fifth ball of this over pitched outside the off-stump and jumped up unexpectedly; scarcely another slow ball in all the match had behaved like this. Bradman could not check his stroke, which, of course, was offensive; he jerked his bat and Verity was a happy, consoled man now – imagine, two chances of return catches from Bradman in one over."

At the close of the second day's play Australia had scored 192 for 2 and Brown had batted reassuringly in completing a century on a perfect wicket. Australia needed only 98 runs to save the follow-on, but more realistically the signs were that England would do well to scramble a first innings lead.

Bob Wyatt recalls that his depleted attack – Hammond, Farnes and Geary were incapacitated by injuries – was unable to contain Australia on the Saturday. "We bowled badly and they were scoring too quickly for my comfort," he says. Douglas Jardine said that the English fielding was "fumbling and slovenly to a degree which would have reflected no credit on a county side."

A severe storm came to England's aid at the weekend. Hedley Verity chuckled with delight at breakfast in a London hotel room on the morning of his triumph. He looked out on a street damp with rain. Turning to his team-mates, he said: "I shouldn't wonder if we don't have a bit of fun today. It looks as though it might turn a little."

It was a prophetic comment but there was a discouraging prelude which might have been construed by a superstitious person as a signal of ill-fortune. On his way by car to Lord's Verity ran down and killed a black cat. Others might have ignored the accident, but he stopped and did not continue his journey until he had found the owner and tendered his apologies. Charles Barnett, in telling this story, says: "Hedley went to all that trouble when he must have been bubbling over with other thoughts of cricket."

Of these cricket events Percy Fender related that they were a tragedy for Australia and a triumph for Verity. "That he took every advantage of the conditions and the limitations of the Australians admits of no argument. I do not think there is another bowler in England who could have done better if as well." Wyatt also thinks that the inexperienced

Australian batsmen were unlucky but wryly adds: "They thought it was a sticky wicket and we kept persuading them that it was." "The batsmen seemed foot-tied," said Jardine, "and Verity was allowed to pitch the ball time and time again on the same spot. He may even have created a pitch for himself by his accuracy."

Wisden endorsed this verdict. "This amazing achievement would probably have been only possible to a man possessed of such length and finger spin as Verity because although the wicket certainly helped him considerably, it could scarcely be described as genuinely 'sticky' except for one period after lunch. Verity's length was impeccable and he made the ball lift so abruptly that most of the Aussies were helpless . . . "

Verity moved eagerly into his stride on the last morning. He took six wickets and was only checked by a gritty partnership between Oldfield and Chipperfield who put on 40 for the seventh wicket. After Oldfield's dismissal, caught high up by Sutcliffe at first slip, Australia still required 33 to avoid the follow-on. Chipperfield defiantly struck a fine boundary off Verity; Grimmett less certainly edged Bowes for more runs through the slips; and then, off the last ball before lunch, he was bowled by Bowes.

The adjournment should have been an anxious time but Verity seemed unperturbed. With the match in the balance, he said: "Well, I really must have another helping of strawberries and cream." The dish was duly replenished and, his appetite sated, he went out to deal the final, conclusive blows. One close friend of the Yorkshireman said afterwards: "I can still see Hedley walking out on to the field of play after lunch on that famous day. I could tell by the look on his face what was coming to Australia."

Australia reduced the margin to 14 runs before O'Reilly, with a scything heave, succumbed to Verity. Wall lasted only two balls before departing lbw to the Yorkshire bowler. Australia had failed by seven runs to make England bat again. It was the first time in England for 29 years that they had been forced to follow-on. Chipperfield, obstinate to the last, was undefeated with 37 runs.

The Australian first innings ended at a quarter-to-three. Before six o'clock the second innings was finished and England had won by an innings and 38 runs. All but one of the 20 Australian wickets were taken by Verity and Bowes. Verity's figures were 7 for 61 in 216 balls in the first innings and 8 for 43 in 135 balls in the second innings. After tea, inspired and irresistible, he took six wickets for 15 runs as Australia declined from 94 for 3 to 118 all out. He had bowled, with only a short rest, for five and a half hours.

Percy Fender considered that Verity's figures in the first innings took precedence over his second innings return. "There is no doubt about the fact that the wicket was slowly getting more difficult as the day went on, and that the wicket was less responsive to him before lunch than it was afterwards. It was the getting of those wickets on the slower and more easy wicket to make Australia follow-on which counted most."

The conqueror of Australia was almost apologetic about his success. "It's a funny game, this cricket," he said. "A funny game and a grand one. I have been lucky today in having a wicket on which I could make the ball stand up a bit."

Douglas Jardine was at Lord's to witness the Yorkshireman's mastery. Twice he sent notes of congratulations round to the England dressing-room for Verity, and when the season was over he penned the following tribute:

"The crowd and the Pavilion were treated to an exhibition of bowling which, whether judged by standards of accuracy or of general ability, may possibly have been equalled, but certainly has never been surpassed. For clear thinking and execution it may stand alone for all time ... Much of Yorkshire's success has been due to the unselfish ability of one bowler in keeping an end closed and quiet while the wickets were being taken at the other end. Bowes did this for Verity on the Lord's wicket which for a fast bowler was unsympathetic to a degree."

Bob Wyatt also places special emphasis on the part played by Bowes in a memorable victory. "Bowes did a tremendous lot to bring about our success. It was most unusual that I should have to go to a fast bowler and ask him to shut up an end. My aim was to block one end while Hedley got them out at the other end, and I had difficulty in doing that because the other supporting bowlers had bowled so badly.

"Then I went to Bill and asked him if he would cut down his pace and just shut them up if possible. He did this magnificently and it made all the difference in forcing the follow-on." The Yorkshire fast bowler, with three for 98 in 31 overs, was a miserly accomplice, keeping the runs down so that Verity could operate with greater freedom.

Bowes recalls: "My job was to hold one end up so that the runs had to be scored off Hedley or he had to get them out." Wyatt and Bowes had adopted the Yorkshire mode of attack which dictated to opponents the message: "If you are going to beat us you will have to get them off him." At Lord's Bowes "bowled for keeps" for Verity and it was a method which might have been employed for the slow bowler's benefit by England on other Test occasions.

Another key factor contributing to Australia's defeat at Lord's was Wyatt's decison, much criticised at the time, not to declare when England's ninth wicket fell at 410. Fender was convinced that Wyatt would declare as he did not believe that Bowes could stay long even if Verity showed signs of repeating his earlier Test batting successes. "It was on the decision that Wyatt took that England should bat after lunch on the Saturday that the ultimate result of the match depended," said Fender. "After the interval Bowes and Verity stayed for 45 minutes and added 30 runs. As the match unfolded that time and those runs were not only the minutes and runs by which England won, but the shortening of the time that Australia had to bat on the Saturday meant everything to England on the Monday."

Wyatt adds his own footnote to the decision. "It would have been very foolish to have declared. If I had played it as a three-day game and declared at lunch, we should never have won the match."

Another memory of a great achievement concerns the trip from London to Northampton, where Verity and Bowes joined Yorkshire for a county game. They took their cricket bags straight to the Northampton ground, where a local game was being watched by a couple of hundred spectators. The players interrupted the game to stand with the crowd and cheer the two England heroes as they walked from their taxi to the pavilion. It was a spontaneous tribute reserved for exploits of a special kind.

9

THE WHITE ROSE
BLOOMS

"Hedley and Bill were marvellous in their encouragement to a young player. You couldn't go wrong with such people." –
Sir Leonard Hutton

HEDLEY Verity and Bill Bowes were the earnest students whose friendship and prowess grew into a masterly alliance during the 1930s. The partnership was forged during their apprenticeship with Yorkshire. They were new boys in an imposing regime. Such was their dominance as bowlers – an adroit mix of spin and pace coupled with formidable tactical acumen – that together they took nearly 2,400 championship wickets for Yorkshire. They provided the impetus for the county's seven championships between 1931 and 1939.

Yorkshire's sequence of successes was interrupted by Lancashire and Derbyshire in 1934 and 1936. Test calls exacted their toll in 1934 when Yorkshire slipped to sixth place, the lowest they had occupied for 23 years. In the nine years of Verity's reign Yorkshire won 153 championship games (out of 260) and were beaten 24 times.

Of Bowes and Verity as a match-winning partnership Sir Leonard Hutton says: "Any captain with a couple of bowlers of their stature is a lucky fellow. Brian Sellers was fortunate that he had two intelligent chaps; they knew how they wanted their field and how to bowl to it when they got it. Bill would get 'one-two-three' out with the new ball and give us a start and Hedley would then take over if the conditions were right for him."

Bowes remembers the comforting attitude of the Yorkshire elders during his early years with the county. "We don't mind you getting hit as long as you're getting 'em out," was the assurance given to the two newcomers. Yorkshire had a stellar cast of batsmen, regularly scoring heavily and quickly. They created the platform and time needed for victory. Bowes and Verity – and their accomplices, Macaulay, Smailes and Ellis Robinson – were expected to bowl out their opponents, particularly on the wet and uncovered wickets of the period, as cheaply as possible, either to set up the target or apply the finishing touch.

The boy in his father's coal cart (Verity senior is pictured far right).

Verity's birthplace at Welton Grove, Headingley, little more than a long cricket throw from the famous Test ground (below) where he achieved his two 10-wickets feats against Warwickshire and Nottinghamshire in successive seasons in 1931 and 1932 (photos: Tony Woodhouse and John Featherstone).

Grace and Hedley.

Edith Verity, one of her son's fiercest critics.

Young Hedley the cricket apprentice.

The Rawdon ground, the scene of Verity's first triumphs.

Duel on the sand at Scarborough: Verity with his wife Kathleen and their eldest son, Wilfred (named after Rhodes).

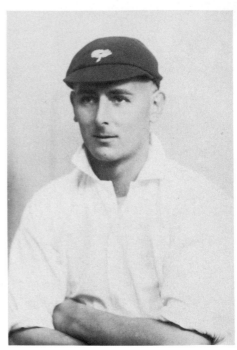

Yorkshire mentors: George Hirst (left) and Wilfred Rhodes together with their pupil, Hedley Verity, soon after he had won his Yorkshire cap.

Ted Peate and Bobby Peel, the first in Yorkshire's left-arm spinning chain. (M.C.C. Collection).

SECOND INNINGS OF Notts

Played at Leeds ... Date July 9 [11-12] 193[2]

Scorers: K. Ringrose / J. Carlin

Order of going in	BATSMAN	RUNS AS SCORED	HOW OUT	BOWLER	Total Runs
1	Keeton		c Macaulay	Verity	21
2	Shipston		c Wood	Verity	21
3	Walker		c Macaulay	Verity	11
4	A.W. Carr		c Barber	Verity	0
5	Staples A.		c Macaulay	Verity	7
6	Harris		c Holmes	Verity	0
7	Gunn G.V.		L B W	Verity	0
8	Lilley		not out		3
9	Larwood		c Sutcliffe	Verity	0
10	Voce		c Holmes	Verity	0
11	Staples S.		st Wood	Verity	0

BYES 2 [ ] LEG BYES [ ] WIDES [ ] NO BALLS [ ]

Runs at the fall of each wicket	1 for	2 for	3 for	4 for	5 for	6 for	7 for	8 for	9 for	10 for	TOTAL
	44	47	51	63	63	63	64	64	67	67	67
Batsman's Number / Order of going out										all out at 3.22 pm 5th day	

BOWLING ANALYSIS—SECOND INNINGS.

NUMBER OF "OVERS" AND "RUNS" MADE FROM EACH BOWLER.

BOWLERS	Wides	No Balls	1	2	3	4	5	6	7	8	9	10	11	12	13	14	15
Bowes																	
Macaulay																	
Verity						WWW	WW W						W		W	W	

	BOWLERS	TOTALS							BOWLERS	TOTALS					
		Overs	Maidens	Runs	Wickets	Wides	No Balls			Overs	Maidens	Runs	Wickets	Wides	No Balls
1	Bowes	5	0	19	0	1		6							
2	Macaulay	23	9	34	0			7							
3	Verity	19.4	16	10	10			8							
4								9							
5								10							

Ten for 10: the historic score sheet from the Yorkshire County Cricket archives.
(Reproduced by kind permission of Yorkshire C.C.C.).

Ten for 36: Verity is congratulated by the Yorkshire and Warwickshire captains, F. E. Greenwood and R. E. S. Wyatt, after his feat against Warwickshire in 1931 (British Library).

Arthur Wood, George Macaulay, Arthur Mitchell and Frank Dennis share Verity's jubilation after his achievement against Nottinghamshire.

An example of Yorkshire's tight field setting for Verity at the Oval (Central Press).

Bill Bowes in belligerent mood against Surrey at the Oval (Central Press).

Yet another spectacular catch by Arthur Mitchell, the vigilant specialist in the gulley, against Middlesex at Lord's (British Library).

"You win a lot more matches," says Bowes, "if you can guarantee, through thick and thin, to bowl the other side out for no more than 200. That was our task."

"Yorkshire had many great cricketers before they became a great team," wrote Jim Kilburn, the county historian. "The championships only began to come home when the individuals grew into something bigger than the sum of themselves. When Yorkshire became a team they became championship winners, not occasionally but time and time again."

The tradition of aggressive fielding, first instituted by Lord Hawke, was the keystone of Yorkshire's triumphs in the 1930s. Kilburn wrote: "The team going into the field at the beginning of a match made an impressive picture; there was a crouching, expectant half-circle from gully to fine leg, a forward short-leg within whispering distance of the batsman, prowling cover point and mid-off, and everywhere an atmosphere of menace. Batsmen were encouraged to think that their chances of survival from the slightest misjudgement were poor indeed, and that very belief was in itself an inducement to misjudgement."

Of Brian Sellers, who took over the Yorkshire captaincy in 1933, Kilburn said he drew loyalty because he gave loyalty. Team interests were paramount and his principles were so clearly illustrated that they could not fail to escape the attention of the established player or newest recruit.

Bill Bowes remembers how Sellers slipped into the experienced Yorkshire team of the 1930s "in his stockinged feet" and quickly earned the respect of an august group of professionals. In his early days, after Yorkshire had won the toss, he would invariably ask Holmes and Sutcliffe to accompany him on an inspection of the wicket. "Then he would return to the dressing-room and Hedley and myself would be asked to join the skipper on another visit to the middle. And then he'd do what he wanted," says Bowes. He adds: "We never knew whether he had taken Percy or Herbert's advice or ours."

It was Sellers' ability to judge the situation and make fewer mistakes than most which enabled Yorkshire to maintain their supremacy. Norman Yardley, the post-war Yorkshire captain, remembers how Sellers assiduously swotted up the cricket rules until he knew them backwards so as to twist the arms of the often inexperienced southern county captains. "He could pull the wool over their eyes but they couldn't pull it over his," says Yardley.

Hedley Verity prospered in this adventurous regime. Making the ball lift and turn, he benefited from the daring support of his fieldsmen.

Sellers, Ellis Robinson, Cyril Turner, and especially Arthur Mitchell resolutely kept their vigil on the edge of the bat to play key roles in Yorkshire's triumphs. Verity frequently caused catches to be edged not so much to the normally stationed slips as towards gully. Mitchell and wicket-keeper Arthur Wood were the attentive waiters, combining agility and anticipation, and they feasted noisily at Verity's table. They assisted in 346 dismissals, Wood with 119 stumpings and 67 catches; and Mitchell with 160 catches.

Mitchell's partnership with Verity began as soon as Verity took his place in the Yorkshire attack. He had fielded in the gully for Rhodes and he went to the position, automatically you might say, for Verity. But there was a difference. "When fielding to Wilfred," said Mitchell, "I used to stand a little squarer. For Hedley, I varied the position, according to the batsman, between square and a foot and a half behind, but mostly I was behind.

"I'd be no more than six or seven feet from the bat to start with, and usually I finished much nearer – only a yard or so from the bat when the ball was played. But Hedley bowled a marvellous direction and there were few occasions when the close-in fieldsmen were in danger. Generally speaking, were were absolutely safe.

"Hedley was easy to field to. I could watch him deliver the ball, judge its length, and then transfer to the bat. By then, I knew what I expected the batsman to do. In a way it was like batting against him, though I have to admit that it was easier to imagine yourself batting against him than it was to do the actual batting."

Bill Bowes, venomous because of his "strength in the back" and armed with his unnerving pace, perfectly complemented his partner, Verity. He was often doubled up with laughter at the disparaging sallies of Verity's victims as they were lured to their doom. "Every batsman fancies his chances against a slow bowler, even on a sticky wicket," he once said. The optimism still flickered however many times they were toppled by Verity. The confidence or foolhardiness was just the incentive Verity needed as he set his traps.

"Time and time again have I seen them beaten by Hedley's skills," says Bowes. "As the batsman passed me he would say: 'I ought to have hit that ball over the pavilion, Bill.' He would go in again for his second innings, make another desperate attempt to hit Hedley for six only to fall into the old snare – c Mitchell b Verity. Once more there would be that look of disgust. On the homeward walk he would say: 'Fancy getting out to him.'" One famous batsman, after being frequently tormented by Verity, expressed the view that all slow bowlers should be strangled at birth. Verity thought this was a fine testimony to the value of his craft.

"We shared an understanding that was absolutely marvellous," says Bowes of his alliance with Verity. It was a product of searching discussions on and off the field. Bowes and Verity hatched their private plots and often baffled not only the opposition but their own team-mates as well. Other Yorkshire players, the shrewdly observant Maurice Leyland among them, would march up and say: "Come on, let's be in on it."

The tactical skills of the two bowlers were so acute that they could judge precisely the time to bowl out their opponents. The day's play would be drawing to a close and Bowes and Verity would debate the question or merits of dismissing a batsman that evening. "Do you want to get rid of this fellow tonight?" one or the other would ask as the shadows lengthened. "No, let's leave him till the morning," might be the response. If it was not imperative to make a swift dispatch, they might take the decision to postpone the overthrow until the morning when the batsman was fresh and more likely to make a mistake.

Bowes and Verity traded their batting rivals like boys with cigarette cards. "There were some batsmen you fancied as scalps and others less likeable," says Bowes. "If they were in the former category I would say to Hedley: 'Get this chap to my end, Hedley!' You had no need to say more than that."

Bowes considers that Verity merged the best characteristics of their mentors, George Hirst and Wilfred Rhodes, in his personality. Lord Hawke said Hirst's smile "went right round his head and met at the back." Someone else poetically described it as a "square-cut smile." Hirst was built like a bull and had a deep, reassuring voice. Bowes says: "George loved his cricket; he was so full of enthusiasm that he took you along with him." Rhodes, on the other hand, could be aloof and brusque. He was a thoughtful master of theory, brilliantly equipped to coach the established county player, but his technical precision could be disconcerting to youngsters. Verity loved these tactical commentaries. They were more to his taste than the most enthralling detective story. Bowes says: "Hedley was not quite so technical as Rhodes. He was a sort of blend of Wilfred and George."

Verity, as a senior player, was only too eager to pass on the benefits of his experience. Another close friend, Sir Leonard Hutton, recalls his early association with the prince of left-handers. "He always impressed me as a man; if you dropped a catch off him he just smiled. I never saw him angry or even agitated at a turn of events in a game. He had a remarkable temperament and it was a privilege to be in his company. Both Hedley and Bill were marvellous in their encouragement to a young player. You couldn't go wrong with such people."

Sir Leonard adds: "I missed them when they were away playing for England. The mere fact that men of their calibre were on the field, even when they were not bowling, was of immeasurable help to the rest of us. Their influence and presence were all-important."

The former England captain wistfully recalls the attitudes of the pre-war Yorkshire eleven. "What I liked so much about players such as Hedley and Bill was the fact that they never sought publicity. They got on with the job of playing cricket and did it in a right and proper way. There was no sharp practice; they were winning, but they were winning without a smell."

One of Verity's Australian rivals has referred to the Yorkshireman's quiet appeals, so quiet that only the umpire and the batsman at his end could hear him. Sir Leonard says that there was never any fear of Verity twisting a batsman out. "He would never jump down an umpire's throat." Bill Bowes remembers his colleague's "nice inquiry". "He didn't scream his head off or throw his arms up, like some of us did. But he didn't miss a chance. He would often make a psychological appeal."

The rapport between Verity and Hutton, a shy youth by his own account, undoubtedly assisted the development of one of the greatest of all Yorkshire batsmen. "If I wanted a bit of practice before a match," says Sir Leonard, "Hedley was always willing to come out and bowl at me in the nets for 10 minutes. He wasn't a duffer as a batsman and he would make many useful points. This was where I found him so helpful. Nothing seemed too much trouble for him."

The association prospered off the field. Golf and motoring were favourite pursuits of the two friends. Verity gave his young colleague his first and only driving lessons around the then quiet roads adjoining the local golf course at Fulneck, near his cricket nursery at Pudsey, Sir Leonard's boyhood home in Yorkshire. "We would have a round of golf followed by driving practice for half an hour. I never had any professional tuition, but I passed my test without any problems," says Sir Leonard.

Hedley Verity was "never a man for the taproom" says the former England captain. "He liked a drink – a glass of wine or a pint of beer at the close of play – but he was really a temperate man. He was fond of a pipe. But he didn't smoke heavily, perhaps just the odd cigarette at the tea interval or after the match."

The cinema, the "pictures" or the "flicks" in the parlance of those days, provided a relaxing interlude for the Yorkshire players. One of the Hollywood pin-up girls of the 1930s was the glamorous Joan Crawford. As an 18-year-old, Sir Leonard doted on the beguiling charms of this screen heroine. Verity never lost an opportunity to tease him about his youthful adoration. "Hedley was so amused that I should be so keen on her. He would look up at a poster advertising the favourite one's latest film role and laughingly say: 'Oh, I see she's on here, your girl friend.'" A fond smile lights up Sir Leonard's face at the remembrance. "Hedley reminded me a lot about Joan Crawford. He could always see the funny side of things."

Sir Leonard, in more serious vein, also remembers the counsel of Verity during his then record innings of 364 against Australia at the Oval in 1938. "I owe him the kind of debt one can never fully repay. As my innings developed it was obvious that something out of the ordinary was in the offing, and the ever kindly and wise Hedley made it his duty to stay with me during every lunch and tea break while I nibbled at a sandwich and sipped tea.

"We both knew that the most likely way I could lose my wicket was by sheer fatigue, or by a lapse of concentration causing a careless stroke. Hedley sat by my side like a faithful ally to make sure that my thoughts did not wander, and that I concentrated and disciplined myself as never before. His quiet, natural dignity was an immense source of strength to me throughout those long hours."

Verity also made arrangements on the rest day on the Sunday for a seaside outing. At the invitation of Stanley Pratt, a London stockbroker and an old schoolfriend of Verity, they visited his home in Bognor Regis for lunch. There they were joined by Dr Swain, another Yorkshire cricket enthusiast, who had a practice at the Sussex resort. The afternoon was fine and sunny and Sir Leonard eased his tension with a game of beach cricket.

A quiet stubbornness could rise to the surface of Verity's personality in situations which riled him. Others have remarked on a reflective state akin to a trance. Norman Yardley speaks of Verity's "daydreams", which, in John Kay's view, simply meant that he was mentally tussling with some deep strategy. R. C. Robertson-Glasgow, a fervent admirer of the Yorkshireman, has noted Verity's rare flat days when, knowing that the match was well won by Yorkshire without him, "he bowled just like a book of instruction and gave his soul a rest."

One day when Yorkshire toiled and Verity had drifted into a lethargic mood, Brian Sellers paused between overs to vent his frustration on Bowes. "That pal of yours, you can't do anything with him. You can't goad him into action." Bowes responded: "Have you ever tried going to him and saying: 'Well, Hedley, I don't think we can win this match. I suppose if we've any hope at all, it will have to be you to get them out. But I don't think you can do it.'"

Sellers duly passed on the message and immediately Verity bristled with energy and purpose. At the end of the over a beaming Yorkshire captain looked round at Bowes and cupped his hands to whisper: "By God, Bill, that system of yours – it works like a charm. If you tell him he can't do it, he shows you he jolly well can."

Verity usually maintained his calm as a cricketer. "Hedley was a nice, solid type of chap and generally very quiet," says Bill Bowes. "He was a patient man." There was, however, one occasion when Verity simmered with uncharacteristic petulance. The match was against Surrey at the Oval, and Yorkshire, without Bowes and Macaulay, could not prevent their hosts from building up a massive total. Verity bowled 57 overs and conceded 115 runs. Squires and Barling both hit centuries and Surrey totalled 560. It was the highest innings against Yorkshire since 1901 when Sussex, in the days of Ranji and Fry, had achieved an identical target at Hove.

Surrey chose to bat on after topping 500 by lunch on the second day and Verity could not hide his disgust at the delayed declaration. The *Yorkshire Post* described his protest in the following terms: "It opened with a slow leg theory attack so genuine that he had not a single fieldsman on the offside. He bowled over the wicket and pitched well outside the leg stump, his attitude being: 'If you want any more runs you must fetch them.' Then, to emphasise his protest, he delivered two balls with an under-arm action, tossing them straight on to the bat." Each of Verity's under-arm deliveries was ruled no-ball by umpire Frank Chester because the bowler had not notified him of his intention to change from over-arm, and each was hit for two runs.

Verity clearly intended to continue his ironic lob bowling excursion, but Sellers called a halt to the charade by insisting that he should revert to his normal style. All tempers were cooled when Barling was dismissed and Surrey at last applied the declaration.

In other trying circumstances Verity usually took the course of polite protest. This was his response when he was called upon to answer charges of unfitness by the Yorkshire committee. He had suffered a painful reaction, a small lump appearing under his bowling arm, to inoculations before an Australian tour. Bill Bowes remembers that he also had sustained a troublesome groin injury, as luck would have it before a Roses match. "I trust you are all fit. If anyone is injured tell me now or forever hold your peace," was the inimitably trenchant greeting of Brian Sellers when the Yorkshire players trooped into the dressing-room.

Bowes did not know that Verity had preceded him in the sick parade when he reported his injury to Sellers. The Yorkshire captain looked sternly at him and said: "What the bloody hell is this? Your mate has just been in. He says he can't play, in a *Roses match*, because he's got a lump under his arm. Inoculations for Australia! [An appalled gasp here.] Yorkshire means more than England. You should know that." There was an awful note of finality in Sellers' next words. "Well, you can both bloody well play," he said.

Bowes and Verity did play and Lancashire had the bonus of unexpected runs against the two Yorkshire crocks. The sequel was a meeting of the Yorkshire committee and Verity was asked to explain why he had played in a match when he was obviously unfit. He replied: "I'm very sorry. I certainly would not have had the inoculations if I'd thought this would happen. But it did and I reported the matter to the skipper." Verity said he had told Sellers that he doubted whether he would be able to bowl properly. The Yorkshire committee expressed their ignorance of this state of affairs. Verity then sought the corroboration of Sellers who was sitting close to him. "Didn't I report it, skipper?" he appealed. Sellers looked straight ahead and did not utter a word.

Bowes says that after the incident and for the rest of the season an air of coolness prevailed between the Yorkshire captain and his premier slow left-arm bowler. "Hedley would not speak to Brian unless he was asked a direct question." The rift was healed in time; but Sellers would often say to Bowes: "I can handle thee, Bill, but thi' mate – well, he's a different matter." In reply, Bowes, remembering the disagreement, would comment: "You weren't too clever, skipper. You must never threaten Hedley."

The ice had to be broken from time to time, but Sellers always saluted the qualities of Verity as a bowler. Such was Verity's importance that he once played for several weeks with a broken finger, fortunately for Yorkshire, on his right hand. During this time he batted at No. 11 and, between spells of bowling, he fielded at third man or fine leg. Sellers told him: "Stop the ball with your bloody boot. Don't break your other hand." Verity was retained in the team entirely for his bowling.

In 1933 Verity and Bowes were already seasoned campaigners with a tour of Australia behind them. Yorkshire won their third successive championship and in May and June they won 12 successive matches, seven in two days and six with an innings to spare. Verity, Bowes and Macaulay were the leading bowlers, not only in Yorkshire, but in the whole of the country, and in championship matches alone they took 391 wickets between them.

At Leyton, on the Essex ground where Holmes and Sutcliffe had established their first wicket record of 555 in the previous season, Verity claimed 17 wickets in a day in July. He took 8–47 in the first innings and 9–44 in the second innings to exceed Tom Emmett's record of 16 wickets for 38 runs against Cambridgeshire at Hunslet, Leeds in 1869. Essex were dismissed for 104 in their first innings and by four o'clock were all out for the second time for 64. Colin Blythe, in 1907, and Tom Goddard, in 1939, are the only other bowlers to have matched Verity's feat. It gave him a total of 44 wickets at a cost of just over seven runs each in three successive games.

"There has never been a match in which the secret of Verity's power has been revealed as in this achievement," reported the *Yorkshire Post*. "The wicket was soft, and there was a strong wind and a warm sun to dry it. But, surprising to relate, the ball at no point in either of the two Essex innings turned, as all expected it would do. There is ready proof of this in the fact that Macaulay, bowling round the wicket, was unable to make his leg-trap into the profitable affair it would have been had the wicket been completely responsive to the spinning ball.

"But the wicket, even though the ball did not turn viciously, was just right for Verity," continued the report. "From the top of his outstretched left arm he delivered the ball to make it rise from the pitch in a way that completely baffled the Essex batsmen. They found it popping so much – there were times when the ball passed them chest high – that while they, sadly puzzled, were trying to decide what to do about it they got out."

The Essex batsmen provided Verity with 50 wickets, 36 at a cost of 6.9 runs each in three matches at Leyton, in his first three seasons with Yorkshire; but they did not see the ball rear so terrifyingly as it did on that dispiriting day in 1933.

Warwickshire also had cause to remember Verity and the rain-affected wickets at Headingley. Only Essex, Glamorgan, Kent and Lancashire suffered worse at his hands. In 1933, two years after his feat against them, Verity's spin contributed to the Midland county's innings defeat. Eighteen of the 20 wickets which fell in four hours were shared by Verity and Macaulay. Bob Wyatt, the Warwickshire captain, was unbeaten with 33, including five boundaries, out of the first innings total of 63. He batted defiantly for 90 minutes but he could not save the follow-on. In the second innings he was second top scorer with 24.

Wyatt, now aged 84 and England's oldest living captain, recalls a wager he made with Verity and Bowes before the start of the 1933 season. The Yorkshire bowlers teasingly told him that he would not get 50 against them, and a five-shilling stake was agreed. "When we went to

Leeds they got us on a sticky wicket," says Wyatt. "Verity and Bowes agreed that as I was not out I hadn't lost the bet and could count 25 towards my second innings score." Wyatt was unimpressed by what he considered an extreme case of Yorkshire parsimony.

"That was not really fair, as my 33 not out on a bad wicket when my side had been dismissed cheaply was worth a good deal more. However, I agreed against my better judgement. In the second innings Hedley got me out for 24, so I lost my bet by one run."

In each of his nine full English seasons Verity took at least 150 wickets, and he averaged 185 wickets a season; thrice consecutively between 1935 and 1937 he took over 200 wickets to equal the record set by Rhodes. His average for Yorkshire ranged from 11.44 to 15.31. He headed the English first-class bowling averages in his first season and in his last in 1939, and he never finished lower than fifth.

The second of Verity's three 200 wickets' seasons, in 1936, brought him an astonishing sequence of 69 wickets at a cost of 8.63 runs each in seven matches. These figures included 15 wickets against Essex and Oxford University and heading the list was a staggering performance against Kent at Sheffield.

The match produced a wonderful triumph for Verity, who took 15 wickets for 38 runs as Yorkshire won by an innings and 153 runs. Kent at the time led the championship and they had won four of their previous five matches. In their second innings at Sheffield Kent were bowled out for 39. The innings lasted 75 minutes and the last five wickets fell for nine runs. Verity took nine wickets for 12 runs and also caught Fagg off the bowling of Smailes. "Yorkshire were incredibly, almost indecently, victorious, and from first to last outplayed Kent who were but a shadow of themselves," wrote Kilburn.

The Yorkshire team of the 1930s were lords of an enviable domain. The county's renown was such that a tour of Australia was mooted at one stage. They did tour Jamaica in the early months of 1936 to earn further distinction and admiration. This was the first overseas tour by an English county since Kent's visit to America in 1903. It was undertaken at the request of the Jamaica Cricket Association who guaranteed the expenses of the tour. Lord Hawke, the Yorkshire president, who had been instrumental in arranging the trip, told the players: "Ahead of you is a difficult task. If you can win where so many teams have failed, I shall be delighted. Dispose of Headley as quickly as you can, then you will probably win." Jamaica had not lost a home match for 10 years and Hawke's warning reflected the worldwide respect for George Headley, who was known as the "black Bradman" and dominated West Indian cricket for nearly 20 years.

Yorkshire, led by Paul Gibb, played three games against Jamaica, winning the first at Melbourne Park by five wickets. Hedley Verity bowled 57 overs in the match and took 10 wickets at a cost of 106 runs. Herbert Sutcliffe, who shared the managerial duties with George Hirst, considered that his colleague bowled better in the West Indies than in Australia three years earlier. "Verity's magnificent bowling amazed not only our opponents, but even the Yorkshire players," he said.

Jamaica prospered while George Headley was at the wicket. "He was in splendid form," related Sutcliffe. "A century from his flashing blade appeared a foregone conclusion, but tactics played a prominent part in his dismissal. Verity, in particular, tied him up for long periods. Headley began to show signs of irritation. We were not averse to allowing the other batsman to score a single to 'collar' the bowling. Our aim was for Headley's downfall because here, we realised, was a super batsman capable of prolific scores. Headley tired of an innings of inactivity, made a rash stroke, and paid the penalty."

Headley's dismissal for 62 restricted Jamaica to 280 in reply to Yorkshire's first innings score of 325. The colony's batsmen seemed likely to deny the Yorkshire bowlers in a spirited start to their second innings. At the end of the third day Jamaica had reached 174 for the loss of only two wickets. The next morning brought a startling change. Beckford was out without scoring and Headley, again frustrated, struck out at a perfect length ball from Verity and was easily caught by Ellis Robinson. Jamaica's last eight wickets fell for 79 runs.

Yorkshire needed 213 for victory in less than three hours and lost three wickets for only 57 runs. Whirlwind hitting by Robinson, who was promoted in a profitable gamble, sealed the issue. Arthur Mitchell, playing one of the finest innings of his career, hit a century and stroked the conclusive runs in the last over of the match.

The exciting finish to this game overshadowed the two remaining games against Jamaica, both drawn, but marked by intense rivalry. The keenness of the cricket in the second game at Melbourne Park, in which Jamaica rallied after following-on, is shown by Yorkshire's bowling figures. In the first innings Bowes bowled 44 overs, Fisher 46, and Verity 59. Of Fisher's overs no fewer than 33 were maidens and only 33 were scored off him altogether. Verity's figures included 30 maidens and his two wickets cost him 91 runs.

"The wickets in Jamaica are much too good," declared Sutcliffe. Verity proceeded to emphasise the point with a century – his only first-class hundred – in the last match at Sabina Park. The innings included 10 boundaries and, reported the Yorkshire Post, "Verity delighted the crowd with his aggressive tactics. So well did he attack the bowling with crisp shots all round the wicket that his second 50 came in just over an hour."

Horace Fisher, another left-arm bowler and a strong contender at one time for a place in the Yorkshire attack, also won high praise on the tour to Jamaica. Fisher was reputed to have demanded his Yorkshire cap before refusing a league offer to take his chance with the county. Horace hotly denied the allegation and said: "Ah were never bothered about a cap. All I wanted was t'brass as went wi' it." Fisher deputised as the Middleton professional when Verity was released for county duties. He always maintained that matters would have been different if the Central Lancashire League club had refused to release Verity. "Ah got mucky end o'stick every time" was his answer to repeated questions about his failure to stay in first-class cricket.

Sir Leonard Hutton, like Verity, was moulded in the furnace of Roses cricket. He remembers the rugged quality of the matches between Yorkshire and Lancashire. "There was a hardness about them you only found elsewhere in Test matches against Australia. The training was very handy for North-country players looking for England recognition."

Verity played in his first Roses match at Old Trafford in 1931, a few days after his 10 wickets' feat against Warwickshire. He took the first of his 89 wickets against Lancashire – five for 54 in 28 responsible overs – and it was the beginning of a notable association with the Manchester ground.

In the years of Verity's supremacy Neville Cardus was moved to write: "I think that when Lancashire batsmen suffer nightmares they moan and turn uneasily in their sleep, while their minds retreat from the dreadful problem of Peel, Hirst, Rhodes and Verity all available at once on a bad wicket, with a Sheffield crowd to cheer on the White Rose, and Arthur Mitchell crouching at silly mid-off. But then Yorkshire's left-arm bowlers deserve a whole book to themselves."

Eddie Paynter, a tiny left-hander whose batting pulsed with ferocity, was one Lancastrian who sought to break the defensive stalemate and lighten the grim battles of attrition of the 1930s. He seethed with the resolution of a born fighter and he once said, in response to the cautionary words of his captain, "I'm not going to pander to them." Paynter's belligerence was particularly addressed to Yorkshire, but it was also a rebuke to those partisans who found his swashbuckling stroke-play unbecoming, even shocking, in a Roses match.

Bill Bowes recalls that Lancashire had so far become embedded in a defensive groove that "even our bad balls weren't hit. They'd stopped thinking they could beat us." Bowes says that it was this resigned approach that Brian Sellers was quick to turn to his advantage. "If a batsman played at one and missed Brian used to try to suggest that the ball had turned many a mile. He would instantly summon up the close fieldsmen to crowd the bat and it often worked the trick."

The twinkling feet of Eddie Paynter expressed his contempt for such ploys on a day of thrilling adventure at Bradford in May, 1932. On a bowler's pitch, potentially treacherous in the warm sunshine, Paynter made it look positively genial as he hit 152 out of 209 in three and a half hours. His third 50 came in less than half-an-hour. He mounted a prodigious attack on Verity who was hit for five sixes. Verity's figures of 8 for 107 in 39 overs reflected his inexperience; but they were dented by a batsman on the rampage, living dangerously where lesser players would have opted for survival.

When the Yorkshire players returned disconsolately to the pavilion at the close of play they were reprimanded by Emmott Robinson. "You've made a mess of it now," was his greeting, "you ought to have batted tonight." The Yorkshiremen had had a busy, tiring day. The old campaigner was in danger of being kicked downstairs for his impertinence. "What on that wicket!" they exclaimed in disbelief. "Yes", said the unabashed Emmott, "if only for one over. Then you could have had the roller on." Robinson was proved right on the Monday morning. The debris of turf loosened by Verity's spinners, which might have been battened down to help bind a deteriorating wicket, was now tossed aside.

Yorkshire were beaten by an innings and 50 runs, their first defeat by Lancashire at Bradford for 40 years. Sibbles, bowling with alarming lift, took seven wickets for 10 runs (he took another five in Yorkshire's second innings) to bowl out Yorkshire for 46. It was Yorkshire's second lowest score against Lancashire, ranking next to their 33 at Leeds in 1924 when Cecil Parkin and Richard Tyldesley bowled them out on another Whitsuntide morning.

Yorkshire – and Hedley Verity – did not dally in turning the tables on Lancashire in 1932. The return trip across the Pennines to Old Trafford produced the inevitable, fiery riposte. Sutcliffe, in captivating mood, hit a century and Leyland scored 91. The Yorkshire stalwarts mocked the slowcoach tradition of Roses matches by scoring 141 together in an hour and three quarters.

Verity and Bowes, shouldering the burden left by the withdrawal from the attack of the injured Macaulay, shared 16 wickets in the match. Between them the two bowlers delivered 80 out of the 101 overs in Lancashire's first innings, taking four wickets each. Verity bowled one ball short of 77 overs, 39 of which were maidens, for a match return of nine wickets for 106 runs.

"The bowling of Verity and Bowes in the half-hour after lunch on the third day made victory certain," commented the *Yorkshire Post*. Lancashire were 118 for 1 at lunch; afterwards they lost five wickets for 25 runs in less than three-quarters of an hour. Verity, with the assistance of Mitchell, broke the threatening second-wicket partnership of Hopwood and Ernest Tyldesley, who had put on 95 in 100 minutes. Bowes, making the ball lift and, in Maurice Leyland's words "not leaving much time for study", quickly dismissed Paynter and Iddon. The big man then brought off a capital catch at mid-on to dismiss Hopwood off Verity. Yorkshire's victory by an innings and five runs was quite a breakthrough. It was their first win in a Roses match since 1926.

Verity and Bowes enjoyed the pleasure of working together during a decade in which Yorkshire beat the old enemy nine times, four times in succession in the last two seasons before the war. Neville Cardus offered one explanation of, what for him – and he was never slow to censure – must have been an unpardonable surrender. Speaking of one instance of Lancashire's nerveless batting in a Roses match he said: "The players probably suffered much when young from eating Yorkshire pudding, or perhaps some of them had their teeth taken out by dentists from Pudsey."

Verity's supple left hand extracted the wickets in more affable fashion. He had match figures of 8 for 53 in 60 overs in the innings victory over Lancashire at Sheffield in 1934. Three years later he claimed 10 wickets in another comprehensive Yorkshire success at Old Trafford. One *Yorkshire Post* editorial was headlined: "Not so bad." It saluted the arrival at a distinctive milestone in Roses match history in 1934. "Our mood is one of quiet satisfaction; after all it is just the 50th time we have done it. We have the right to say it is not so bad."

The artful persuasiveness of Verity combined with the ebullient leadership of Brian Sellers produced a kind of dementia in Lancashire cricket circles in the last years before the war. Yorkshire's sporting instincts in this grave time did not permit the indulgence of appeasement. If Hitler had played cricket, they would probably have called his bluff too. Yorkshire exuded an icy calm in keeping with their all-round deterrents and they brought the curtain down on this Roses decade with a flourish.

The first of Yorkshire's four pre-war victories over Lancashire was gained at Bradford in 1938. Verity took four wickets for nine runs in 28 balls to exploit faint-hearted Lancashire batting. This was a game which seemed doomed to stalemate. "In the first hour," wrote Kilburn, "the match was clearly labelled 'drawn with care'. Paynter and Iddon paid not the slightest attention to suggestions by Yorkshire that the ball was turning or about to turn dangerously.

"At half-past twelve Paynter was so convinced that the day was drifting to a certain draw that he scampered down the wicket to hit Verity for six. He then tried again and was stumped by Wood." Lancashire were 86 for 2 but had seemingly no cause for alarm. Their complacency was to be rudely shaken. Sellers, like a circus ringmaster, now took a grip on the situation. The hitherto carefree batsmen were pressed into a strokeless diffidence.

"In the early afternoon," wrote Kilburn, "the Lancashire innings passed to a dramatic and pitiful end. In 45 minutes the score changed from 120 for 4 to 138 all out. Nature was never responsible for all the dust thrown into the batsmen's eyes, but Verity and Smailes were, naturally, only too ready to enhance the illusions created."

At 2.20 a superb diving catch by Sellers at silly mid-off dismissed Nutter and 10 minutes later, in one over, Smailes gained lbw decisions against Phillipson and Lister. Hopwood, playing over a ball pitched well up to him, was bowled at 130, and after one despairing boundary by Pollard, Verity ended the innings with two wickets in successive balls. The Yorkshireman had taken another six "cheap and surprising" wickets against Lancashire to complete a task which had looked beyond even his formidable talents.

There was another overwhelming victory in the return match at Old Trafford where Yorkshire won by an innings and 200 runs. The pitch did this time come to Yorkshire's and Verity's aid. Sunshine after rain ensured that the match was over by 12.30 on the third day. "Verity was accounted the indisputable master and no-one so much as offered a challenge to his throne," said one writer. "Verity and Robinson bowled at once with a close-set field and a general air of appointments elsewhere."

Lancashire lost their last nine wickets for 51 runs and Verity moving in, high on his toes, took five of them with superb delicacy and refinement. The unluckiest Lancastrian on another dire day for the county was Paynter, who was out to a vicious ball. He had batted with great determination and deserved to retain his wicket. He was the ninth man out as he played defensively at a ball from Bowes, which rose sharply from the pitch. It just glanced his glove and Robinson took the catch at short-leg.

Warm sunshine graced the setting as the players left the field. A radiant day had been spoiled for the spectators, particularly those in the

Lancashire section. "Old Trafford was left in its green graciousness," wrote Kilburn, "and so intrinsically attractive was the scene that hundreds of people stayed to take their lunch and perhaps hoped that Lancashire would be given another innings."

Yorkshire emphasised their superiority with another double success against Lancashire in 1939. Verity assumed the role of supporting bowler with five wickets at Manchester where a magnificent performance by Bowes carried Yorkshire to another innings victory. It was achieved on a flawless wicket on which, so it was said, another game could have started when stumps were drawn.

Over 800 runs, a frenetic flurry of activity in a Roses match, were scored on the first two days. It was the highest total that had then been recorded in the holiday games between the two counties. Sutcliffe, who scored his ninth century against Lancashire, and Mitchell actually put on a hundred before lunch on the Whitsuntide Monday. They added another 161 runs in the afternoon session. Yorkshire, with commendable haste, spurted to a total of 528 – the first score of 500 or more against Lancashire for 52 years.

At lunch on the Tuesday Lancashire were 124 for 2, and Paynter and Oldfield had completed militant fifties without any sign of strain. Sellers still dared to hope with a cussedness which was his trademark. Before the restart he called for one last, defiant assault. "Now, lads, let's get stuck in; we can do 'em all right. Come on, let's go."

Bowes led the rally and, said Kilburn, "a great bowler suddenly found great inspiration and triumphed principally because of the virtue within himself." In an hour and a half Lancashire catastrophically lost their eight wickets for 61 runs. In his last eight overs Bowes took five wickets for 21 runs to finish with a return of 6 for 43.

The best for Yorkshire was still to come; the finale under the dark skies of Headingley was one of the most memorable in the Roses match annals. Lancashire went down with their pride intact, beaten by superlative bowling and a batsman at the height of his mastery. Lancashire, in fact, led Yorkshire by 54 runs on the first innings and it needed a touch of genius to tip the scales against them. It was forthcoming in the off-spin of Ellis Robinson, who took eight wickets for 35 runs in the finest performance of his career. Robinson and Verity bowled unchanged on the last morning. Lancashire lost five wickets for nine runs and were all out for 92.

Yorkshire needed 147 to win and the game was struck at its most exciting stage by an extraordinary freak of weather which drenched the pitch when Yorkshire were six short of victory. "It seemed impossible to complete the game in such a cloudburst but that is what the players, to their infinite credit, did," wrote A. A. Thomson.

The stately calm of Leonard Hutton, who played an innings which he today considers was probably the best of his career, was the deciding factor. He had worthy adversaries in Garlick and Pollard who bowled themselves to a standstill during the course of a nerve-racking afternoon. Yorkshire lost five wickets for 106 and their alarms continued as the angry clouds built up over Headingley. At 129, Sellers played a ball from Garlick wide of mid-on and such confusion arose over the second run that by the time the ball was in the bowler's hands Sellers was sprawled flat on his face and yards out of his ground. Garlick, his back to the pitch, knew nothing of this and discovering that Hutton was safely home did no more, while Sellers thankfully scrambled to his feet to make good his escape.

"Hutton, growing greater by the minute, drove Garlick for four to the off, balanced and serene for all his opportunism," wrote Cardus in the *Manchester Guardian*. "Only eight wanted and the heavens ready to burst. Several boys screamed; their elders roared; caps went on high when Hutton got his century; umbrellas were opened desperately: a match and a crescendo in a thousand."

Mine was one of the schoolboy caps hurled aloft when Hutton reached a remarkable hundred. The rain streamed down our faces as the scattered drops became a downpour. Hutton now drove wildly at Pollard, his first uncontrolled shot in an innings lasting three hours and a quarter.

The ball swirled through the rain and darkness and high over cover. Hutton and Sellers scampered the two runs needed for victory. The catch, if it ever was one, fell to ground behind Washbrook splashing vainly in pursuit of the ball. Had he caught it there could have been no more play, for the ground was swiftly transformed into a river amid the torrents.

One apocryphal story concerned an Ilkley man who watched the dramatic events at Headingley. He was sitting in his armchair at home, 15 miles away, when he heard the lunchtime broadcast and realised the possibility of an exciting finish to the game. He turned to his wife and said: "I can't miss this." He walked straight out of the house in his slippers, without a hat or coat, jumped on a bus, and reached the ground in time to witness a famous victory.

He may have been the man who was seen just below the Press box dribbling a cushion about in the drenching rain, hatless and soaked to the skin and laughing with hysterical joy.

Hedley Verity, like Rhodes, opened the batting for England in a Test match. His average in Tests against Australia was higher than in matches for Yorkshire. Gubby Allen, the England captain in the 1936–7 series, promoted the Yorkshireman when the regular openers had failed to prosper on that tour. In the fourth Test at Adelaide, Verity went in first with Charles Barnett and together they scored 53 and 45, the best opening partnerships up to that point in the series. There were other even more stirring deeds in company with Eddie Paynter and Les Ames in Test cricket.

Verity scored 5,605 runs for Yorkshire and England, with an average of 18.08 in first-class cricket. Of these 3,898 were made for Yorkshire. There were some rousing moments at the crease, notably in 1936, when at one stage he headed the Yorkshire averages. Against India at Bradford he shared a seventh wicket partnership of 128 with Frank Smailes. He was unbeaten on 96, his highest score in England.

In Yorkshire there were many good judges who felt that had he cared to develop his batting Verity could have achieved distinction as an all-rounder. Jim Kilburn said: "As a batsman in any other company but Yorkshire he might well have been a leading run-getter." The occasional batting treats were, for Verity, pleasant diversions amid more pressing duties. He did not dwell upon his unfulfilled batting hopes. Brian Sellers was, we can be assured, not joking when he said: "You may open for England, but you bat No. 10 for Yorkshire."

T. C. F. Prittie believed that Verity was underrated as a batsman. He wrote: "Verity learnt to bat much as the writer of a short story learns his trade – by eliminating every frill and embellishment, weeding out the phrase for effect and the extraneous gesture, pruning with rigorous economy. He found that a purely utilitarian method was most often in the best interests of his side."

Bob Wyatt considers that the batting mannerisms of Verity pointed to the fact that he had modelled himself on Herbert Sutcliffe. R. C. Robertson-Glasgow said that, in common with Sutcliffe, Verity could make his dismissal from the wicket seem due to a regrettable lapse on the part of Providence. He whimsically noted that a casual observer might easily have mistaken Verity for Sutcliffe a little out of form, for he seemed to have caught something of the master's style and gesture. Like Sutcliffe, he could be clean bowled in a manner that somehow exonerated the batsman from all guilt.

"On the field," said Robertson-Glasgow, "both these Yorkshiremen stood halfway between grand opera and high drama. Only Verity did not make so many runs. The most he scored in a season was 855. But he was apt to make runs when they mattered most."

In the matter of plain arithmetic, so often torn from its context to the confusion of judgement, Verity showed by far the best average during this century, wrote Robertson-Glasgow in his obituary tribute in *Wisden* in 1944. He was referring to Verity's achievement in taking 1,956 wickets at 14.90 runs each in 10 years of first-class cricket.

Verity's efficiency in tailor-made conditions was unanswerable. He was psychologically as well as technically the master. Yet he was unmoved by the ease of such performances. His favourite saying was: "Do not praise me when I have taken 8 for 20 on a sticky wicket, but when I have got 2 for 100 on a perfect wicket." He remembered the blank days when he bowled his marathon spells with no luck at all.

Robertson-Glasgow delighted in the memory of an artist at work, and of the way Verity "peered down the pitch after each ball, suggesting a chemist watching the perilous crucible, the connoiseur nosing the dubious vase, or even a conjuror investing simplicity with mystery."

There was so much to treasure in Verity's genius. Another man intent on watching the marvels, which became a part of his cricket education, was Sir Leonard Hutton. It was a heritage upon wich he looks back with keen pleasure. These were great years for Yorkshire cricket and Sir Leonard says: "I missed people like Hedley after the war. You can never recapture such moments. You never get it back."

10

MISADVENTURE AT MELBOURNE

"Verity was magnificent. Nothing but consummate length and flight could have checked Bradman, in circumstances made for Bradman." – Neville Cardus.

AUSTRALIA, two down in the series, were on their knees in the third Test at Melbourne in January, 1937. It was a match they had to win in order to save the Ashes. Torrential rain came to their aid to produce a heart-breaking wicket which might have been designed by the witches of Macbeth so preposterous was its behaviour.

The savagery of the wicket was a demoralising setback for the England captain, Gubby Allen. Allen's potential matchwinner Hedley Verity had to watch, with sickened eyes, the discomforture of his batting colleagues on a wicket upon which he would surely have sealed the outcome of the series. One writer said: "You did not want batsmen on that wicket. You wanted the Crazy Gang, Mickey Mouse, Einstein and Euclid!"

It was a cruel match for England, for it also marked the resurgence of Don Bradman, hitherto in the doldrums, who rallied his team with resolute batsmanship. He was only just in time. Bradman had scored only 133 runs in five innings before the Melbourne misadventure: afterwards he unfurled his stroke-play to make glorious amends with 677 runs, including two double centuries, in four innings. At Melbourne he scored 270 out of 564 and in the fourth Test at Adelaide (a match in which England briefly held the ascendency) his contribution was 212 out of Australia's second innings total of 433.

"The unkind thing about the Melbourne Test," says Gubby Allen, "was that we lost the toss on a good wicket and at the close of play on the first day Australia had lost six wickets for 181." Bradman was one of Verity's two wickets on a day when England seemed to be moving remorselessly towards a conclusive victory. "We had done marvellously well to reach this position, for we had bowled when the ball was wet and rather awkward," comments Allen. The rains started to descend in earnest towards the end of the first afternoon and tumbled pitilessly and with increasing ferocity throughout the night. Play did not resume until after lunch on the second day when the impact of the deluge was confirmed in horrific terms. Hugh Trumble, the former Australian spinner and secretary of the Melbourne Club, considered it the worst wicket he had seen. "The behaviour of the ball on this terrible Saturday went beyond all I had expected," wrote Neville Cardus. "I could scarcely believe my eyesight. The pitch grew fiercer over by over."

Australia declared at 200 for 9, amid an atmosphere bordering on the slapstick. On this crazy pitch many observers felt that Allen should have declared as soon as Hammond, after his near miraculous 32, had been dismissed. "The chance was there to get Bradman out for next to nothing," said Cardus, "I doubt if any Australian batsman could have stayed in 10 minutes."

According to one observer, Australia were so anxious not to bat again in a hurry that Bradman spread his fielders out wide and, in the end, his bowlers were directing the ball off the wicket. Allen remains adamant that an early declaration would have been meaningless. He gives this explanation of his decision: "England had scored about 60. We were still 140 behind. The clouds were rolling across the ground. Only one of these had to open and the rest of us would then have batted on a perfectly good wicket on the Monday.

"Furthermore, if I had declared, the Australians would have appealed against the light, which wasn't good, and their appeal would have been upheld." Allen believes that even if he had declared earlier Australia would not have subjected their major batsmen to the perils of the wicket. He argues that Bradman would have sent in only his tailenders and then made a light appeal to avert disaster.

England finally declared at 76 for 9 and Sievers, a medium-pace bowler of no great pretensions, took five wickets for 21 runs. Sievers did not play again in the series, which may mean that he was lucky to bowl on the Melbourne wicket, or that he should not have been picked in the first place. Even at the last the fates were against Allen. His bowlers had to grapple with a wet ball amid the persistent drizzle after they had taken five Australian second innings wickets for 97 runs. Bradman and Fingleton (136) seized their chance to drive home their advantage as the weather relented on the fourth day. They scored 346 together in six hours and effectively won the match.

"Verity was magnificent," wrote Cardus. "In his absence Bradman might have scored another 100 runs. Nothing but consummate length and flight could have checked Bradman, in circumstances made for Bradman. Verity's accuracy made the position of silly point as safe as it was necessary, technically and psychologically, all day. Every run from Verity had to be earned. It was beautiful bowling, delightful to the eye and intellect." Verity's figures in the Australian total of 564 were three wickets for 79 runs in 37.7 overs.

Before the trauma of Melbourne England were buoyant and revelled in this peacemaking tour which attracted record crowds. The goodwill after the disharmony of the previous "bodyline" tour was such that less truculent Australians thought it would be beneficial for the game if England won the series. One man went so far as to say: "It would do us good to lose. We are a bit too cocky, and a kick in the pants wouldn't do us any harm."

At Brisbane, in the first Test of Hedley Verity's second Australian tour, the pitch was tailormade for him and yet he did not get a chance to bowl on it. Australia were bowled out for 58 and Allen and Voce took the wickets. "Verity," said William Pollock, "was like a dog watching two other dogs with a succulent bone."

Gubby Allen says that the wicket had disintegrated after rain. "The foothold had gone and I had a very hard bang down on my front foot, as indeed all fast bowlers should have, and I was skidding a bit and bowling some bad 'uns. Maurice Leyland said: 'Put Hedley on.' I said: 'No, I'm not going to put him on. I don't want them to see Hedley on a turner. We can keep him in reserve – we're winning the match.'" Verity had, in fact, made a substantial contribution to England's victory in Australia's first innings, bowling in his implacable run-saving style. Verity bowled 28 overs for 52 runs and so difficult was he to score from that the batsmen in desperation tried to get runs off Voce. The Nottinghamshire man bowled magnificently; he did not miss his chance; but he was almost obliged to take six wickets at the other end.

Allen and Voce took 18 wickets in the match but Verity prized out the Australian opener, Jack Fingleton, who had defended stoutly to score a hundred in the first innings. Charles Barnett presents the story of Fingleton's dismissal as another example of Verity's expertise and planning. "We could not prevent Fingleton from reaching his century, but Hedley got him next ball with his 'quickie'. Maurice Leyland came to me and said: 'Charlie, there's real brains. If Hedley had bowled that quickie all the way up through the nineties, Fingleton would have seen it.'" Barnett adds: "Fingleton was just a shade relaxed, and having made his hundred, he was caught napping. This was a perfect example of a bowler who can 'think out' a batsman and carry it through at the right time."

Bob Wyatt also remembers his former Test colleague as a perceptive man and a master in spotting a batsman's weak points. He cites one example of Verity's acumen in a match against South Africa at Trent Bridge in 1935. Dudley Nourse was the batsman and he had just arrived at the wicket. Wyatt recalls Verity coming up to him and saying: "I've played against this chap before and tied him up. I don't think he likes batting against me." Wyatt immediately brought Verity into the attack and he says: "Nourse managed only four runs and he never looked like getting any more against Hedley." He remembers Pelham Warner, who was chairman of the Test selectors, congratulating him on the dismissal. He explained to Warner that it was Verity who deserved the congratulations. "The reason I'd put Hedley on was due to *his* confidence that he could dismiss Nourse." Wyatt adds: "Verity bowled intelligently and was always thinking of the best way to get batsmen out."

Gubby Allen recalls the intelligence of a cricketer to whom he invariably turned for advice. "Hedley always gave 100 per cent and you knew perfectly well that he would give everything from first to last."

Verity took three wickets, including that of Bradman for the seventh time, in the second Test at Sydney in the 1936–7 series. This was a match which was again dominated by England's fast bowlers. At Adelaide, in the fourth Test, England squandered their last opportunity to regain the Ashes with a batting decline after bowling out Australia for 288 on a perfect wicket. "That's where we lost – at Adelaide," said Allen after the series. "It has been our batting more than our bowling that has let us down in the Tests."

Allen and Voce, so commanding as bowlers before Christmas, were victims of the injury malaise at Adelaide. Allen says that he was over-ruled by the selection committee and that Voce was picked despite suffering from a back injury. Allen also pulled a muscle and only bowled 14 overs in Australia's second innings. Verity had to perform another of his holding operations as Bradman, with a double century made dourly by his standards, imposed his stamp on the match. Verity's figures in difficult circumstances underlined his accuracy. They read: 0-37; M–17; R–54. He bowled unchanged after tea and sent down 13 overs for only seven runs. "All the pressure was on Hedley," says Allen, "and he blocked it up very effectively."

In the Adelaide Test Verity was pressed into service as an emergency opener and he shared partnerships of 53 and 45 with Barnett, the best for England up to that point in the series. His promotion was a surprise choice but Allen says: "We were struggling and I considered that Hedley had the ability to do the job." Verity himself, despite his fine efforts, later acknowledged that he did not have the strokes for the position of a Test opening batsman. "There are half-a-dozen youngsters at home who know more about batting than I do," he said.

Charles Barnett tells the amusing story of Verity's dismissal in the Adelaide Test. "Hedley had that bloody 'dog-leg' shot – he must have copied it from Sutcliffe. Like Herbert he would take a run at the ball and lift his left leg out. The ball missed the bat, hit his leg and went straight back into the stumps. It was a pity because we were going very well."

Australia retained the Ashes in England in 1938 and the catalyst was a magnificent innings by Stan McCabe in the first Test at Nottingham. "McCabe changed the gravest situation with the ease of a man using a master key," wrote Neville Cardus. "In an hour he smashed the bowling and decimated a field which had been a close, keen net." McCabe scored 232 out of 300 in less than four hours. In the last 10 overs bowled to him the Australian took strike in eight and hit 16 of his 34 fours. In the last wicket stand of 77 with Fleetwood-Smith he actually scored 72 in less than half an hour. "The dear valiance of his cricket won our hearts," enthused Cardus. McCabe's blazing stroke-play saved the game for Australia after England had run up a total of 658. Before the 903 at the Oval this was the highest innings total against Australia.

Hedley Verity bowled only 45 balls, during which he eventually took McCabe's wicket, at Nottingham. Some commentators have said that the probability of a follow-on influenced the England captain, Wally Hammond's decision to conserve Verity's energies. Charles Barnett, however, firmly believes that this was a match England should have won. He attributes Australia's reprieve to appalling captaincy by Hammond.

Barnett had watched McCabe's trials against the Gloucestershire off-spinner, Reg Sinfield, in the Australians' previous match at Bristol. He recalls: "When Stan came in I said to Wally: 'Stick a short-leg up there. This feller can't play spin.'" Hammond replied: "Mind your own business." Barnett persisted. "I am minding my own business or yours," he said. He remembers that another 90 minutes elapsed before Hammond decided to put Verity on to bowl. "Eventually someone did get through to Wally that he had Hedley in the side and he might as well bowl him. But the damage had been done then."

Douglas Wright was the unluckiest of the England bowlers. He conceded 153 runs in 39 overs. It was one of those less happy days when his eccentric spin was mauled by a batsman at the height of his powers. Brown and Bradman duly expressed their gratitude for McCabe's lifeline with match-saving centuries. Despite Barnett's indictment, it needs to be stated that England still had the scent of victory on the last day on a wearing pitch. Bradman marshalled the tactical plan to deny England;

he curbed his natural aggression with an innings of grim watchfulness. In six hours he hit only five boundaries. It was the slowest century of his life. England did not get him out. His chanceless 144 was one of his most valuable innings for Australia. It was a long, laborious and futile day for English supporters. Bradman smothered Verity's spin and the Yorkshireman had to be content to run through his precise skills in taking three wickets for 102 runs in 62 painstaking overs.

Charles Barnett considers that later in the series, at Headingley, Verity, had he been given a fair crack of the whip, would have improved on his one epic feat against Australia. "He took his chance at Lord's in 1934 and he had another at Leeds in 1938 when he did not have a captain astute enough to let him operate." Barnett says that most of the England team believed that the Yorkshire combination of Verity and Bowes would have beaten Australia at Headingley. "They were on a crumbled wicket," he says, "and if Wally had shown any aptitude at all *Yorkshire* would have defeated Australia that day. All that was wanted was for Bowes to close up one end and Verity would have got them out at the other end."

The facts of the Leeds game are that Bowes and Farnes bowled 62 overs between them, Verity severely taxed Bradman in the 19 overs allotted to him, and that the Australian scored yet another century (103 out of 153) on an overcast afternoon. One writer said that the light was as sepulchral as for any Test played in England. Cardus likened the Australians to "lost souls in a November fog being led by Bradman and his torch." Sir Pelham Warner said: "I believe Bradman would make a hundred in a blackout."

Barnett remembers that Verity had spotted a mark around the leg stump and he said to Hammond: "I'm going to bowl over the wicket." Verity knew that from round-the-wicket he could not aim the ball in the direction of fine leg to hit the rough. Over the wicket he considered that he could create problems for the Australian batsmen. Hammond, according to Barnett, refused to allow the tactic.

England's misjudgement and the emphasis on fast bowling was O'Reilly's gain. He took 10 wickets in the match on a pitch which always responded to his spin. "The air was electric as those long arms and legs came whirling down to the crease," said one writer of O'Reilly. The Australian was nicknamed "Tiger" because of the belligerent manner in which he attacked batsmen. He was like a demon at the kill. O'Reilly's menace soared to a nightmarish crescendo at Leeds when he overwhelmed England with a thrilling piece of bowling. He took five wickets for 45 runs in 15 overs. England lost 10 wickets for 74 runs in less than two hours and were all out for 123. It was England's lowest score against Australia since 1921 when they were dismissed for 112 by McDonald and Gregory at Trent Bridge.

Australia moved on tenterhooks to victory, but Cardus said: "It was not deadly spin which brought our five wickets; Hammond's faith in fast bowling rather exceeded his faith in the arts of Verity and Wright. The result was sad disillusionment."

Hedley Verity may have been denied the opportunity to take the initiative in the crucial Tests at Nottingham and Leeds, but his bowling retained its lustre. In the 1938 series against Australia he bowled 154 overs, including 53 maidens, for 354 runs. He conceded only 2.30 runs an over. It was an economy to be wondered at when it is set against another remarkable statistic. Bradman's average in the series was 108.50.

Jim Kilburn has said that Hedley Verity's idea of a cricket heaven was to bowl against Australia, with Bradman, of course, when the conditions gave batsman and bowler an equal chance. Norman Yardley, who captained England against Australia after the war, says: "I think the greatest pleasure Hedley got in his whole life was bowling to Don Bradman. No-one who did not watch him closely can realise the time and thought he gave, off the field, to working out a method of attack that would find a chink in the Australian's armour."

Verity bowled more balls in Tests – 932 – to Bradman, who scored 401 runs against him, than any other bowler sent down to the Australian and it was largely due to the Yorkshireman that Bradman's Test average was kept under 150. Verity was one of the few bowlers who refused to be over-awed by a cricketing genius. He dismissed Bradman 10 times, eight times in 16 Test meetings and twice in each innings in two matches. No other English bowler can match this achievement. His nearest English rivals were Alec Bedser, with eight dismissals, including six in post-war Tests against Australia, Larwood and Tate (seven times), and Bill Bowes with five dismissals, all in Tests. Clarrie Grimmett, the Australian leg-spinner, also took Bradman's wicket 10 times, on each occasion on the hard Australian wickets.

Leo O'Brien, who played in the 1932–3 series against England, pays tribute to his two contemporaries and comments that Verity and Grimmett had wonderful and consistent success against a formidable opponent. Bradman once said: "I think I know all about Clarrie, but with Hedley I am never sure. You see, there's no breaking point with him."

As testimony to Verity's feats against Bradman I append details of the dismissals: 1932–3: Combined Australian XI v MCC (Perth): c Hammond b Verity 3. Australia v England, 3rd Test (Adelaide): c and b

Verity 66. Fifth Test (Sydney): b Verity 71. 1934: England v Australia (Lord's): c and b Verity 36; c Ames b Verity 13. H. D. G. Leveson-Gower's XI v Australians (Scarborough): st Duckworth b Verity 132. 1936–7: Australia v England, 2nd Test (Sydney): b Verity 82. 3rd Test (Melbourne): c Robins b Verity 13; c Allen b Verity 270. 1938: England v Australia, 2nd Test (Lord's): b Verity 18.

Don Bradman always treasured his association with Yorkshire in Test and county rivalry. His record at Headingley was truly phenomenal. In six innings there between 1930 and 1948 he scored 963 runs, with an average of 192.60. His overall record in Yorkshire was 1,804 runs (average: 120.26) and his only real failure was at Park Avenue, Bradford in 1930 when he was bowled by Emmott Robinson for one. The Yorkshire committee saluted his supremacy by bestowing on him honorary life membership of the club after his last tour in 1948. It was a tribute which reflected the respect and admiration of thousands of North-country followers and it was one which would have been endorsed by Hedley Verity.

Sir Leonard Hutton, who, as a 14-year-old schoolboy, saw Bradman's then record Test score in 1930, remembers Verity's assessment of his Australian rival. "Hedley said Bradman was so difficult to bowl against because he was so quick on his feet. Bradman was always looking to attack the ball and he played shots that other batsmen would not even have attempted."

Wilfred Rhodes considered Bradman the finest batsman he had encountered in his long and distinguished career. During the Australian's second triple hundred at Leeds in 1934 Rhodes described Bradman as the "best scoring batsman" he had seen. "He has all the shots; he can apparently use them at will; he has wonderful strength in his wrists and forearms, and his timing is so perfect that one knows the quickest of eyesight is allied with lightning footwork and an astonishing judgement of the length of the ball; and with all this, he has a determination that enables him to do almost as he pleases."

One story which epitomised Bradman's confidence was his response to one questioner at lunchtime on the day of his record Test innings. He was asked how he felt after his morning's exertions. Bradman replied, with typical candour: "Good for the day."

Bill Bowes today says it would be worth going into training just to bowl at Bradman again. "Hedley and I talked about our duels with a marvellous batsman many times. I think the two of us got more pleasure, with all the stick he gave us and all the problems he set us, bowling to Don than any other batsman."

Talking about their strategies against Bradman, Bowes remembers the ploys used in an attempt to disrupt the rhythm of their rival. Verity would pitch on the off-stump and seek to make the ball turn, just slightly, away towards the slips. "You would leave the opening on the on-side, with a fieldsman deepish at mid-on," says Bowes. "Don then had to go against the spin. There was always a single, but he was playing a shot that had a certain element of risk to it. The ball had only to turn a little bit and it would take the edge. There was a *chance* of getting him out."

At other times Verity would bowl "seam up" – beautifully accurate inswingers – and he would then leave a gap at extra cover in the hope that Bradman would try to force the ball away on the offside and thus exaggerate the impetus of the ball swinging in on him. Bowes adds: "We would, of course, adopt such tactics against all good batsmen but, above all, with Bradman you had to keep him quiet at the same time." Their tactics were designed to throw the ruthless machine out of gear as Bradman looked for easy runs.

Bowes remembers how his great adversary, perhaps within sight of yet another century, would impatiently prowl at the crease when Verity and himself made adjustments to their fields. "If you moved a man from the covers to the legside or out of the slips into the covers, you could bet that the next ball would go like a bullet past the fieldsman you'd put in, or it was cut through the vacant slips."

"We used to win the odd psychological battle against Don, but he was a far better batsman than I was a bowler, and I think Hedley would have said the same in his case."

Bowes adds, with a wonderment undimmed by the passing of time: "Don hit all your bad balls for four and an awful lot of your good ones as well."

11

DOMINANT IN A
BATTING ERA

*"Verity's greatness was demonstrated in an inopportune time
for bowlers. He shone triumphantly in a bleak landscape."*

GUBBY Allen had, in fact, taken over the England captaincy, before the
1936–7 tour of Australia, for the first home Test series against India in
the preceding summer. It was a sad tour for India, riven by internal
troubles which culminated in disciplinary action being taken against Lala
Amarnath who was sent back home just before the first Test.

The team was captained by the Maharajkumar of Vizianagram,
known to cricket as "Vizzy". The appointment of "Vizzy" as captain was
generally regarded as a sign of deference to the princely patrons, who
virtually sustained cricket in India and had a number of cricketers on
their payroll. C. K. Nayudu, an outstanding cricketer and respected
leader, was subjected to the indignity of playing under a captain who did
not merit Test status.

India played 31 matches in all, winning five, losing 13 and drawing 13.
England again won the Test series with two victories at Lord's and the
Oval. Commenting on India's performances in England, *Wisden* said:
"Without wishing to be unfair or ungenerous, one has to state that, for
the chosen cricketers of a country admitted to Test status, the playing
results were most disappointing."

The first Test at Lord's opened in bright sunshine after two days of
heavy rain. Verity and Langridge were both selected, together with
Middlesex leg-spinner, Walter Robins, for the match. Under the hot sun
the wicket seemed likely to be one which a left-arm bowler would be
pleased to have at his service. Allen recalls: "I won the toss. The wicket
was wet and I went out to look at it with Hedley." Verity urged his
captain to put India in to bat. "We'll bowl them out before lunch," he
said. The confident forecast rebounded upon the Yorkshireman with a
vengeance. Allen says it was one of the few times that he saw Verity
bowl "thoroughly badly." He adds, in retrospect, that there was not quite

as much turn in the wicket as they had expected. "Merchant and Hindlekar hit our spinners all over the place."

The Lord's wicket was soft, but whenever a spinning ball dropped on a good length it invariably jumped and, said Neville Cardus, "it behaved like a bluebottle in a window pane". "But no England bowler could achieve a length, least of all Verity, whose attack before lunch was so inaccurate that Wilfred Rhodes could not have equalled it bowling right-handed from a bathchair."

Allen was a worried man after the high expectations before the start of play. The England captain did, in fact, use five bowlers – himself, Wyatt, Verity, Langridge and Robins – in the first hour of the morning. At one o'clock Allen took matters into his own hands. He bowled Merchant with a full toss and in the same over he persuaded Mushtaq Ali to present a catch to Langridge at short-leg. Robins then bowled Hindlekar and Allen trapped Nayudu leg-before-wicket. India thus lost four wickets for four runs. "The collapse was psychological as much as technical; I saw little or nothing in England's bowling to account for the falling wickets," wrote Cardus.

India, after scoring 62 for the first wicket, subsided to 147 all out. Allen took five wickets in the innings. "I often ragged Hedley about his indiscretion," says the former England captain. "But he did, in fact, bowl much better in the second innings." Verity regained his poise to take four wickets for 17 runs in 16 overs and shared the bowling honours with Allen. Gimblett hit 67 on his Test debut, the highest score of the match, as England won by nine wickets.

Verity headed the England bowling averages in the three-match series with 15 wickets at a cost of just over 15 runs each. In the second drawn Test at Manchester he took four wickets for 41 runs in 17 overs in India's first innings and then joined Robins in a century partnership for the eighth wicket. It was the third three-figure stand of the innings. Verity (66 not out) and Robins added 138 runs in 70 minutes. England, scoring at the rate of 91 runs an hour, relentlessly built up a total of 571.

Hedley Verity missed only seven Tests in 12 series in his nine years of international cricket and during a time when Australia were the principal rivals. His solitary demotion in four series against Australia occurred in the second Test, which England lost, at Melbourne on the 1932–3 tour. Even if one allows his distinctive attribute as a superb defensive bowler to be his prime claim, and that is a curt recognition of his genius, it has to be set alongside the plain fact that the 1930s were dominated by supremely talented batsmen with Bradman and Hammond as the gods.

In addition, the wickets, pledged to "last a fortnight" in the words of

Test groundsmen, provided another major burden. As testimony to how all but the very best bowlers were defeated by the shirt-front wickets the comments of *Wisden* in 1934 are worth repeating. "How often does one see nowadays a real 'sticky' wicket," commented the august almanack. "It is impossible to ignore the evidence, afforded year after year and even in a wet season, that the batsman definitely holds the upper hand." Verity's greatness was demonstrated in an inopportune time for bowlers. He shone triumphantly in a bleak landscape.

His dominance as a bowler in England was only rarely challenged by the eccentric merchants of leg-spin, with the dynamic Robins (64 wickets in 19 Tests) and later the extravagant Douglas Wright (108 wickets in 34 Tests) as the more successful exponents. Tommy Mitchell, a lovable man of Derbyshire, and the contrastingly lugubrious Jim Sims, of Middlesex, failed, in the long term, to match their considerable county achievements at Test level. Of the left-arm contenders Jim Langridge, like Robins a punishing batsman, shadowed Verity with some persistence through the 1930s. Langridge's all-round ability did, in fact, usurp Verity in the Oval Test against the West Indies in 1933. Ironically, Langridge bowled only seven overs for 23 runs and the match was won for England by Kent leg-spinner, C. S.('Father') Marriott, who claimed 11 wickets for 96 runs in his one and only Test.

Despite this omission, Verity took 31 wickets, including seven in two Tests, against the West Indian tourists. At Harrogate, in July, he masterminded Yorkshire's victory with 14 wickets for 83 runs in the match. His sensational coup enabled the county to make light of the absence of Bowes and Macaulay. Verity applied his corrective measures again for Leveson-Gower's XI in the tourists' last match at Scarborough. He obtained another 10 wickets (five in each innings) to seal the bewilderment of a chastened opposition. Jim Langridge was his ally on this occasion, taking four wickets as the West Indians lost by 125 runs.

Two years later, against the victorious South Africans at Lord's, Langridge and Verity were unable to prevent the tourists achieving their first win in England after striving for 28 years. This was the season of Cameron's magnificent onslaught against Yorkshire at Sheffield. Cameron's second hundred of the tour included 30 runs in one over off the bowling of Verity. He struck 81 runs in an hour and then, as if startled by his impudent, calculated hitting, spent 75 minutes crawling to his century on the following morning.

Cameron's breathtaking assault started with three fours and ended with three sixes. "With each shot the applause of the crowd increased, until the last and most towering six of all, was greeted with an ear-shattering roar," reported the *Yorkshire Post*. "Verity could, without doubt, have put a stop to the hitting by bowling his fast inswinger close to Cameron; but he persisted, as he said afterwards, in trying to pitch the ball on the spot which he thought would cause the batsman trouble," the report added.

In later years, when one interviewer pardonably dwelt upon his achievements against Bradman, Verity replied: "You did not see that South African get at me! Now that was champion hitting." Verity's figures on that gruelling afternoon ought charitably to be consigned to oblivion. They were 0–87 in 18 overs. South Africa won by 128 runs. It was only the tourists' second victory over Yorkshire and leg-spinner Balaskas, with 12 wickets, vied with his googly counterpart Reggie Schwarz, who had helped to overthrow Yorkshire in 1907.

South Africa were the opponents for Hedley Verity's last Test series. It was a tedious farewell, a series governed by caution or perhaps, in fairness to the antagonists, by mattress-like wickets. *Wisden* reported that the games were "played on pitches which, like certain triumphs of chemistry in England, had so far overstepped perfection as to be of little use to the bowler and to impose some inexplicable narcotic on the batsmen."

Verity's figures were costly by his standards; but he was the most economical of all the England bowlers and headed the Test averages with 19 wickets at just over 29 runs apiece. Amid his marathon spells there were moments of elation and chagrin. In the innings victory over Griqualand West at Kimberley, Verity took 11 wickets, including 7 for 22 in the first innings, after Hutton, Paynter, Edrich and Yardley had scored centuries in the MCC total of 676. On a wearing wicket at Bloemfontein, Verity paved the way for another innings victory over Orange Free State. Before he completed this conquest he had to suffer some drastic punishment from the last batsman, the appropriately named Sparks. The blissful Sparks scored 57 out of 260. His innings included seven 6's and three fours, and 42 of his runs came off Verity in three overs. The last wicket yielded 68 runs in 24 minutes. The thrashing tailender severely bruised the Yorkshireman's analysis. Verity's figures were seven wickets for 75 runs.

England led by one match in the series after four had been played. The solitary victory by an innings and 13 runs was in the third Test at Durban where Paynter scored a double century and Hammond his 20th in Test cricket. The alliance of Paynter and Hammond proved to be a match-winning partnership. But it was a rare interlude of freedom and gaiety.

The fifth Test at Durban was to have been played to a finish. It never ended. Some wished it had never started. It lasted 10 days, the longest match ever played, and after the sixth day the spectators were let in free. The duration of the match surpassed the previous longest between England and the West Indies at Kingston, Jamaica in April, 1930 when rain prevented any play on the eighth and ninth days. A total of 1,981 runs were scored at Durban. South Africa's first innings total of 530 was their highest in Test cricket and lasted 13 hours. Verity bowled 766 balls (95.6 overs and 23 maidens for 184 runs and four wickets) in the two South African innings, 17 more than J. C. White against Australia at Adelaide in 1929.

England were set the colossal target of 696 runs for victory. "Quite soon as 'soon' went in this match, with 250 for 1 on the board it was obvious that England had a strong chance of victory," related *Wisden*. "The world of cricket, till now uninterested, suddenly became wildly excited at the prospect of victory in this weird battle. The days went on, and at last that victory was almost in sight. But in the end all the taking of guard, retaking of guard, walking, running, limping, talking and throwing went for nothing." England left for home, 42 runs short of victory. Jim Swanton reported that by the end "neither side seemed to care a jot. The match in the steamy heat of March had left them drained and exhausted."

Swanton related that the key to the extraordinary lasting power of the pitch – and therefore to the course of the game – was that one of the playing conditions empowered the groundsman to roll before a day's play began any time after rain, if the pitch could be improved by the action. Before the third, fourth, sixth and ninth days the Durban groundsman used the heavy roller at dawn "and in effect made a new cake which the tropical sun had dried out before the start of play."

England still had five wickets in hand when a thunderstorm prevented any play after tea on the 10th day at Durban. The South African Board of Control and the two captains conferred before issuing a statement that the game had to be called off. The reason given was that the England team had to catch the 8.5 train that Tuesday night in order to reach Cape Town – a journey of around 1,000 miles – in time to sail home on the *Athlone Castle* on the Friday. A flight was considered impracticable. English cricketers were then thought too precious to be entrusted to the care of an aeroplane.

Hugh Bartlett sighs with disbelief at the waste of England's endeavours. "The sailing could not be postponed. We had to get back because of contracts with the counties. It was a terrible labour in vain for 11 chaps who had strived so hard to win a Test match."

A Tom Webster cartoon exults in yet another championship in 1935 (*Daily Mail*).

The Yorkshire team which won the first of the county's seven championships in 1931, Verity's first full season. Back row, left to right: W. Barber, A. Mitchell, F. Dennis, W. E. Bowes, H. Verity, A. Wood, W. Ringrose (scorer). Front row: G. G. Macaulay, E. Oldroyd, P. Holmes, F. E. Greenwood (captain), H. H. Sutcliffe, E. Robinson, M. Leyland.

A railway halt in the desert: Verity relaxes with his Australian rivals Stan McCabe, Don Bradman, and Vic Richardson (1932–33 tour).

A 1932 Christmas card, designed by the former Australian Test cricketer and journalist and cartoonist Arthur Mailey, and including the autographs of the England team.

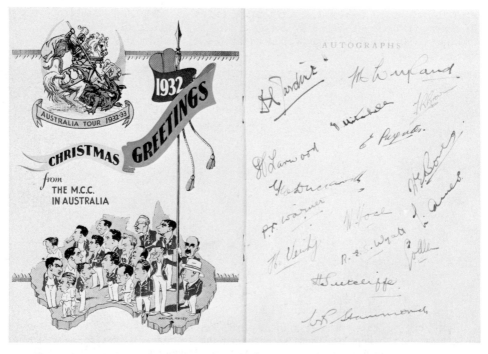

T. W. WALL (S. AUSTRALIA)

W. M. WOODFULL (VICTORIA)

W. A. BROWN (N. S. WALES)

D. G. BRADMAN (N. S. WALES)

W. J. O'REILLY (N. S. WALES)

S. J. McCABE (N. S. WALES)

C. V. GRIMMETT (S. AUSTRALIA)

W. A. OLDFIELD (N. S. WALES)

L. S. DARLING (VICTORIA)

E. H. BROMLEY (VICTORIA)

A. CHIPPERFIELD (N. S. WALES)

A resolute Verity walks out after lunch in the Lord's Test match of 1934. The Yorkshireman took 14 Australian wickets for 80 runs, six of them in the last hour of a momentous Monday. His victims were Woodfull, Brown, Bradman, McCabe, Darling, Chipperfield, Bromley, Oldfield, Grimmett, O'Reilly and Wall.

Bradman was twice dismissed by Verity in the Lord's Test match of 1934. The English fieldsmen, Sutcliffe, Ames, the catcher, and Hammond, wait underneath the towering mis-hit which brought about Bradman's downfall in the second innings (British Library).

Verity in action: the Test match at Leeds – 1938. Bradman is the non-striker (Central Press).

A batting flourish against
Sussex at Hove in 1932
(Central Press).

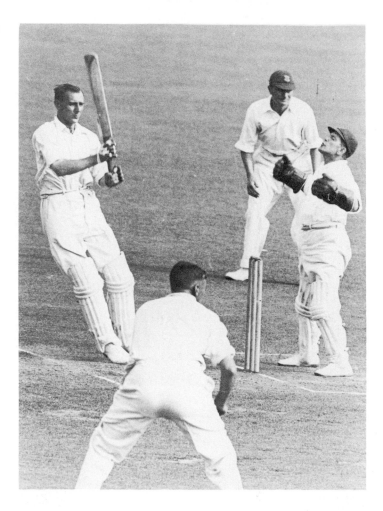

A stunning piece of fielding to dismiss Australian Keith Rigg off Allen in the third Test at
Melbourne in the 1936–7 series. (Melbourne C.C.)

A Yorkshire line-up in uniform.

Inspecting the wicket at the Tyrone and Fermanagh hospital ground which was requistioned by the Green Howards in 1941. Left to right: Captain Verity, Louis Walsh senior (lay administrator at the hospital), Captain Borwick (adjutant) and Lieutenant-Colonel Shaw.

Last cricket action in Ireland, 1941. Norman Yardley, the post-war Yorkshire and England captain, with Verity.

Cricket in Omagh: Top: Green Howards XI: Back row (left to right): Lt. W. D. Thomas, Lt. K. E. Kissack, Lt. P. D. Wild, W. Burke (rank not known), RSM F. Broad, L/Cpl. E. S. Pawsey. Front row: Lt. G. R. Hovington, Capt. Verity, Lt-Col. A. L. Shaw, Lt. N. W. D. Yardley, Pte. G. Mortimer. Below: North-West Ireland XI: Standing: R. M. Miller, Resident Magistrate in Omagh, Lt. H. Morgan, Cpl. J. Brockway, Lt. R. Morgan, J. L. Rankin. Front Row: V. A. Craig, H. Donaghey, Dr. J. M. Johnston (capt), Dr. A. H. Montgomery, A. McFarlane. Seated: J. W. Walsh.

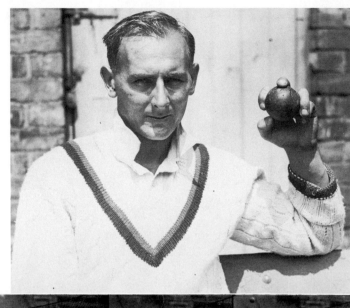

The powerful fingers and the swift, decisive action of a master bowler. The four action pictures of Verity encompass one stride and were taken with an ultra-rapid continuity camera (Central Press).

The immaculate lawns of the military cemetery at Caserta in Italy, where Hedley Verity is buried (Commonwealth Graves Commission).

Hedley Verity, despite his toils and torment on unyielding wickets, revelled in the harmonious spirit prevailing on his last cricket tour to a beautiful land. As he looked back at Cape Town in the shadow of its majestic mountain, he dreamed of his return. He had received many offers of coaching appointments, including one at the King Edward VII School in Johannesburg.

Verity's own influence on the South African tour was readily recalled by two of the younger members of the England team, Bartlett and Leonard Hutton. Bartlett remembers how "this great spinner from Yorkshire" took him, as a Test novice, under his wing during the early days of the tour. The former Sussex player says he was having difficulty in judging the bounce and pace of the ball. "He took the trouble when he saw me practising in the nets at Cape Town to pull me aside and say: 'You're not getting used to the rarefied atmosphere here. Let me bowl to you for a little while.' I thought it was a wonderful gesture." Bartlett adds: "If you played a good shot in the nets, he would say 'that's better. You must do that again. I will bowl the same ball to you' – and he could do that – to sharpen up a particular stroke. Hedley was a marvellous, steadying influence on people."

Though the sounds of war were muted for a brief time by the end of the tour, Verity was sorely troubled by his wife's persistent ill-health. The family doctor thought the voyage and a holiday in a warm climate would hasten her recovery. Plans were laid for a journey to South Africa in the winter of 1939. The benefits of this convalescence unhappily had to be abandoned. The world was pitched into a conflict bearing other scars and wounds that would never be erased.

12

FINALE AT HOVE

"There was a blazing sun and the wicket was ready for Hedley. It really suited him but you've also got to be a good enough bowler to take advantage of it, which he did to our cost." – Hugh Bartlett.

IT was one of those lovely summer days when the sea at the bottom of the road from the Tate Gates rolled along the shore like a soothing lullaby. The serenity of the September day at Hove in 1939 was matched by exhilarating, astonishing cricket – or cricket that would have been astonishing had everyone present not been too distracted by other events to appreciate what they were seeing. It was the last game of the season and in Sussex's second innings Hedley Verity took seven wickets for nine runs, the second best analysis of his career, in 48 balls.

Norman Yardley recalls a fitful concentration on the game which was fluctuating enough, in normal circumstances, to make sporting head-lines. Verity was unusually subdued, not even offering the characteristic twinkle of a smile at his latest conquest. His nine wickets in the match gave him 191 for the season and he headed the English bowling averages as he had done in his first Yorkshire campaign in 1930.

Amid the congratulations on his performance against Sussex Verity observed: "I wonder if I shall ever bowl here again." The tentatively expressed premonition that he would never again play first-class cricket reflected the sadness of a generation of sportsmen whose world was to be consumed in the fires of a terrible war. Throughout this oppressed summer, happy and glorious in its many achievements, followers had turned to cricket, in the words of R. C. Robertson-Glasgow, "as to an old friend who gives you a seat, a glass of beer and something sane to talk about." But sombre issues now hung in the balance.

On what should have been a gala occasion, the Brighton and Hove Cricket Week, with the cherished visit of Yorkshire, the county cham-pions, as its highlight it was no longer possible to ignore the ominous news bulletins.

"War was upon us and the guns had started in Poland," remembered the late George Cox, one of the three century-makers in Jim Parks' benefit game. "The tension was awful, there was a feeling that we shouldn't be playing cricket. Yet there was also a festive air. We knew that this was to be our last time of freedom for many years and so we enjoyed ourselves while we could."

The Hove committee room was festooned with newspapers carrying their grim tidings, while outside on the green field the band played and teas were served in the shade of the marquees. The sounds of bat and ball mingled strangely with talk of other things beyond the boundary.

Before their arrival at Hove Yorkshire had sealed their seventh championship of the decade with victories over Kent and Hampshire at Dover and Bournemouth. One of the greatest county teams of all time was entering the final straight. At Dover Verity took nine wickets in the match as Yorkshire won by an innings after being put in to bat. Jim Kilburn recalled the sequence of successes in matches played in the "strangest atmosphere that ever encompassed first-class cricket." "At Dover the outbreak of war seemed imminent every minute. Telegraph boys came to the ground almost in procession with orders for reservists to report for duty. Cricket was a secondary topic of conversation among players and spectators."

At Bournemouth Hampshire were dismissed for 116 in each innings, Verity taking 6 for 32 in the first innings, and Yorkshire's total of 243 was sufficient to gain yet another victory. The shrill cries of the impending conflict buffetted the anxious cricketers; but even in late August one popular newspaper was still plaintively insisting: "There will be no war." There was now a direct military intervention in Yorkshire's cricket affairs. Herbert Sutcliffe, who was an officer reservist, received his calling-up papers and did not travel on to Hove. The others did, because there was nothing else to do, and at an impromptu team meeting Brian Sellers summed up the situation by saying: "We are public entertainers and until we have instructions to the contrary we will carry on as usual." "Sellers was putting on a bold mask on a bleak outlook," said Kilburn. Before long the Scarborough Cricket Festival had been cancelled; the West Indian tourists had sailed for home with seven matches unplayed; and other county matches were abruptly called off.

Yorkshire's cricketers moved on along the south coast. At Hove, on the Wednesday before war was declared, Sussex won the toss on a perfect wicket and scored 387, the highest total of the season against the champion county. The innings was dominated by George Cox whose scintillating 198, a collection of powerful drives and elegant deflections, occupied three hours and 20 minutes and brought him 28 fours and one six, struck fiercely off Verity over mid-on. Cox was especially severe on the Yorkshire left-hander. Verity's figures were 18 (eight ball) overs and two wickets for 108 runs.

With his typical, wry sense of humour Cox recalled that he was top scorer in both innings. He actually shared the privilege with Harry Parks in the Sussex second innings. Each batsman scored nine as Sussex were bowled out by Verity and Robinson for 33. Cox's first innings *tour de force* during a wonderful day's cricket which produced nearly 500 runs, drew high praise from Dudley Carew, the former *Times* cricket correspondent. Carew described the scene on the Hove ground in the following words: "It was crowded but nothing like so crowded had there been no threat to Poland. Groups of people were gathered around cars parked in the ground listening to the wireless as it spoke of the hopeless, last-minute efforts to save a peace that was beyond aid.

"Concentration on the cricket was fitful and disjointed. Yet Cox's strokes through the covers insisted on drawing attention to themselves. They were played in the grand manner, and again and again the ball came rattling up against the pavilion rails." Jim Kilburn said of the innings: "At times Cox knew fortune, but then his method invited the co-operation of fortune. When he could not reasonably drive he was prepared to cut, and if the slips once or twice stretched up expectant hands, many of the boundaries gathered were as faultless as they were beautiful."

A thunderstorm flooded the ground overnight and play did not restart until 3.30 on the Thursday afternoon. "All through the morning in our hotel we were anxiously discussing the cables from Poland and Germany, which made it plain that a world war was just about to begin," recalled Norman Yardley. "We managed to restart a game that was played with many men's minds elsewhere. But to Yorkshiremen cricket is cricket, and when we get out on to the field our job is to win the game, no matter whether the heavens are falling."

Yorkshire, 112 for 1 overnight, reached 330 for 3 at the close on the rain-affected wicket. Hutton was his masterly self on the difficult pitch. He nullified the spin of Jim Langridge, another superb left-arm bowler whose career unfortunately coincided with that of Verity. Langridge always acknowledged the superiority of his Yorkshire rival for whom he had a deep respect. "Hutton changed the principles of his batsmanship to meet the changed situation. Langridge was not allowed to spin the ball because he was not allowed to pitch, except in the form of a long hop, and he had no allurement of flight with which to deceive the magnificent Hutton," wrote Kilburn.

Norman Yardley said: "Len ran down the wicket to Langridge, drove and pulled, square-cut and late-cut when Langridge changed his length, and we were edified by the sight of a great bowler on a heaven-sent wicket being slammed all over the place." Langridge's figures were redeemed by avenging wickets on the following day and his final analysis of four wickets for 84 runs in 20.4 overs was commendable in the circumstances.

Hutton duly reached his second century of this southern tour before he was dismissed by George Cox. Cox's bowling accomplishments often surprised himself as well as his opponents. As Sussex's fifth bowler, he gained an unexpected prize when Hutton tried to sweep him, missed, and was leg-before-wicket.

Shortly before six o'clock on Friday, September 1, the news of Hitler's latest intransigence was revealed. Germany had invaded Poland. Neville Chamberlain, the Prime Minister, announced that Britain's commitment to come to the aid of a stricken country would be fulfilled. War was now certain. At Old Trafford, where Lancashire were playing Surrey, the match was abandoned early that morning though as yet there had been no formal declaration of hostilities. The only other county match in progress was also abandoned, and all matches due to start on the following day were cancelled. Meanwhile the Yorkshire committee wired Sellers to suggest that the game at Hove should be called off. The Yorkshire captain said that as the match was a benefit for Jim Parks the players would prefer to continue, if at all possible, and this was agreed.

Yorkshire lost their last seven wickets for 62 runs on that fateful Friday morning. Langridge, relieved of the presence of Hutton, reasserted his command with four wickets. Jim Parks also took three wickets and Yardley was ninth man out, caught and bowled by Langridge for 108.

Hugh Bartlett, the pre-war Sussex batting cavalier, today remembers the amazing finish to the game. The light billowing clouds of mist which so often curl in from the sea at Hove were absent on the day of Hedley Verity's last cricket triumph. "There was a blazing sun," says Bartlett, "and the wicket was ready for Hedley. It really suited him but you've also got to be a good enough bowler to take advantage of it, which he did to our cost." The Hove wicket, drying and cutting up badly, must have seemed possessed by a thousand imps to the hapless batsmen. Sussex never looked like saving the game. Verity and Ellis Robinson bowled unchanged. Sussex were swiftly 18 for 5 and 33 all out. The innings lasted less than 12 overs and Yorkshire needed only another 13 overs to achieve their nine-wicket victory.

By mid-afternoon the green Southdown coach carrying the Yorkshire team was heading northwards along the quiet Sussex lanes. Sir Leonard Hutton remembers the sadness of their forlorn journey home. "There was no guessing precisely what the future held, but there was no escaping the reflection that a well-loved way of life was being shattered, perhaps beyond repair," wrote Jim Kilburn. "The anxiety of the uncertain hung heavily in the air. Scarcely anyone mentioned cricket, though the past few days had brought cricket of uncommon quality.

"For a mile or two the route led down the Great West Road towards London. In that direction there was no other traffic; the opposite path was crowded to danger point with every conceivable kind of vehicle carrying every conceivable cargo. Perambulators, bedding, household goods, food hampers were piled on the passing cars which were hastening out of London as precaution against bombing. Coach-loads of children swept by to unknown foster homes. Urgency covered the earth.

"An experimental black-out had been ordered throughout the country for that Friday night and it was felt advisable not to attempt to drive through the darkness. Like Cardinal Wolsey on another significant journey, Yorkshire halted at Leicester. Luggage was left in the coach overnight; thoughts were beyond the creature comforts of shaving tackle and a clean collar, and the journey was to be continued soon after dawn. In any event there was little sleep. Half the night was spent in awaiting delayed telephone calls to explain revised arrangements, and before eight o'clock on the Saturday morning Yorkshire were in Yorkshire again.

"Halts began, one passenger dropping off here, another there. Finally came journey's end in City Square, Leeds, and thence departed their several ways one of the finest county teams in the history of cricket. It never assembled again."

There was an intriguing postscript to Hedley Verity's last championship wickets at Hove. The story has the impact of a delayed letter from a dear, departed friend. In the opening match of the first post-war season in 1946 the Yorkshire captain Brian Sellers donned his blazer again. He put his hand into the top pocket of his blazer and pulled out a tiny slip of paper. "Good God, Norman, look at this," he said to Yardley. It was the scorer's chit, handed to him by Billy Ringrose seven years earlier at Hove. The fading but still legible figures on the paper provided a poignant reminder. They recorded Hedley Verity's final bowling analysis – 6–1–9–7.

13

THE PATRIOT GOES TO WAR

"There was short shrift for the man who shirked his duties but with others, the slow and persevering, he displayed infinite patience." – fellow Green Howards officer.

HEDLEY Verity always believed in the rightness of a cause in war as he did in peace. He was to become, in the words of his Green Howards batman, Tom Rennoldson, as fine a soldier as he was a cricketer. "He was a wonderful tactician and a master of his job," said Rennoldson.

At the time of the Munich crisis in 1938 Verity was reunited with an old friend whom he had first met on the tour of India in the winter of 1933-4. Lieutenant-Colonel (later Brigadier) Arnold Shaw was to become his commanding officer in the Green Howards. The meeting took place in the pavilion at Headingley and Shaw recalled: "Hedley asked my advice on what he could do and how best to prepare for it, if war should come. His profession prevented him from joining the Territorial Army or any civil defence organisation, as his cricket travels would make it impossible for him to fulfil his obligations; so I made an alternative suggestion: I promised and subsequently gave him a collection of military text books, advised him to study them and arranged that when war did come he would get in touch with me."

This was the beginning of an ill-starred odyssey which was to take Hedley Verity to the heights of heroic endeavour and on to his last battleground. He brought his finely tuned intelligence to his military reconnaissance and worked at it with all the thoroughness and thoughtfulness which he applied to his cricket. Sir Leonard Hutton, one of his colleagues on the 1938-9 tour of South Africa, remembers how Verity spent his time aboard ship and during his hours away from cricket voraciously assimilating army tactics and manoeuvres. Verity had embarked on an urgent course of action. His leisure reading on that tour was a small library of infantry manuals and training pamphlets supplied by Colonel Shaw.

Bill Bowes also speaks of his friend's earnest preparations for the impending conflict. "As early as 1937 he was certain that war was coming and he said it would last six years." Bowes recalls how, after Yorkshire's last game at Hove, they sat up into the small hours discussing the future. "We had done most things together and we were going to join up. But my wife Esme was expecting another kiddie in the October, and we decided that until that event was settled we would join the ARP." Bowes and Verity spent the interval as assistants to the controller of a command post at Guiseley, near Leeds. The new arrival in the Bowes household – a baby girl – was given little time to get to know her father. Mrs Bowes came out of hospital on the Friday and on Saturday her husband joined up. "Hedley and I went down to the recruiting office in Bradford and they told us that lorry drivers were required for a searchlight unit at Selby." They were sent out on to a detachment with members of the Harrogate Rugby Club, all of whom had had a convivial night at a social function and decided, in a haze of alcohol, to offer their services.

The two Yorkshire cricketers had planned to take infantry commissions but as a result of a knee operation Bowes realised that he would be unfit for lowering himself along hedge bottoms. He would later become a gunnery officer and take part in the North Africa campaign before being captured at Tobruk. Bowes, despite his misgivings at the parting, persuaded Verity to accept the chance of a commission. He knew it was his friend's ambition and he had no wish to deter him.

In one of their last conversations Bowes reminded Verity of other heartsearchings when the Test selectors had ignored the claims of one or other of them. It was a moving little episode which conveyed the depth of comradeship between the two men who had learned and prospered together with Yorkshire and England. "This is war, Hedley," said Bowes. "When there has been a Test match and I've not been picked you have still gone and done your damnedest. It's the same way here. It's a pity we can't both go. But, look, don't bother about me. If you want to join the Green Howards, and I know you do, you must follow your inclination." Verity expressed his doubts about the decision. "You're sure you don't mind?" he said. Bowes replied: "I shan't mind a bit."

Verity was gazetted in the Green Howards at the end of 1939 and, after a period at ITC under Lt Col E. V. B. Ramsden, he was posted to the 1st Battalion commanded by Colonel Shaw. Some time afterwards Bowes was on duty at his searchlight detachment. "This fellow came walking down with his three pips up. It was Captain Hedley Verity. I was able to throw one up for him without my hat on." Verity roared with laughter. They both instantly remembered their nervousness as recruits at Selby when they encountered their first officer. Hats were off on that occasion, too. In an ill assortment of clothes, lacking any vestige of order, they did not know whether to salute or not.

One of the less salty adjectives in common usage in the Yorkshire dressing-room in the 1930s was the word "chuffing". Grace Verity remembers the warning of her brother as Britain drifted uncertainly, even reluctantly, into war. "This is no chuffing garden party," said Hedley. "This fellow, Hitler, means it if we don't stop him. We have got to stop him." In a wartime letter to his two boys, Wilfred and Douglas, Verity issued another urgent instruction. "Always remember to do what's right," he wrote, "and to fight for what's right if necessary."

That Verity, indisputably a man of peace, could so far step out of character as to ally his gifts to the horrors of war was a testimony to his beliefs. It was also another example of his singlemindedness, this time in the role of patriot. A fellow officer in the Green Howards remembers his brief association with Verity at the regimental depot at Richmond in North Yorkshire. As young subalterns and members of different battalions, they had been posted there for attachment to a company engaged in training young recruits. The company commander was Sir William Worsley, the former Yorkshire captain and later president of the county club.

The portrait of shyness as a product of Verity's modesty is retained by the former Green Howards officer. At Richmond Verity maintained sporting fitness and impressed the need for it on his charges. He was a keen disciplinarian but he was a kindly and fairminded superior on the parade ground. There was short shrift for the man who shirked his duties but with others, the slow and persevering, he displayed infinite patience. At the end of the day's training Verity would often turn out to bowl to his recruits in the nets.

Verity's responsibilities in training the young NCOs were eased because his men idolised him, not only because of his reputation as a cricketer and merits as a teacher, but for his fine character and sympathy. He was, for these reasons, able to get more out of his recruits than many other officers.

In those early days of the war many distinguished Yorkshire cricketers passed through the Green Howards depot at Richmond. Among them were Leonard Hutton, Herbert Sutcliffe, Maurice Leyland and Arthur Wood. During this time Verity was moved to say with a fierce pride in his regiment: "I reckon we can put out a team from this depot to beat any county side in England." Then, remembering his other allegiance, he added: "Except Yorkshire, of course!"

Colonel Shaw considered that Verity had a natural aptitude for military tactics, developed, he believed, by constantly and rapidly appreciating situations in first-class cricket. He established an affinity between tactical principles at the bowling crease and those in battle. "He was by no means hidebound in his tactical methods, and in spite of his gentle nature, he was essentially an 'all-in' fighter," said Colonel Shaw. "His attitude to the enemy was: 'They started it, now let them take it.' And he had some good ideas as to what to give them!"

Verity, it would appear and it seems a surprising defect for an outstanding sportsman, was bereft of manual dexterity. "To watch him stripping a Bren gun," said Colonel Shaw, "one would think he had two right hands, mainly consisting of thumbs." Verity never acquired a barrack square polish. "Drill and the strict routine of a regular battalion were alien to Hedley's nature," said his commanding officer. "He would have preferred more 'irregular' methods of achieving the same end – to beat the enemy – but he loyally accepted a system of which he had become a part."

The 1st Battalion of the Green Howards ended their manoeuvres in defeat in Northern Ireland in the summer of 1941. They were beaten at cricket by a North-West Ireland eleven at the garrison town of Omagh in Hedley Verity's last game on a British field. Verity took eight wickets for 55 runs to dismiss the Irishmen for 112 but the Green Howards, cloaked in the anonymity of a "Military XI", lost by 21 runs.

The hiccup could not this time be excused on the grounds of an excess of hospitality in the pavilion. On other less important occasions it was not uncommon for these wartime games to be punctuated by extended refreshment breaks. "There was always half-time", says one local cricketer. Even then Verity would show his irritation if a game was spoiled because one or other of the team had succumbed to what has been described as the opposition's "secret weapon." He could make allowances and take a more relaxed attitude, perhaps because he had taken a couple of drinks himself, when the opposition was less than strong. Then he might suggest to his captain that a declaration was in order to make a match more even.

The match between the North-West Ireland team and the Green Howards took place on September 20, 1941. The scorebook of the match records that it was between the Green Howards and Mr Walsh's XI. The latter title was clearly adopted by the scorer because Louis Walsh senior, as the lay administrator at the local hospital, had made all the ground arrangements and had collaborated with the battalion in the preparation of the pitch at the Omagh ground. The local weekly newspaper, *The Tyrone Constitution*, chose the name of an "Army XI" in the interests of security although everyone living in and around the county town of Omagh could readily identify them as the Green Howards. The celebrities, Verity and Norman Yardley, were unacknowledged as England cricketers. Another local newspaper confusingly observed: "X will have the assistance of those well-known players, Yardley, Hedley and Verity."

The North-West team included four players who had represented Ireland. They comprised Charlie Brockway, the professional at Trinity College, Dublin; the Morgan brothers, Reggie, who was killed while serving with the Royal Ulster Rifles in the Normandy landings and Harry who lost a leg in the same campaign; and Andy McFarlane, a reputed local cricketer and a stalwart of the Sion Mills club. Other members were Jim Rankin, an Irish badminton international as well as a keen cricketer, and Pat Kelly, an all-rounder and a seam bowler with a natural swerve whom Verity considered good enough to have played for an English county side. Kelly was the bowler who began the unexpected march to victory after the Green Howards had been set a modest target of 113. He took the first four wickets, including the prized ones of Yardley and Verity.

The fifth Green Howards' wicket fell at 72 and the collapse continued despite a stubborn innings of 25 by the battalion opener, G. R. Hovington. Hugh Donaghey, from Sion Mills, was brought into the attack late in the innings and proceeded to take four wickets for nine runs in four overs. The all-out score of 91 was an incredible turn of events. The famous victory over a famous regiment still evokes a surge of pride among the people of Tyrone.

Colonel Shaw remembered the arrival of the 1st Battalion in Omagh in the spring of 1941. "The town had no cricket ground, but local admirers, and wherever we went there were always plenty, told Hedley that cricket had been played at the lunatic asylum. There was a well-supported school of thought in the neighbourhood who believed that this was a very suitable place for it." The ground at the Tyrone and Fermanagh Mental Hospital was small but attractive and it was described by the superintendent, Dr Moore Johnston (later to become the linchpin of the Green Howards cricket in Ireland) as "nice and springy".

Norman Yardley, who served with Verity in various parts of the world, says the discovery of the ground resolved one of their major priorities. "The ground was tiny, only about 40 yards wide, with a running track outside it. The width of the track was included in the field to make a little more room for boundaries, but even so it was one of the easiest grounds upon which to score fours.

"The arrangement suited everybody, and Hedley most of all, for he could walk abstractedly up to the wicket and deliver what looked like an innocuous ball. The batsman would see those tempting boundaries hardly beyond the bat's end and take a swing – and there would be a deathly rattle of wood behind him."

The Green Howards battalion, apart from inter-unit contests, were largely opposed by club cricketers in Londonderry, Sion Mills, Strabane, Armagh and Ballymena throughout a perfect summer. It was a happy diversion before the grimmer struggles which lay ahead of them. Yardley recalls: "We won most of our matches fairly easily, mainly because of Verity's bowling. Indeed, throughout the war, if a side that contained Hedley in it got 60 runs, it reckoned that the match was won."

The appearance of the Green Howards and their two England cricketers in Omagh sent local youngsters cartwheeling with excitement along the pavements. The Walsh family were especially thrilled. The presence of the battalion was first spotted by an awestruck Louis junior, the youngest of the three Walsh boys. He arrived home one day to announce: "Hedley Verity is here. I'm sure I've seen him bowling in one of the gardens."

Verity was indeed among the Green Howards officers newly billeted in the town and before the summer was over the Walsh boys had ample cause to remember his kindness and patience. Frazier Walsh, a retired doctor now living in Newfoundland, believes that Verity's sojourn in Ireland was a tranquil time for him. "He could be a player or a gentleman as the occasion warranted. You had to watch his face carefully to see the smile lurking behind his eyes. There was a wee small devil hidden behind the outward show. But he was always quiet, controlled and in charge."

The Walsh family home at Omagh was an ideal setting for the resolute boys growing up in a fervent sports atmosphere. The freedom of its spacious acres was a blessing for aspiring cricketers. The practice grounds became even more rewarding when the boys came under the guidance of Hedley Verity. There were double tennis lawns lovingly tended by Walsh senior. Special permission was normally required to pitch cricket stumps on the lawns but it was quickly forthcoming when Verity arrived in the town. On the other side of the house was a concrete pitch and nets. "As boys we would be out at 6.30 in the morning all trying to out-do each other," says Frazier Walsh. "Father would throw balls over the house on to the tennis courts and we became tremendous outfielders."

The practice sharpened when Verity made the Walsh house his cricket home. Training was serious; there could be no slackness; and among other lessons learned by the Walsh boys was that you could be nice but still tough. Frazier Walsh remembers how their hero treated them as adults and only acted the comedian with the grown-ups. Any frivolity in the garden came after the cricket groundwork. Then Verity would play the jester, stumbling as he ran and pretending to miss a catch. He would look bemused and begin to search for the ball. The boys would pounce on his pockets and pull out the ball. Other tricks were reserved for members of his own team in their matches against local clubs. "How else could they have had a chance?" says Frazier Walsh.

Another member of the Omagh family to profit from Verity's coaching was Jim Walsh, then a 17-year-old schoolboy and a persevering slow left-arm bowler. Mr Walsh, who now lives in Zimbabwe and is a former agricultural college principal, recalls that he was enlisted into the victorious North-West Ireland eleven largely on the merits of his fielding. One of his proudest memories is being bowled second ball by Verity in the match.

When the Green Howards arrived in Omagh Verity rallied to the aid of the untutored Walsh whose bowling attempts up to that time had been frustratingly unsuccessful. "Hedley was told about my limited efforts and he typically and generously offered to coach me and eliminate some of the more obvious faults." The absolute importance of a smooth, controlled run-up to the delivery stride was first of all stressed by Verity. "Having observed him in action," says Jim Walsh, "I felt I could not do better than model my run-up on his – and so began many hours of practice until I could do it without having to look down and, more important, without having to think about it.

"Then I took the ball and began bowling at a single stump on the lawn at home. Hedley had told me that the best ball was the one which pitched middle and off and just in front of the batsman's front foot and outstretched bat and spun away into the slips."

Many years before Verity had followed the ritual of his own master, Wilfred Rhodes. He had also spent painstaking hours pitching the ball on a piece of newspaper and slowly shredding the sheet to reduce the target. "As Hedley had done," says Jim Walsh, "I pinned the paper on the turf on that spot and bowled, again for many hours, trying to drop the spinning ball as close to the paper as possible."

Frazier Walsh believes that the war hurt Hedley Verity in the sense that it destroyed everything he had worked so hard to achieve. "It took him into a different field where he had to use all he had learned for Britain – and he gave this sterner struggle his all." Other people have said that Verity accepted the role of soldier as a job that had to be carried out to the best of his considerable ability. Verity also accepted, with equanimity, that his life would never be the same, whatever the outcome of the war. Yet he was optimistic for the future which, in his opinion, had to be secured for the younger generations. Another Omagh host, Mrs Emma Wilson, with whom Verity was billeted in 1941, remembers him saying: "After the war I would like to go into politics to make this world a better place to live in."

Norman Yardley affectionately recalls the happy interlude in Ireland where the pitches were "sometimes more suitable for fox-hunting" and he says that Verity reaped a rich harvest of wickets. At Ballymena the Green Howards men arrived asleep on their bus, having come off a five-day exercise the previous night. It was a typical Irish wicket, very wet, but the battalion players did not appear to be unduly taxed by the conditions. Colonel Shaw recalled: "Norman, Jimmy Gundill and I put on 100 before lunch. We were all out for 130 afterwards, due I may say to the state of the wicket and not to the hospitality of our hosts, though this may have contributed."

During the interval between the innings Jim Rankin turned to Verity and said: "Hedley, do you think we have enough runs?" Verity rubbed his hands in anticipation of the pleasures to come, and replied: "I wish I had the Aussies on that wicket." In the afternoon, on a drying wicket, he twice bowled out the opposition for less than his team's total.

The Green Howards battalion included within its ranks Cambridge cricketer Laurie Hesmondhalgh, later to become Verity's second-in-command in Sicily and who was killed in the action on the plain of Catania. Gundill, another Cambridge man and Yorkshire Colt, was also prominent in the team's many runaway victories. Verity and Yardley, happy in the knowledge that the men they left behind them could hold the cricket fort, also assisted Strabane. Their presence in the team in key games undoubtedly contributed to the success of the club in winning the North-West Ireland league and cup trophies for the first time since 1912.

Hedley Verity, bronzed and fit after his training in County Tyrone, returned to Lord's for the last time in 1941. It was his final meeting with Charles Barnett and the occasion was a charity match against the Royal Air Force. Barnett recalls that his old friend did not take kindly to the frolics at Lord's. "Do you know, Charles," said Verity, "I've come all these miles and bowled just a few overs. They don't want my type of bowling. They want something they can slog around." One can imagine the furrowed brow. Cavalier cricket even in wartime seemed to Verity unwarranted and undignified. It was beyond his understanding.

Sharing Verity's summer idyll in Ireland was his wife, Kathleen. It was a contented time and the longest period the Veritys had spent together during their marriage. "I wonder am I doing wrong staying here with Hedley and leaving my sister to look after our boys at home," remarked Kathleen to her hosts. Hedley replied: "Stay where you are, I need you. The boys are all right." After her husband's death Kathleen said she was glad they had had that time and found joy in the memories.

The Veritys revelled in the charms of Tyrone's rolling hills where, as one traveller described the scene, "the late afternoon glowed with gold and the harvest fields were gilded and men, women and children moved about the meadows winning hay."

Emma Wilson remembers her guests in Omagh as a quiet couple – "cricket and nature were their main pursuits outdoors" – during their stay in the Irish town. When petrol supplies were available they would take a short car ride "down the Glens" into the countryside. One of the highlights of that treasured summer of 1941 for the Wilson children was to take a picnic hamper down to the river bank at Sion Mills and watch their hero "bowling 'em out." The Veritys loved to spend days among the farming folk of the area. Mrs Wilson, herself the daughter of a farmer, remembers how Hedley would often slip away with her brothers and earnestly question them about their crops and animals.

The summer, a time of good fellowship, drifted to a close and the Veritys returned to England and a sad leavetaking. Grace Verity recalls: "Kathleen was with Hedley in London. She knew that it wouldn't be long. He had been issued with his tropical kit but he didn't say anything about his impending departure.

"One night he said: 'Kathleen, I'm going now.' He put his arms round her and repeated: 'This is it, I'm going. I must go tonight.' And he went. It was a frosty night and she could hear his footsteps right away down the garden path until they died away in the distance."

14

VALOUR ON A SICILIAN PLAIN

"Get them out of the farmhouse and get me into it." – Hedley Verity.

THE preparations for a campaign which was to end on the banks of the River Elbe in Germany began early in 1942. The 1st battalion of the Green Howards was then stationed in the vicinity of Walton Heath in Surrey where arms, equipment and transport were overhauled. The battalion was inspected by King George VI on Epsom Downs racecourse and soon afterwards embarked at Liverpool for the journey to India. In India Verity suffered very badly from dysentery and the doctors wanted to send him to a better climate.

In a letter to his wife in November Verity spoke of his illness. "I continue to improve in health but it is a slow job in this climate. However, it is merely a case of regaining strength and weight – and I'm doing it gradually." On a resilient note he added: "The good war news means a shorter and quicker route home for mail and one for mail through to us."

Grace Verity recalls that the drugs used to combat the dysentery had sapped her brother's strength; but despite his low state he stubbornly insisted on rejoining his battalion before being declared fit. "He met up with his men on manoeuvres and told them he was taking over command," says Miss Verity. "They asked him if he had got clearance from his doctor. He replied: 'No, I'm not waiting any longer. I'm signing on again.'" Colonel Shaw never ceased to reproach himself for not demanding that Verity should return home.

Verity's determination to resume his duties prevailed; but one of the saddest features of his subsequent death, as Norman Yardley relates, was that Lt General Miles Dempsey, the 13th Corps Commander, had told Colonel Shaw that he had planned to withdraw Verity from active service after the Sicily campaign. The Yorkshireman would have been given a post on the headquarters staff. General Dempsey said later how much he admired Verity for doing a front-line fighting task when he could so easily have found a softer job. "Hedley was getting a bit old. He was struggling a bit and he wasn't 100 per cent fit," says Yardley. "In a matter of a week or so he would have been safe and able to play for Yorkshire again after the war."

Before the Sicily action the Green Howards battalion had spent a bitterly cold winter in 1942 in the highlands of Persia which was in sharp contrast to the intense heat of Ranchi in the Eastern Provinces in India where it had been stationed in the previous summer. The battalion arrived at Kabrit on the shores of the Bitter Lakes in the Suez Canal zone in March, 1943. Over the next three weeks, training exercises in assault landings and combined operations were carried out. In the following month they moved to Qatana, near Damascus. Here they were housed in a good camp of timbered huts, the nearest approach to permanent dwellings since landing in India a year earlier. The camp was situated in hill country, fresh and green, with the towering snow-clad height of Mount Herman across the valley. The surroundings were a refreshing change from the bare plains, the freezing tablelands of Persia and the scorching sands of the desert.

The blueprint for the invasion of Sicily was drawn up at Qatana. The brigade commander, Brigadier G. S. Rawsterne, who had been informed where the landings would take place, explained his plan of operations to the battalion commanders only, but he did not give them any date. An operations room was set up complete with maps, aerial photographs and plastic models of the beaches and the hinterland; but these contained no place names and the grid lines on the maps were not numbered. Every officer and man had the opportunity of studying the maps and models. Colonel Shaw gave detailed operation orders at Damascus on May 28. They were to be carried out at a time and place which his officers did not know, and at a time which he did not know. These orders were fulfilled to the letter six weeks later on the Sicilian beaches.

In Egypt, as Colonel Shaw recalled, the battalion was able to take time off from their training exercises to play in a cricket match against the Gezeira Sporting Club in Cairo. Gezeira, with its perfect and lavishly watered turf, was the mecca for every first-class cricketer who could obtain leave. On the lovely palm-fringed ground the Green Howards' opponents included Lt Col Johnson (Hampshire); Sandy Baxter (Middlesex); and Bob Crisp and S. K. Coen, of South Africa.

"We won in the last over," said Colonel Shaw. "The position was last man in and eight runs to win. Two runs were needed off the last ball and

Laurie Hesmondhalgh got them with a slashing drive which soared high over the slips to the boundary." Verity and Yardley also made significant contributions to the victory, the former with five wickets and the latter a fiercely hit 71.

The battalion was encamped at El Shatt on the east bank of the Suez Canal before the invasion. They were addressed by General Montgomery on June 28. In the words of one officer present at this rallying speech, "I think it is true to say that he got it across all right – that magic personality and ability to inspire us with confidence, and to make us feel that he had the whole thing taped, which indeed he had."

Norman Yardley recalls how the battalion went to camp in a "sealed area". "According to the strictest possible orders, nobody was allowed out, and every minute was devoted to preparations for the push." But with Colonel Shaw in command there was still time for one last cricket match. "It was memorable to those who took part, not particularly as a match, or because of who won, but for the atmosphere in which it was played," said the battalion commander. "We had a feeling of being on the eve of a tremendous adventure, to which we were looking forward, and everyone was in terrific heart."

One Yorkshire soldier, who was also based at El Shatt, remembers how his regiment came to supply the pitch for the match. "Life for us was fairly undemanding at that time but swimming day after day, although not boring, needed some variation. It was suggested that since we were a Yorkshire unit (the old 66th Leeds Rifles) cricket was the obvious answer.

"And so in a very short time, as things did in the army, cricketing tackle including matting and an Egyptian railway sleeper put in an appearance. The sleeper was attached by a chain to the rear of a 15cwt truck and then dragged round and round on the flat area of salt and sand until a very acceptable site was created. We might possibly also have borrowed a mixer and cement to make a solid base for the matting."

Shortly after these enthusiastic labours El Shatt and the surrounding area began to fill with troops, a large concentration of men, which was obviously an invasion force. "I can only speculate on how the Green Howards were made aware of our 'cricket field'", says this onlooker. "But I think it highly likely that an approach was made to our commanding officer. The fact that he was a Leeds solicitor whose home was at the Kirkstall Lane end of the Headingley cricket ground doubtless had some bearing on the matter."

The fortuitously designed pitch was a handsome deed in the circumstances. It ensured that Colonel Shaw would have his cricket match before the embarkation for Sicily. A sporting challenge thrown down by Major Pope, of the King's Own Yorkshire Light Infantry, whose ambition it had always been to defeat the Green Howards, was swiftly accepted. Major Pope failed to achieve his ambition largely because Hedley Verity once again rose to his last cricket occasion. "He was just as usual, bowling imperturbably and as near perfectly as made no difference," says Norman Yardley. In the opposition ranks was General Dempsey and Verity saluted his Corps Commander by bowling him out. He took six wickets for 37 runs, dispatching his victims with ridiculous ease. In this brief hour of peaceful combat his bowling was as poised as ever.

The Green Howards launched their attack on the blazing plain of Catania in Sicily in the early hours of July 20, 1943. It was a close-range, bitter duel against the crack troops of the Herman Goering Division.

Verity's Green Howards company was entrenched for more than an hour, watching a creeping barrage infiltrate into the German lines, watching the dust spit and flash under the distant artillery fire. When the barrage ceased the company moved forward more than half a mile in the moonlight, into a belt of deep shadows cast by the hills on either side of them. As they wriggled through the summer corn, tracer bullets whistled across the fields and came at them from three sides. "We were more or less surrounded by Germans," said one of the attacking soldiers. "There were Germans in front and on either side of us."

Captain Verity, having screened his company as much as possible in the corn, gave the signal to continue the advance. The men dropped in their tracks and started crawling towards the enemy gun positions. Mortar fire began to fall as soon as they neared the target. Flares and shell explosions illuminated the battleground, turning night into day, and the trees and corn behind the troops caught fire, silhouetting Verity and his men as they penetrated the last defences below a railway embankment.

Opposite the enemy lines, where the fire was at its heaviest, Verity studied the position. The danger point was a farm building away to the left; if he could silence the guns he could carry the position. Accordingly, he ordered one platoon round to the farmhouse, while another platoon gave fire cover. Almost immediately he was hit in the chest, but still at the head of his men he shouted: "Keep going. Get them out of the farmhouse and get me into it."

The landings and initial stages of the Sicily campaign had been completed successfully and it was not until the Catania plain was reached, five days after the invasion, that the enemy was able to regroup its forces and put up an organized resistance. The Allied army had chased the Germans northwards from the beachheads south of Syracuse and across the broken, rugged plain towards Catania. "The enemy had their backs to the wall," wrote Capt W. A. Synge, "but they were holding a strong position on high ground to the north of the railway crossing the Catania plain. The position was guarded by forward machine gun posts, dug every 20 yards into the side of a steep embankment."

In the fiercely fought battle the attacking force of the 15th Brigade consisted, on the left, of a battalion of the York and Lancasters; and on the right the 1st battalion of the Green Howards of which Captain Verity was in charge of "B" company. At 5 p.m. on July 19 orders were issued for the brigade to make a night attack. "Darkness was approaching and it was not possible to make a ground reconnaissance before the attack," wrote Synge. "This, together with the difficult terrain, helped to contribute to its ultimate failure. Canals and ditches that had looked shallow and easy to negotiate through binoculars in the daylight proved unexpectedly difficult in practice in the darkness.

"All went well until the leading companies were within a few hundred yards of the railway line. Here they encountered deep fosses which held up the advance to such an extent that the barrage ran away from them."

The delay alerted the enemy and as the force approached the forward defence line the Germans emerged from their dug-outs and manned their guns. The leading companies came under withering fire but they pressed on right up to the German posts. In the confusion of an ill-conceived attack (some reports alleged that an order to withdraw was made but never received) Verity's company lost its position. Working its way round the right flank, it had overtaken the leading company in the darkness. It was decimated by the full impact of the enemy's fire.

The remnants of the force withdrew leaving behind many casualties, including Verity, his senior subaltern, and his second-in-command and close friend Laurie Hesmondhalgh who, it later transpired, was killed outright in the attack. One of the platoon commanders, Lieutenant Bell, who was awarded the Military Cross, successfully carried out the retreat but next morning, when he returned to the scene and rescued the wounded subaltern, he could find no trace of Verity or Hesmondhalgh.

At Verity's side when he fell was his faithful batman, Private Tom Rennoldson. He stayed with his captain throughout a harrowing ordeal. Rennoldson had become Verity's batman in November, 1940. They had first met at Bury in Lancashire and had served together in Ireland, India, Persia, Egypt, Syria – and finally in Sicily. "I'd never seen any first-class cricket," later recalled Rennoldson. "And I used to say to the captain that I couldn't understand how anyone who bowled 'em so slow as he did could get anyone out. He would laugh and say that some day he would show me.

"He had his cricket kit with him everywhere we went until we moved into Sicily, and then I took it down to PRI. We left it behind for the last time. Often I watched him at practice – sometimes I'd field when he was bowling at the nets – and often I'd get his boots and flannels ready for games."

Rennoldson remembered the events of his night-long vigil on the Catania plain and how he had hoped to bring Verity back to the safety of their own lines on the following morning. In his account of the ill-fated attack he said: "We were up against it and we went right into it. They set the corn alight and they gave us everything they'd got. They had a strong trench down one side, too, and we were trapped.

"When the captain was wounded a sergeant came with a field dressing. We used that and my own. I never saw the sergeant again, but I saw the company runner and I said to him: 'Get back to company headquarters for stretcher bearers, the captain is badly hurt.'" There was a sequel to this conversation on Rennoldson's return home to England. As he changed trains at York, he met on the platform a RAMC man, who pointed to the Green Howards' flash on Rennoldson's battledress. He said: "Heard of your lot in Sicily. I was among the stretcher bearers sent out to look for Hedley Verity and his batman." Rennoldson replied: "You've been a long time in finding me."

Continuing his version of the Sicily attack Rennoldson said: "It would be as near as I can say between half-past three and half-past four in the morning. Some of our fellows smothered the fire in the corn and there we stayed. When the captain asked for water I raised him to give him it, and each time the Germans saw the movement they let us have it. Worst of all that night was the mortar fire.

"With the morning came the Germans. They made me leave the captain and took me to their headquarters, where I asked at once: 'Does anyone speak English?' A young officer, a nice fellow, said: 'I do.' When I explained that I had been compelled to leave my captain behind on the field he said: 'I will go with you.'

"And he did, though for him there was the danger that our men might attack over the ground again. I was away from the captain for only about 10 minutes and when we got to where he was and the German officer saw him he said: 'We must find something to carry him in on.'"

From near the farmhouse they found a broken mortar carrier. They packed the carrier with sheaves of corn, put the severely wounded Verity on to it, and took him to a field hospital. Verity underwent an emergency operation in the afternoon. "I was with the captain when they attended to his wounds," Rennoldson continued, "and in that improvised dressing theatre there was a scamper when, after we had lifted him on to the table, a grenade fell out of the pocket of his bush shirt.

"A German orderly who spoke a little English ordered me to pick it up, saying 'unprime it', and there in the operating theatre, I removed the detonator and made it safe. I made some soup for the captain, getting a tin from the Germans, and he said: 'I will try to get you kept with me in hospital.'

"I stayed with him until late that afternoon and then I was ordered away with the others who were not wounded. I thought I was going out on a job of some kind and that I would be taken back to the captain; but they took me away with the others and I never saw him again."

Captain Verity was well treated by the Germans despite the intensive battles then raging and the fact that they were in a tight spot with the imminent prospect of surrender or evacuation across the Straits of Messina which they later accomplished. The dressing station where Verity received his first treatment was a bleak farm stable. The roof of the stable was shattered by shrapnel and the tiny windows were glassless and draughty. On a dirty cobbled floor a mass of old straw had been trampled to mud by the boots of the German stretcher-bearers. Over a table under the flickering lights of oil lamps, two German doctors worked ceaselessly on the wounded soldiers, German and British alike.

One of the Green Howards survivors of the battle, Corporal Harry Walker, remembered waiting for treatment, along with Captain Verity, outside the dressing station. As they waited there shells were continually falling from an artillery bombardment as the British troops resumed their offensive. One of them hit a German ambulance which exploded in front of them. Walker recalled: "I saw the captain was wounded in the chest and my stretcher was placed next to his. He became unconscious and then he came round, turned his head, and said: 'Hello, Walker, are you there?' I said: 'Yes' but neither of us was in much state to talk. Captain Verity took it very well. The attention was good, and directly the Germans knew he was an officer they placed him among the officers. I was given a cup of tea, but the captain could not take one."

Private Tom Moody, a keen Yorkshire cricket supporter, was among the contingent of British prisoners, including Verity, which was ferried in open railway trucks across the Straits of Messina to Reggio in Italy. In happier days, on a cricket journey to Australia, Verity had described in his tour diary another voyage along this stretch of water.

"It is the usual blue sky and sunshine," he wrote. "We caught a distant glimpse of Mount Etna. An old-time sailing ship making its way through the straits added to the picturesqueness of the scene, with the mountains of Italy on the left, Messina at their foot and Sicily on the right. We were close enough to make out the vines growing in the valleys and on the lower slopes."

The sunshine mocked the prisoners of war as they slept fitfully, often swooning with pain, before landing in Reggio. "We spent one night in a military hospital," said Moody, "and then with 1,500 German wounded, we were bundled into a goods train, on straw, and began our weary journey, which took nearly two days. Captain Verity became very ill. We reached Naples on July 26 and from there they took us to a German hospital. It was so full that they turned us over to the Italians at the military hospital at Caserta."

The last hours of Hedley Verity's life were recalled by another survivor, Leeds medical orderly, Corporal Henty, who met his fellow Yorkshireman when he arrived at the Caserta hospital after the long and agonising journey by sea and ambulance train. "I asked him his name as he lay on the stretcher," said Henty, "and when he gave it I remarked: 'Are you the Yorkshire cricketer?' He replied: 'Yes, that's me.'

"Immediately there was a great bond of sympathy between us because Hedley Verity was a name to conjure with, and I was anxious to see that everything was done to make him comfortable. His wounds were badly infected and he was in great pain. It was clear that he would need the greatest care and attention."

Verity was given a dressing for a shoulder wound caused by shrapnel and he sat on the bed while it was being done. Henty said he talked about his home at Rawdon and about his cricketing days and how he was looking forward to returning to his family, and to another glimpse of the Headingley cricket ground. "The captain showed me a photograph of his wife and their two boys. It was very touching and he was clearly proud of them," said Henty.

Three days after Verity's arrival at Caserta it was decided to operate to remove part of a rib pressing down on his lung. The task was undertaken by the director of the hospital, Colonel Musto, who specialised in chest operations, and it was carried out with great skill. Sergeant-Major Morrison, who was in charge of the prisoners at the hospital, said: "The surgeon did a good job. As it was a chest case, he could not use a general anaesthetic. He had to use a local, the standard local anaesthetic issued to Italian field hospitals."

Captain Verity lived only three days after the operation and died on the afternoon of July 31. He was watched night and day by an Italian Red Cross nurse and the doctor and the soldier who had been appointed his batman slept in the same room. The operation at first seemed to have been a success. The medical group orderly said Verity had weathered it well and was comfortable when he spoke to him after the operation. The first sign that his recovery was in doubt occurred when he suffered the first of three haemorrhages on the Friday night. One observer said that some of the British contingent raided the hospital food store for ice to stem the flow of blood. It was checked but the gallant soldier became weaker as each hour passed.

Throughout the tense hours Verity, suffering as he was, steadfastly looked forward to his repatriation. "We took him out on to the verandah into the warm sunshine as often as we could," said Corporal Henty. "But it was obvious that he was declining and his death shocked every Englishman at the hospital." Henty today says that the passing of a great cricketer angered the prisoners of war. It was, of course, an emotionally charged situation; but the soldiers were aghast at the poor treatment Verity had received prior to his arrival at Caserta. Drugs and pain-killers were in short supply and the post-operative care was basic in the extreme, said one observer. Sergeant-Major Morrison, however, was adamant that everything possible was done for Captain Verity. "Nobody was to blame for his death," he said.

"I suppose I heard the bad news before anyone in England," says Bill Bowes. Bowes was then in a prisoner-of-war camp at Chieti on the Adriatic coast. At the camp they welcomed two Canadian airmen who had been shot down over Naples a few days before. The Canadians had spent a couple of days in the Caserta hospital and then, after interrogation, had been sent to Chieti where, for over an hour, they were subjected to more friendly questions.

"I listened for a while until the questions were being repeated and was halted at the door by one of the Canadians," recalls Bowes. "And say," he said, "there was some cricketer guy at Caserta." The airman puzzled over the name for a moment and then went on: "Verity . . . yeah, that's right, Verity."

Bowes was instantly on the alert. "Do you mean that Hedley Verity was in hospital at Caserta?" he asked. "Yeah, that's the feller," the Canadian responded. "But he's not in hospital now. He was buried yesterday. He must have been some important guy. The Italians gave him military honours."

In his book *Express Deliveries* Bowes relates how he walked out into the deserted roadway through the camp. "The wind was cold but I did not notice it. Hedley . . . dead! It was unbelievable. For a long while I walked up and down that road, time stilled, living again the many incidents and hours we had shared together.

"I was roused from my reverie by a tug at my elbow. 'Say, feller,' came the Canadian voice again. 'I'm mighty sorry. I'd no idea that Verity was your cobber. Would you like to hear all about it?' The airman fell into step beside me and told me the story. He ended with the words: 'He seemed a great guy.'"

Bowes says he often wondered what a certain Yorkshireman thought when he heard the news of Verity's death. "Not knowing that both Hedley and I had already visited the recruiting office at the beginning of the war, the man said: 'And what about you? I reckon that anyone who
is good enough to play for England can fight for England.'" Bowes adds: "Perhaps he got his answer. Hedley was good enough to die for England."

Hedley Verity was buried with full military honours; officers at Caserta acted as bearers; and his coffin was draped with the Union Jack. He was first laid to rest in the cypress-shaded town cemetery situated above the town off a peaceful country lane. His grave at one time had a stone with a white rose. Frank Smailes, another Yorkshire cricketer, who also fought in Sicily but with a different regiment, and Phil King, a Yorkshireman who played for Worcestershire and Lancashire, later erected a simply inscribed cross as a memorial. Smailes and King met in Italy – one a captain and one a sergeant – in April, 1944, and hitch-hiked to Caserta to stand by the grave.

Another Yorkshireman, then serving with the Royal Engineers, re-members visiting the grave towards the end of the war. "There was an atmosphere of ineffable peace in what, at that time, was a period of turmoil for Italy." He had heard that Verity had been killed in action in Sicily and did not expect to see his grave at Caserta. He stepped into an adjoining meadow where wild flowers grew in profusion and then returned to place a posy beneath the cross and stood for a moment to pay his respects.

"The morning was one of brilliant sunshine and blue skies after what had been a grim winter in Italy. I am not sure mere words can convey my feelings (wartime seemed to have deepened rather than diminished one's awareness of eternity); but I am sure my little gesture was some-how accepted as a tribute to a man who, quite frankly, stood head and shoulders above some of our so-called sportsmen in the 1980s."

Caserta lies some 16 miles inland from Naples, and established a place in history in the 18th century, when the Bourbons built a royal residence there. The palace they constructed in golden coloured Bellona stone became the headquarters of Field-Marshal Alexander during the Italian campaign. It was to Caserta that the German General von Vietinghoff flew to surrender the German forces in Italy.

Hedley Verity is now buried in the immaculate military cemetery built and maintained by the Commonwealth War Graves Commission. The cemetery stands on the slopes of a hill, not far from the royal palace. It is a garden of smooth lawns, clean paths and simple gravestones ranged in a simple pattern. Mature trees now shade the boundary walks and tended flowers grace every stone, and in the background stand the watching hills. It has been a point of pilgrimage for many Yorkshire folk.

One reflective group stood there in the autumn of 1954. They were Yorkshire cricketers, including the MCC captain, Leonard Hutton, and journalists. The party left the *Orsova* when she called at Naples en route for Australia. Abe Waddington, who had bowled for Yorkshire in the decade before Verity's, joined them in the rush by car to Caserta.

John Kay was also there in his capacity as a family friend as well as a journalist. "It was one of the most touching moments of my life," he says; "Abe Waddington draped a Yorkshire tie around the gravestone and said: 'Well bowled, mi' old cobber.'"

A family mission of tribute was later made by Mary Winfield, Verity's niece. She remembers the uniformity and vastness of the Caserta cemetery and yet, despite its size, that it had the appearance of an English garden in Italy.

Miss Winfield also remembers her feelings of regret in visiting the grave of a man she had never met and yet felt as though she knew him, having grown up with pictures and talk about him. "The family picture of a kind, sincere man but suffering from basic shyness fits so well with my knowledge of the rest of the family. I could feel the closeness of us all as a result of my visit to the grave.

"I regret never having known Hedley for myself but perhaps more than that, never having lived through the war. My visit to Italy gave me an insight through personal experience of an even greater regret. My uncle was one of so many people who died, and yet my generation have not grasped how many; but I have, as a result of the fact that Hedley was sufficiently special for people so many years later still to care."

Throughout the long anxious weeks of August, 1943, Verity's family and friends fervently prayed that he had survived the action in Sicily. He was variously reported as wounded or missing. In a letter to a friend

Norman Yardley wrote: "We have great hopes that Hedley has been evacuated by the Boche. He was most certainly wounded while leading his company. A search has been made of the area and there is no trace of him – and no trace of a grave. Another thing that makes us think he was wounded is that his batman stayed with him, has never been seen since, and so he is presumed to be a prisoner. I saw Hedley about an hour before the attack and had a word with him as I went past. He was fit and in good spirits."

Colonel Arnold Shaw, the commanding officer of the 1st Battalion of the Green Howards with which Verity had served since being commissioned early in 1940, also expressed a guarded optimism. In a letter to Mrs. Verity he told of a night attack "which did not succeed owing to the enemy's strong position and heavy opposition." "Hedley," he wrote, "led his company gallantly into attack against this opposition, and was hit in the chest." Colonel Shaw added: "There is a slender ray of hope that if his wound was not fatal Hedley may be a prisoner."

During this lingering time of uncertainty there were numerous messages of sympathy, including one from Douglas Jardine. "I know something of your well-justified pride in him, and his in you," wrote Jardine. "It may be of some consolation in your anxiety to know that there are so many folk like myself the world over grieving with you and sharing your anxieties and hopes. I hope you will soon have better news of the cricketer and man I most admired."

The news, when it came on the morning of September 1, confirmed the worst fears. Communications from the War Office and the Red Cross, two days later, announced that Verity had died from his wounds in an Italian military hospital at Caserta. Grace Verity remembers: "I will never forget the sight of father's face when he received the news of the death. We had been assured that Hedley had been picked up and was a prisoner of war, and then came the letter from the Red Cross to tell us that he had died in hospital."

The first world war deprived England of her slow left-arm bowler, Colin Blythe, of Kent, who was killed in action in France at the age of 38. Verity was also aged 38 when he died in the Italian hospital. Norman Yardley recorded his tribute after the war. "England lost perhaps the greatest cricketer of the inter-war period, modest, thoughtful, greatest in a crisis, a man who never did a bad turn to anybody, and who was liked and trusted by everyone.

"Yorkshire missed him terribly after the war," said Yardley. "We missed him as a bowler, as a tutor to our younger men, but most of all – just as a friend."

"Wherever good cricket is appreciated, wherever sportsmanship is accepted as an indication of character, wherever men are honoured not because they are wealthy or gifted, but because they are in the true sense of the word men, here will the name of Hedley Verity be ever respected."

This eulogy in the *Bradford Telegraph and Argus* was one of the many expressions of homage to a treasured sportsman. Wilfred Rhodes, in voicing his sense of personal loss, told the bereaved Verity family: "I know you were proud of him. He was worth it and that makes it all the harder to bear." From another of Verity's cricket teachers, George Hirst, came the message: "Anyone who came into contact with Hedley had but one thought: he may be a good bowler but he is certainly a fine man. I am so glad that I knew him so well and will cherish his memory as long as I live."

On the fifth anniversary of the outbreak of war Rhodes and Emmott Robinson were the umpires in a memorial cricket match at Roundhay Park, Leeds. It was arranged by a prominent local charity committee which had staged so many wartime games in this magnificent arena. The practical purpose of the match was to endow a Hedley Verity bed at the Leeds General Infirmary.

Men who had played with and against Verity and men who had supported him in the field in his triumphs for Yorkshire and England travelled to Leeds to pay their tributes. Wally Hammond led one team and he had in his ranks players from Australia, New Zealand, Lancashire, Derbyshire, Middlesex, Hampshire, Notts and Leicester-shire. The other team, captained by Herbert Sutcliffe, brought together again many of Yorkshire's victorious team of the 1930s. The players wore black armbands and before the match they observed, along with the big crowd, a two-minute silence as a mark of respect to an old friend.

Two influential cricket comrades were missing from the line-up of celebrities at Roundhay Park. They were Douglas Jardine and Brian Sellers under whose leadership Verity had produced so many of his sterling performances. Jardine was to supply an intriguing postscript to the death of a great cricketer in recounting the story of his own survival in the war. He had become separated from his batman during the retreat from Boulogne in 1940. The batman got off the last destroyer to look for his officer. At last he found him and as they came aboard he said to Jardine: "We're bound to be all right now, sir; she's called after your favourite bowler." The pair sailed home safely on *H.M.S. Verity*.

15

APPRECIATION OF HIS CRAFT

"He honours the craftsmanship of the game, making it beautiful to see and stimulating to think about." – C.B. Fry.

THE boy who came under the spell of a master identified so closely with him that he became uncomfortable at his impersonation. So keenly did the young Hedley Verity try to emulate Wilfred Rhodes that spectators in local league cricket were amazed at the resemblance. "Hedley had watched Rhodes so intently," said his father, "that subconsciously he went through the same evolutions in his efforts to become a bowler. When he became aware that he was imitating he grew uneasy. Then someone suggested that he should take a longer run and he accepted the proposal with alacrity and nothing would persuade him to do any other."

There was an acknowledgement in Verity's youthful embarrassment of the futility and dangers of aping a creative genius. His task was to build his own style and profit from the accomplishments of a bowling pioneer. Verity was to prove not just a follower but the product of his own age and a deep student of the problems of his own era. It was, however, much in his favour that Rhodes liked him; the two men shared a similar temperament; and Rhodes bequeathed to his young successor many of his secrets. If ever a torch burned with a pure, gem-like flame it was the torch handed on by Rhodes to Verity, said A. A. Thomson.

Rhodes was Verity's prototype but the younger man's place in the Yorkshire spinning chain was assured by different means. Rhodes dismissed his victims before the ball pitched; his spin, as Neville Cardus said, "was an accessory after the act of flight." Verity, as a much taller man, was never, in the true sense, a flight bowler. They did, however, share, as a priceless asset, what has become known as the left-hander's master ball. This was the ball which curves wickedly through the air and pitches on the leg and middle stumps and glances almost inevitably off the batsman's outstretched bat and into the waiting hands of the expectant slip catcher. Verity learned how to bowl this ball from Rhodes and he practised it for three years before he dared to use it in a match.

Anyone who ever saw him on the field of play will retain a clear picture of Hedley Verity as a tall figure with frank, friendly eyes characterised by a shy fearlessness. He ran up to the crease lightly and decisively over seven paces, like a perfectly choreographed dancer. After each dismissal he would press his thumb into his cheek as a gesture of contemplation over his conquest. Then he would throw a catch to a nearby fieldsman with a little jink of joy. It was the nearest he got to self-congratulation.

Verity began with the advantage of height and a length of arm not common among left-arm spin bowlers. The ball, tightly gripped across the seam by three fingers, scarcely touched the palm of his hand, thus allowing free play of all the muscles. His third finger was bent almost double beneath the ball. The pressure upon it was such as to form a patch of hard skin, the impact upon which brought a special force in sending the ball down. Out on the field Verity gave the impression of being slim, but in fact he turned the scale at a considerable weight. A well-braced right knee carried his body through with splendid balance. With feet and toes, shoulder and body (joined to the height of the arm), his bowling delivery was one of beautiful concentrated action.

Verity was an imperturbable bowler. "He tackled every job studiously and quietly," says Bill Bowes. "If you saw nothing but his poker face it would be impossible to tell whether the ball had been knocked for six or had spreadeagled the stumps." Bowes says that his old bowling partner was always confident that he could bowl against anybody. Verity himself said: "By unflinching purpose and accuracy of execution a grip can be maintained on any batsman. If he does not risk anything, then deliberate attempts can be made to obtain his wicket. The bowler is then in a position to attack, to call the tune, and decide which ball the batsman shall be offered as an inducement to make a stroke." He did concede that the Australians might take a little longer to deal with but, he said, "everybody gets out sooner or later," and, with a laugh, "in any case 6.30 comes round and we all go home."

The essence of Verity's art was "a marvellous control of length" and a direction "as straight as an arrow," to quote the words of Bowes. Bob Wyatt, Verity's captain in the time-hallowed Lord's Test in 1934, says: "One of Hedley's chief assets was his ability to make the ball lift on a wet wicket and bounce on a dry one. Batsmen frequently found themselves playing the ball in the air when they thought they had got well over the top of it."

Verity's "perching ball", as one contemporary observer neatly described it, led to the downfall of many of his victims. But in a decade dominated by batsmen it was the ever-present guile and one of the most acute brains in the history of the game which accounted for his tally of 1,956 wickets, costing under 15 runs each, and including 144 for England, in less than 10 years. Few could challenge Verity's record on a bowler's wicket; but his value was highest on a batsmen's wicket where he bore the heat and burden of the day in a manner which the figures could never convey to anyone not on the field. His name as a potential menace was linked, in the opinion of many good judges, to one other only – that of Harold Larwood.

Like all bowlers of subtlety and persistence Verity did not escape the charge of monotony and lack of penetration; but he was respected by Bradman and feared by nearly all other batsmen. Verity especially relished his duels with Bradman. Sir Leonard Hutton says: "Bowling against Bradman made Hedley concentrate perhaps more than against any other batsman, with the possible exception of Wally Hammond. He enjoyed bowling against good players. He had a marvellous temperament for these contests." Charles Barnett remembers one episode of uncertainty against Hammond in Verity's early years with Yorkshire. Such was Hammond's command on this occasion that Verity wondered whether his length was at fault. "One of the older Yorkshire players told Hedley: 'Nay, lad, there's nowt wrong. You keep it there, lad. It's the batter. He's that good.'" Barnett adds: "Wally was a really great player on sticky wickets."

T. C. F. Prittie wrote of Verity: "More than other contemporary, he could meet the Australians on a common psychological plane. He was one of the few English players who continued to believe in their own self-sufficiency and the efficacy of unyielding, uncompromising hostility. Verity never flagged and his face never betrayed the slightest emotion. The figures on the scoreboard played no part in his calculations.

"His bowling has always lacked the appearance of conscious striving. No cricketer I have seen preserves so even and unbroken a tenor. Beneath an August sun his face and the great prominence of his forehead glistened with the sweat of long hours of labour. Otherwise he was exactly the same man who had bowled his first over at ten minutes past 12. His tread was the same, light and dancing, well on his toes, effortless and unbroken in its swift rhythm. His arm swung as freely as ever, came over as high as before in that smooth, well-rounded action which seemed to grow out of his run and melt back into it once more."

Sam Davis refers to Verity's photographic memory, an ability which brought commendation from many of his contemporaries and served Yorkshire and England so well. "It often happened, after the drawing of stumps, that he would take himself to a quiet corner of the hotel lounge and there visualise again the details of the long, tiring day," wrote Davis. "Sometimes, as a result of the application of his mind in this way, he could suddenly and clearly see how the employment of a certain stratagem might lead to a batsman's fall, and so upon the morrow he would emerge from the pavilion and take the field already sure of what his course of action should be."

Another aspect of Verity's bowling philosophy was shown during the bombardment by the South African, Herbie Cameron, who hit the Yorkshireman for 30 in one over at Sheffield in 1935. This was the occasion when wicket-keeper Arthur Wood banteringly told Verity: "Go on, Hedley, you've got him in two minds. He doesn't know whether to hit you for four or a six." Bill Bowes says that Wood's droll sally turned the over into a comic interlude when, in fact, Verity's response to the onslaught was anything but funny.

"Is there another bowler who, having been hit for three fours, would not have put the brake on?" asks Bowes. "It never occurred to Hedley that he was bowling badly, or using the wrong tactics. As he tossed up the rest of the over invitingly, and as six followed six, he still thought the batsman was having a bit of luck." The tactics of the 1930s allowed the hitter the opportunity to attack on good wickets. The real point of the story is that Verity did not consider the hammering by Cameron an affront to his skills. In later years he described the assault as "champion hitting." Verity had lost that particular challenge but he was still able to praise the adventure of his opponent.

Norman Yardley's most prized memory of Verity is his former colleague's action. "One of the most delightful things was just to see him run up and bowl. His action was almost perfection, the left arm clipping the left ear and really straight over the top." Yardley says: "Hedley was great on a 'sticky'. After his Australian tours, where conditions forced him to become a length-and-line bowler, he did not spin the ball a lot. But he turned it enough and his height enabled him to make the ball stay up. On a 'sticky' he did not bother much about flight. He tended to push it through on a length and let the pitch and the ball do the work. Hedley never bowled with more than two men on the onside, at midwicket and mid-on, with perhaps another fielder back straight for the hitter. He kept his line around the middle or middle and off stump." Gubby Allen also makes the point that Verity turned the ball enough because he did bowl such a good line and length. "If this is the case, you don't have to turn it quite so much." Ellis Robinson, Verity's Yorkshire spinning partner, says it was the fact that Verity did not spin the ball excessively which enabled him to find the edge of the bat.

Bill Bowes also stresses Verity's control of length as opposed to flight. "He had three paces, a slow one, a normal delivery – one which he could bowl without thinking – and a slightly faster one. He also had a very fast ball. I've seen him knock the stumps flying with this one. Hedley used this delivery about 16 times in a season and it gave him 16 wickets."

One of the most telling tributes to Verity's accuracy was paid by Stewart Dempster, a New Zealander and one of the finest batsmen to be produced by that country. In 1938, at Bradford, Yorkshire caught Leicestershire on a wet wicket. It signalled one of Verity's most commanding performances. He took seven wickets for 18 runs in 15 overs, Ellis Robinson taking five catches at first slip. Leicestershire lost their first wicket at 23, and an hour later they had collapsed to 62 all out. "Verity bowled for almost half an hour before he could persuade the ball into anything resembling unorthodox behaviour," related the *Yorkshire Post*. "Thereafter the batsmen bowed down to him in the deepest humility." Dempster was the only Leicestershire batsman ever to resist Verity. He went in first and was undefeated with 28 runs, nearly half his team's score.

Dempster was so impressed by Verity's control that he took the entire Leicestershire team out to inspect the wicket after the match. He took with him a sheet of newspaper and covered three black indentations near the off-stump where Verity had broken the wet surface during the course of the innings. The marks showed the evidence of an extraordinary piece of precise bowling. Dempster considered it the finest display of controlled bowling he had seen. The sheet of paper covered all three patches and beside them was a little space of grass which had not been touched.

Verity, in his own cricket treatise, dwelt in detail on the importance of length bowling, which he defined as "the shortest length at which a batsman should play forward." "Here you have the ABC of bowling," he said. "The breaks and swings are very important but no break, however huge, is of the slightest use unless the ball is pitched on a good length. Length is of paramount importance and the foundation of all good bowling."

Shortly after Verity's death in July, 1943, Arthur Mitchell sadly commented: "I'd made up my mind that Hedley was booked to play for Yorkshire until he was 50." Mitchell considered that Verity and Leonard Hutton would have provided the foundation on which the post-war Yorkshire team would be built. "It would have been a fair start for the side with the two of them there."

Others have judged that, if he had not been killed in the war, Verity had the tactical acumen and intelligence to become a first-class captain, if not of Yorkshire, then quite probably as England's leader. Verity was so highly regarded that his opinion was one of the first to be sought by pre-war England captains.

In his assessment of his colleague as a bowler Arthur Mitchell re-iterated the importance of Verity's height. "He didn't spin the ball a lot; but the combination of finger spin and his height made the ball get up, and there it was that the batsmen were worried. He made the ball get up so much higher than any other bowler of his type. His record shows that he didn't hit the stumps often when bowling on a sticky wicket. But, as we all know, most batsmen were helpless against him on a sticky 'un."

Mitchell remembered how Bill Bowes would banteringly suggest that opposing batsmen simply gave themelves up to Verity as soon as the ball began to turn. Bowes bragged that if he ever had the chance to bat against his colleague on a sticky wicket, he would have a go at everything because he would be certain that Verity would not hit the stumps.

"But, you know," continued Mitchell, "Bill knew better than that. He knew that if ever he faced Hedley on a sticky 'un, Hedley would soon see to it that Bill was on his way back to the pavilion. Hedley knew his men, and learned to know them quickly. He studied them, knew what they could do, what they might attempt. And he bowled to them accordingly.

"Even on a good 'un, when all he could look forward to was a long and hard day's work, he kept the batsmen at it, and I've heard them say often that, try as they could, they couldn't get after him."

Mitchell recalled Verity's 10 wickets' feats and pondered on the numerous occasions when it seemed likely that the achievement would be recorded again. "He'd take five, six, seven and eight wickets, and when it was over and someone else had nicked in to take a wicket, you'd look back and wonder why he hadn't snapped all 10 once more.

"Yet some of Hedley's best bowling was done on wickets which hadn't any encouragement for him. I remember a game in Jamaica where there was a wicket like a table top. He had five or six wickets for 40 runs when it didn't seem possible to get anybody out. He made himself into the great bowler he was. He put some time in, I know, studying the job and he put hours in – winter and summer – practising."

Mitchell's memories of a great bowler were aligned to watching Verity bowl thousands of overs and judging his skills on good wickets where batsmen had to be lured to their destruction, and of his colleague's command on a pitch where the spin was unanswerable. Then Mitchell would be up there, crouching in his own specialist short gully position, Sellers would be a silly mid-off, and between Mitchell and Wood there would be Turner and Robinson, eager and ready to pounce in the slips.

"Then", said Mitchell, "Verity would bowl straight as an arrow. He would spin the ball, and the batsmen would know just what they were up against. But Hedley was like Bill Bowes – they could bowl on owt. They came into the side almost together, and I do not suppose Yorkshire will ever find at the same time a pair to equal 'em."

Verity's own thoughts on his singular, perplexing art drew attention to the fact that to gain maximum turn the slow ball should have all the bowler's energy behind the spin. "Energy used for the development of speed in the fast bowler is converted – in this case – by grip and action into spin instead of pace.

"The arm should be as high as possible; a striving after additional height being the hallmark of the perfect action; the body on and after delivery swinging forward up, on to, and over the toes of the front foot.

"The ball should go up from the hand, travelling in a curve on to a good length. Not to do this means pitching short, or not spinning the ball properly – sometimes both." Verity recalled the expression by one old coach. "Get it up; tha's burying it again," he said.

In his description of perfection in the left-hander's action, with Rhodes as the model exponent, Verity said: "The left foot is behind the bowling crease, the right foot out on the offside. Then, just before the arm comes over to deliver the ball, the batsman should get a glimpse of the right shoulder blade of the bowler.

"The ball is spun on a line from mid-on to third man. On delivery, the wrist turns and the knuckles go up and out from the head, the ball being spun from the first finger. The momentum of the run-up, through arm, shoulder, body and turn of the wrist, should go into the action." A famous portrait of Rhodes in masterly action was etched on Verity's memory. It appeared to him to portray the ideal lines upon which to work. In such an action, he said, there was both ease and power, and the curving flight, with the ball travelling upwards from the fingers, served spin better than straight flight.

Hedley Verity, a diligent and observant cricketer, deserved to prosper as a pupil of Wilfred Rhodes. One friend said: "Just as there was something poetic about his slow bowling, so was his whole being in tune." "He had the look and carriage of a man likely to do supremely well, something that would need time and trouble," commented another writer. "His dignity was not assumed; it was the natural reflection of mind and body harmonised and controlled. He was solid, conscientious, disciplined; and something far more. In all that he did, till his most gallant end, he showed the vital fire, and warmed others in its flame."

APPENDIX 1

ASSESSMENTS OF CAPTAINS

R. E. S. WYATT – "Hedley Verity was an ideal cricketer who always played the game in the spirit in which it was originally intended it should be played. He was a keen student of theory and practice and never ceased to try, whatever the state of the game. He had a fine control of length and direction, with the ability to make the ball lift which proved to be a great asset on all wickets. Hedley was an observant cricketer. As his captain in many matches I felt it was always in my interests to have his views."

G. O. ALLEN – "Hedley was a splendid man in every way and I became very fond of him. He had a good cricket brain, not only with regard to his own bowling, but in terms of the game as a whole and I respected his judgement. He had a lovely high action. He did not spin the ball an enormous amount but he turned it enough to get wickets because of his accuracy and variation of pace. There have not been many eras in which he would not have been first choice as England's slow left-arm bowler."

D. R. JARDINE – "He has been perpetually compared with the past Yorkshire masters, Peate, Peel and Rhodes. Without being in a position to speak from personal experience of two of these three bowlers I should require a lot of convincing before awarding the palm to any of them in preference to Verity. I venture to doubt whether any other bowler of his type has proved such a master on all wickets."

SIR DONALD BRADMAN – "Undoubtedly he was one of the greatest slow left-handed spinners of all time. His record testifies to that. No Australian left-hander of that type was Verity's equal and of the Englishmen I saw, White, Rhodes and Underwood, there is no doubt that Hedley was as good or better than the others. His run to the wicket was amiable and just long enough to get him into a perfect delivery position. His control of length and flight was immaculate. He had a placid temperament and was a fine sportsman with none of the tantrums one sometimes sees from others."

BRIAN SELLERS – "His character and disposition never changed amid all his triumphs; he just remained Hedley Verity. He was an ideal fellow and a charming personality. His bowling action indicated his character: no fuss, hurry or rush. He worked hard all day with steadiness and determination."

WALTER HAMMOND – "Now hostility is not at all the same thing as say 'bodyline'. It marked Verity's bowling – he talked with his fingers – and he was a man who bowled as if in a mental abstraction, the batsman being just the obstacle. He had that quality which never lets a batsman rest, never allows him an easy stroke, pinches him for foot space, makes him uneasy to step out in case he is stumped, and haunts him with the feeling that he is going to be bowled round his legs by something he tries to ignore altogether."

TRIBUTES FROM OTHER CONTEMPORARIES

FREDDIE BROWN – "On a wet, turning wicket he was almost unplayable. He bowled from such a height and he really did push the ball along and made it bite. But one of his greatest assets was that lovely run-up – fairly long for a slow left-arm bowler. When he got to the wicket he was all in flow; his line and length was awfully good and he kept most batsmen pretty quiet."

LES AMES – "He had the most beautiful delivery. He trotted up to the wicket and over came his left arm in perfect rhythm. He never really bowled a bad ball. There were a few half-volleys but I cannot remember in any Test match seeing him bowl a long hop. All batsmen respected Hedley and feared him if the ball was going to turn. As an orthodox spinner he was in a class of his own. No other left-hander, in my time, came near him."

SIR LEONARD HUTTON – "You could run down the wicket to Rhodes and some people did. But Hedley was a quicker bowler and he was difficult to knock off his length. Patsy Hendren once told me that he found batting against Hedley harder than against Wilfred. If a fellow started hitting Hedley he wouldn't bowl short. He'd still 'give him' the ball, he would still pitch it up. Hedley did not spin the ball as much in the late 1930s as he did earlier. Mind you, he did a lot of bowling and he always retained his accuracy. You could field close to the wicket and feel safe."

SIR PELHAM WARNER – "Verity dismissed Bradman more frequently than any other English bowler. He was always planning and thinking. He used his brains as well as his fingers, and was ever ready to discuss how and why to bowl to various batsmen and the placing and necessary alterations to the field under varying conditions. As a man he was absolutely first-class, quiet and gentle, with a very nice smile. He was a rare companion on tour abroad, and always a happy influence."

HERBERT SUTCLIFFE – "He lived a grand life, always playing the game in a dignified sense. By his example, personality and demeanour, he left a deep impression on the minds of those fortunate to know him. Like many Yorkshiremen, Hedley, when once he had made up his mind to do something, would leave no stone unturned until his ambition was achieved."

. . . AND IN AUSTRALIA

BILL O'REILLY – "His strength was his mechanical accuracy and ability to bowl directly at the middle and leg stumps all day long if need be. He never thought a great deal of a bowler who sacrificed accuracy for experimental purposes. Indeed he despised him as I did too. All Australians admired Verity immensely as a fully involved opponent demanding careful attention at all times."

LEN DARLING – "Verity was one of England's really great bowlers before the second world war. I was one of his regular 'rabbits'. He took my wicket six times in the 12 knocks I had in Tests against England. I can honestly say that prior to Hedley and even after him, I had not had any great difficulty with left-arm bowlers, or with any spin bowlers. However, his accuracy, persistance and general mixture of flight, spin and guile often proved too much for my batting. I played too many strokes so often at the wrong ball."

LEO O'BRIEN – "He had a high action with skilful variations of pace and spin – never far away from a good length, with a well-disguised fast ball which he used sensibly and sparingly. He would have been an automatic selection in most, if not all, Test teams from any country since 1930."

BILL BROWN – "Where he really was supreme, in my opinion, was on a wet or wearing wicket. He usually bowled at exactly the right pace to extract the utmost from the wicket. On a wet wicket, as at Lord's in 1934, he bowled flatter and faster, not giving the batsman any time to change his shot. On a wearing wicket or where a spot appeared he would never leave the damaged bit alone, and adjusted his pace accordingly. Hedley was always a gentleman on the field, a most respected and admired opponent. He was sadly missed in post-war cricket."

APPENDIX 2

HEDLEY VERITY
in
FIRST-CLASS CRICKET
Compiled by
Roy D. Wilkinson
and L. F. Hancock

ALL FIRST-CLASS MATCHES

Season	M	I	NO	Runs	HS	Avge	Overs	Mdns	Runs	Wkts	Avge	5 in Inns	10 in M'ch	Ct
1930	12	14	3	164	32	14.90	411.1	154	795	64	12.42	6	2	5
1931	36	25	6	234	28	12.31	1137.3	359	2542	188	13.52	18	4	17
1932	35	33	7	494	46	19.00	1117.5	401	2250	162	13.88	14	5	24
1932–33 (A.)	13	17	3	300	54*	21.42	190.2+ 135 ‡	119	698	44	15.86	3	—	16
1932–33 (N.Z.)	2	1	0	0	0	0.00	36	9	111	1	111.00	—	—	—
1933	34	42	6	620	78*	17.22	1195.4	438	2553	190	13.43	18	8	27
1933–34 (I.)	13	16	4	364	91*	30.33	466.2	176	1119	72	15.54	5	2	6
1933–34 (C.)	1	2	0	20	15	10.00	21	3	61	6	10.16	—	—	2
1934	33	41	11	520	60*	17.33	1282.1	500	2645	150	17.63	8	2	25
1935	38	45	8	431	35	11.64	1279.2	457	3032	211	14.36	22	7	34
1935–36 (J.)	3	4	0	195	101	48.75	204	85	360	16	22.50	2	1	3
1936	36	41	14	855	96*	31.66	1289.4	463	2847	216	13.18	17	7	22
1936–37 (A.)	11	20	2	164	31	9.11	365.2	94	861	28	30.75	1	—	10
1936–37 (N.Z.)	2	2	0	16	10	8.00	70.1	24	182	10	18.20	1	—	—
1937	33	37	14	335	76	14.56	1386.3	487	3167	202	15.67	20	8	20
1938	31	34	11	385	45*	16.73	1191.4	425	2476	158	15.67	12	4	22
1938–39 (S.A.)	12	12	2	245	39	24.50	428 +	132	937	47	19.93	3	1	7
1939	33	30	15	263	54	17.53	936.7+	270	2509	191	13.13	14	3	28
Totals	378	416	106	5605	101	18.08	1920.3+ 11224	4596	29145	1956	14.90	164	54	268

+ 8 ball overs ‡ six ball overs in Tests

Overseas Tours
1932–33 M.C.C. to Australia and New Zealand
1933–34 M.C.C. to India and Ceylon
1935–36 Yorkshire to Jamaica
1936–37 M.C.C. to Australia and New Zealand
1938–39 M.C.C. to South Africa

ALL FIRST-CLASS MATCHES FOR YORKSHIRE

Season	M	I	NO	Runs	HS	Avge	Overs	Mdns	Runs	Wkts	Avge	5 in Inns	10 in M'ch	Ct
1930	12	14	3	164	32	14.90	411.1	154	795	64	12.42	6	2	5
1931	30	22	5	199	28	11.70	988.5	320	2149	169	12.71	17	4	14
1932	32	31	6	452	46	18.08	1046.1	377	2059	146	14.10	12	4	20
1933	29	36	3	572	78	17.33	1031.3	391	2136	168	12.71	16	7	23
1934	23	28	5	378	38	16.43	833.3	361	1577	100	15.77	5	1	17
1935	33	39	8	378	35	12.19	1097.2	377	2761	199	13.87	22	7	28
1935–36 (J.)	3	4	0	195	101	48.75	204	85	360	16	22.50	2	1	3
1936	30	34	12	716	96*	32.54	1069.3	385	2332	185	12.60	16	7	19
1937	29	30	12	300	76	16.66	1257.3	445	2777	185	15.01	19	8	16
1938	25	26	8	281	45	15.61	965	344	1952	137	14.24	12	4	18
1939	32	30	15	263	54	17.53	906.7+	263	2455	189	12.98	14	3	27
Totals	278	294	77	3898	101	17.96	906.7+ 8904.3	3502	21353	1558	13.70	141	48	190

COUNTY CHAMPIONSHIP MATCHES

Season	M	I	NO	Runs	HS	Avge	Overs	Mdns	Runs	Wkts	Avge	5 in Inns	10 in M'ch	Ct
1930	10	11	2	133	32	14.77	317.	122	595	52	11.44	5	2	5
1931	24	18	3	183	28	12.20	789.2	253	1703	138	12.34	13	3	12
1932	26	25	4	384	36*	18.28	948.1	339	1856	135	13.74	11	4	19
1933	26	31	3	528	78*	18.85	924.4	359	1826	153	11.93	14	6	19
1934	18	22	4	309	38	17.16	632	280	1210	79	15.31	5	1	14
1935	27	28	3	258	35	10.32	906.3	306	2196	161	13.63	18	5	22
1936	25	29	9	535	89	26.75	866.5	311	1942	153	12.69	13	6	16
1937	24	24	9	229	76	15.26	1078.3	395	2270	157	14.45	16	6	12
1938	20	20	5	176	41	11.73	746	260	1523	111	13.72	11	3	14
1939	28	27	13	248	54	17.71	797.6+	236	2095	165	12.69	12	2	25
Totals	228	235	55	2983	89	16.57	797.6+ 7209	2861	17216	1304	13.20	118	38	158

+8 ball overs

WICKET ANALYSIS – ALL FIRST-CLASS MATCHES

	Wickets	Percentage of total
Bowled	393	20.09
LBW	250	12.78
Stumped	148	7.57
Caught	1075	54.96
Caught & Bowled	82	4.19
Hit wicket	8	0.41
Total	1956	100.00

COLLABORATORS WITH VERITY IN ALL
FIRST-CLASS MATCHES FOR YORKSHIRE

Arthur Wood, who kept wicket for Yorkshire in 222 consecutive championship matches between 1928 and 1935, and Arthur Mitchell were Verity's key fielding accomplices. They assisted in 346 dismissals in all first-class games. The best Wood-Verity season was in 1933 when the Yorkshire wicket-keeper took 15 catches and stumped 18 opponents off Verity's bowling. Mitchell's best year was 1936 when he took 25 catches. In seven other seasons he took between 16 and 19 catches.

CATCHES

A. Mitchell 160; A. B. Sellers 100; C. Turner 72; A. Wood 67; H. Sutcliffe 64; G. G. Macaulay 50; W. Barber 48; E. P. Robinson 41; L. Hutton 38; W. E. Bowes 37; M. Leyland 35; T. F. Smailes 32; P. Holmes 21; N. W. D. Yardley 17; F. E. Greenwood 15; E. Robinson 11; A. C. Rhodes 10; Substitute 10; F. Dennis 8; H. Fisher 8; A. T. Barber 5; P. A. Gibb 5; H. Crick 3; K. R. Davidson 3; E. Oldroyd 2; C. H. Hall 1; H. Halliday 1; A. Hamer 1; H. S. Hargreaves 1; T. A. Jacques 1; W. Rhodes 1; F. Wilkinson 1.

STUMPINGS

Wood 119; K. Fiddling 2; Gibb 1.

POSITIONS IN BOWLING AVERAGES
(ALL FIRST-CLASS MATCHES) 1930–1939

Season	Position	Bowler	Overs	Runs	Wkts	Average
1930	1.	H. VERITY	411.1	795	64	12.42
1931	1.	H. Larwood (Notts)	651.3	1553	129	12.03
	2.	D. S. Hiddleston (Scotland)	62.5	200	15	13.33
	3.	H. VERITY	1137.3	2542	188	13.52
1932	1.	H. Larwood (Notts)	866.4	2084	162	12.86
	2.	H. VERITY	1117.5	2250	162	13.88
1933	1.	G. O Allen (Middx)	66.0	117	13	9.00
	2.	F. Edwards (Bucks)	36.0	110	10	11.00
	3.	A. D. Baxter (Scotland)	101.4	240	19	12.63
	4.	H. G. Owen Smith (Oxford Un)	173.3	466	35	13.31
	5.	H. VERITY	1195.4	2553	190	13.43
1934	1.	G. E. Paine (Warwicks)	1285.5	2664	156	17.07
	2.	H. Larwood (Notts)	512.2	1415	82	17.25
	3.	H. VERITY	1282.1	2645	150	17.63
1935	1.	G. O. Allen (Middx)	39.1	74	11	6.72
	2.	A. D. Baxter (Scotland)	200.0	550	42	13.09
	3.	H. VERITY	1279.2	3032	211	14.36
1936	1.	H. Larwood (Notts)	679.1	1544	119	12.97
	2.	H. VERITY	1289.3	2847	216	13.18
1937	1.	J. C. Boucher (Ireland)	75.0	155	27	5.74
	2.	A. D. Matthews (Glam)	253.3	680	47	14.46
	3.	H. VERITY	1386.3	3167	202	15.67
1938	1.	A. D. Matthews (Glam)	180.5	395	30	13.16
	2.	W. E. Bowes (Yorks)	932.3	1844	121	15.23
	3.	H. VERITY	1191.4	2476	158	15.67
1939	1.	H. VERITY	936.7	2509	191	13.13

SEVENTEEN WICKETS IN A MATCH (1)
17 for 91   Yorkshire v. Essex, at Leyton 1933

FIFTEEN WICKETS IN A MATCH (4)
15 for 104 England v. Australia, at Lord's 1934
15 for 129 Yorkshire v. Oxford University, at Oxford 1936
15 for 38   Yorkshire v. Kent, at Sheffield 1936
15 for 100 Yorkshire v. Essex, at Westcliff 1936

FOURTEEN WICKETS IN A MATCH (6)
14 for 54   Yorkshire v. Glamorgan, at Swansea 1931
14 for 83   Yorkshire v. West Indians, at Harrogate 1933
14 for 78   Yorkshire v. Hampshire, at Hull 1935
14 for 92   Yorkshire v. Warwickshire, at Leeds 1937
14 for 132 Yorkshire v. Sussex, at Eastbourne 1937
14 for 68   Yorkshire v. Glamorgan, at Bradford 1939

THIRTEEN WICKETS IN A MATCH (7)
13 for 83   Yorkshire v. Hampshire, at Bournemouth 1930
13 for 97   Yorkshire v. Warwickshire, at Leeds 1931
13 for 145 Yorkshire v. Sussex, at Hove 1931
13 for 102 Yorkshire v. Northamptonshire, at Leeds 1933
13 for 97   Yorkshire v. Leicestershire, at Leeds 1935
13 for 107 Yorkshire v. Hampshire, at Portsmouth 1935
13 for 88   Yorkshire v. Worcestershire, at Stourbridge 1936

TWELVE WICKETS IN A MATCH (7)
12 for 117 Yorkshire v. Glamorgan, at Swansea 1930
12 for 74   Yorkshire v. Nottinghamshire, at Leeds 1932
12 for 53   Yorkshire v. Derbyshire, at Hull 1933
12 for 137 Yorkshire v. Kent, at Dover 1933
12 for 96   Yorkshire v. M.C.C., at Lord's 1935
12 for 85   Yorkshire v. M.C.C., at Lord's 1939
12 for 114 Yorkshire v. Leicestershire, at Hull 1939

ELEVEN WICKETS IN A MATCH (14)
11 for 168 Yorkshire v. New Zealanders at Harrogate 1931
11 for 86   Yorkshire v. Northamptonshire at Northampton 1932
11 for 69   Yorkshire v. Derbyshire, at Leeds 1932
11 for 100 M.C.C. Australian Team v. Rest of England, Folkestone 1932
11 for 74   Yorkshire v. Essex, at Dewsbury 1933
11 for 92   Yorkshire v. Middlesex, at Lord's 1933
11 for 153 England v. India, at Madras 1933–34
11 for 73   Yorkshire v. Middlesex, at Leeds 1935

11 for 111   Yorkshire v. Glamorgan, at Swansea 1936
11 for 90   Yorkshire v. Nottinghamshire, at Bradford 1936
11 for 128   Yorkshire v. Kent at Tonbridge 1937
11 for 181   Yorkshire v. M.C.C., at Scarborough 1937
11 for 88   Yorkshire v. Cambridge University, at Cambridge 1938
11 for 66   M.C.C. v. Griqualand West, at Kimberley 1938–39

TEN WICKETS IN AN INNINGS (2)

10 for 36   Yorkshire v. Warwickshire, at Leeds 1931
10 for 10   Yorkshire v. Nottinghamshire, at Leeds 1932

NINE WICKETS IN AN INNINGS (7)

9 for 60   Yorkshire v. Glamorgan, at Swansea 1930
9 for 44   Yorkshire v. Essex, at Leyton 1933
9 for 59   Yorkshire v. Kent, at Dover 1933
9 for 12   Yorkshire v. Kent, at Sheffield 1936
9 for 48   Yorkshire v. Essex, at Westcliff-on-sea 1936
9 for 43   Yorkshire v. Warwickshire, at Leeds 1937
9 for 62   Yorkshire v. M.C.C., at Lord's 1939

EIGHT WICKETS IN AN INNINGS (13)

8 for 33   Yorkshire v. Glamorgan, at Swansea 1931
8 for 107   Yorkshire v. Lancashire at Bradford 1932
8 for 39   Yorkshire v. Northamptonshire, at Northampton 1932
8 for 60   M.C.C. Australian Team v. Rest of England, Folkestone 1932
8 for 47   Yorkshire v. Essex, at Leyton 1933
8 for 43   England v. Australia, at Lord's 1934
8 for 28   Yorkshire v. Leicestershire, at Leeds 1935
8 for 56   Yorkshire v. Oxford University, at Oxford 1936
8 for 40   Yorkshire v. Worcestershire, at Stourbridge 1936
8 for 42   Yorkshire v. Nottinghamshire, at Bradford 1936
8 for 80   Yorkshire v. Sussex, at Eastbourne 1937
8 for 43   Yorkshire v. Middlesex, at The Oval 1937
8 for 38   Yorkshire v. Leicestershire, at Hull 1939

SEVEN WICKETS IN AN INNINGS (34)

7 for 26   Yorkshire v. Hampshire, at Bournemouth 1930
7 for 77   Yorkshire v. Essex, at Leyton 1931
7 for 64   Yorkshire v. Gloucestershire, at Sheffield 1931
7 for 62   Yorkshire v. Northamptonshire, at Bradford 1931
7 for 93   Yorkshire v. Sussex, at Hove 1931
7 for 37   M.C.C. v. Combined Australian XI, at Perth 1932–33
7 for 29
7 for 54   & Yorkshire v. West Indians, at Harrogate 1933

7 for 35	Yorkshire v. Northamptonshire, at Leeds	1933
7 for 37	M.C.C. v. Viceroy's XI, at Delhi	1933–34
7 for 49	England v. India, at Madras	1933–34
7 for 61	England v. Australia, at Lord's	1934
7 for 75	Yorkshire v. Essex, at Hull	1934
7 for 39	Yorkshire v. Cambridge University, at Cambridge	1935
7 for 31 & 7 for 47	Yorkshire v. Hampshire, at Hull	1935
7 for 53	Yorkshire v. Kent, at Tonbridge	1935
7 for 55	Yorkshire v. Hampshire, at Portsmouth	1935
7 for 55	Yorkshire v. Glamorgan, at Swansea	1936
7 for 35	Yorkshire v. Glamorgan, at Hull	1936
7 for 74	Yorkshire v. Warwickshire, at Bradford	1936
7 for 73	Yorkshire v. Oxford University, at Oxford	1936
7 for 38	Yorkshire v. Worcestershire, at Bradford	1937
7 for 39	Yorkshire v. Cambridge University, at Cambridge	1938
7 for 40	Yorkshire v. Essex, at Sheffield	1938
7 for 63	Yorkshire v. Glamorgan, at Cardiff	1938
7 for 18	Yorkshire v. Leicestershire, at Bradford	1938
7 for 22	M.C.C. v. Griqualand West, at Kimberley	1938–39
7 for 75	M.C.C. v. Orange Free State, at Bloemfontein	1938–39
7 for 48 & 7 for 20	Yorkshire v. Glamorgan, at Bradford	1939
7 for 47	Yorkshire v. Gloucestershire, at Bristol	1939
7 for 35	Yorkshire v. Warwickshire, at Scarborough	1939
7 for 9	Yorkshire v. Sussex, at Hove	1939

THE VERITY/BOWES PARTNERSHIP
IN THE COUNTY CHAMPIONSHIP

Season	Wickets taken by all Yorkshire bowlers	Wickets taken by Verity/Bowes	Percentage
** 1930	373	128	34.3
1931	386	247	64.0
1932	445	295	66.3
1933	503	276	54.9
1934	439	176	40.1
1935	521	299	57.4
1936	456	262	57.5
1937	477	223	46.7
1938	488	211	43.2
1939	505	261	51.7
Summary:	4593	2378	51.8

** Of the 28 Championship matches scheduled for this season two were abandoned without a ball being bowled. Of the remaining 26, Verity bowled in only 9. Bowes, still under contract to M.C.C., bowled in 18.

BOWLING PARTNERSHIP WITH BOWES (COUNTY CHAMPIONSHIP)

		Overs	Mdns	Runs	Wkts	Average
1930	VERITY (1)	317.0	122	595	52	11.44
	BOWES (2)	625.5	169	1317	76	17.32
1931	VERITY (1)	789.2	253	1703	138	12.34
	BOWES (2)	731.3	177	1667	109	15.29
1932	VERITY (2)	948.1	339	1856	135	13.74
	BOWES (3)	992.1	218	2364	160	14.77
1933	VERITY (1)	924.4	359	1826	153	11.93
	BOWES (3)	778.0	179	2139	123	17.39
1934	VERITY (1)	632.0	280	1210	79	15.31
	BOWES (2)	677.5	189	1530	97	15.77
1935	VERITY (2)	906.3	306	2196	161	13.63
	BOWES (1)	811.0	223	1819	138	13.18
1936	VERITY (2)	866.5	311	1942	153	12.69
	BOWES (1)	720.3	227	1344	109	12.33
1937	VERITY (1)	1078.3	395	2270	157	14.45
	BOWES (2)	593.1	158	1330	66	20.15
1938	VERITY (1)	746.0	260	1523	111	13.72
	BOWES (2)	752.5	249	1424	100	14.24
1939	VERITY (1)	797.6	236	2095	165	12.70
	BOWES (2)	549.7	112	1389	96	14.46

Figure in brackets after bowler's name indicates position in 'All Yorkshire Matches' bowling averages.

Acknowledgements to Mr. E.L. Roberts and Mr. J.M. Kilburn.

BOWLING PARTNERSHIP WITH BOWES
(ALL YORKSHIRE MATCHES)

		Overs	*Mdns*	*Runs*	*Wkts*	*Average*
1930	VERITY (1)	411.1	154	795	64	12.42
	BOWES (2)	648.5	176	1380	76	18.16
1931	VERITY (1)	988.5	320	2149	169	12.71
	BOWES (2)	787.1	193	1764	117	15.08
1932	VERITY (2)	1046.1	377	2059	146	14.10
	BOWES (4)	1018.1	220	2454	168	14.60
1933	VERITY (1)	1031.3	391	2136	168	12.71
	BOWES (3)	847.0	192	2372	130	18.25
1934	VERITY (2)	833.3	361	1577	100	15.77
	BOWES (1)	761.1	219	1706	109	15.65
1935	VERITY (2)	1097.2	377	2761	199	13.87
	BOWES (1)	925.1	258	2106	154	13.67
1936	VERITY (2)	1273.3	470	2692	201	13.39
Includes three	BOWES (1)	899.3	281	1748	124	14.10
first-class						
matches versus						
Jamaica)						
1937	VERITY (1)	1257.3	445	2277	185	15.01
	BOWES (3)	688.1	188	1553	78	19.91
1938	VERITY (1)	965.0	344	1952	137	14.24
	BOWES (2)	818.5	271	1542	106	14.54
1939	VERITY (1)	906.7	263	2455	189	12.98
	BOWES (2)	617.3	132	1538	107	14.37

TEST MATCHES

Season	M	I	NO	Runs	HS	Avge	Overs	Mdns	Runs	Wkts	Avge	5 in Inns	10 in M'ch	Ct
1931 (N.Z.)	2	—					34.4	12	85	4	21.25	—	—	—
1932–33 (A.)	4	5	1	114	45	28.50	135	54	271	11	24.63	1	—	3
1932–33 (N.Z.)	1	—					26	8	64	1	64.00	—	—	—
1933 (W.I.)	2	2	1	21	21	21.00	79.1	28	153	7	21.85	—	—	3
1933–34 (I.)	3	3	1	121	55*	60.50	157.5	61	387	23	16.82	1	1	2
1934 (A.)	5	7	3	103	60*	25.75	271.2	93	576	24	24.00	2	1	5
1935 (S.A.)	4	4	0	42	17	10.50	172	78	250	12	20.83	—	—	3
1936 (I.)	3	3	2	72	66*	72.00	114.1	44	228	15	15.20	—	—	1
1936–37 (A.)	5	9	2	75	19	10.71	195.7+	57	455	10	45.50	—	—	4
1937 (N.Z.)	1	1	0	3	3	3.00	39	20	81	2	40.50	—	—	3
1938 (A.)	4	6	2	52	25*	13.00	154.1	53	354	14	25.28	—	—	2
1938–39 (S.A.)	5	4	0	66	29	16.50	283.2+	89	552	19	29.05	1	—	3
1939 (W.I.)	1	—					30 +	7	54	2	27.00	—	—	—
							509.1+							
Totals	40	44	12	669	66*	20.90	1183.2	604	3510	144	24.37	5	2	30

AUSTRALIA

Year	Test	Ground		Overs	Mdns	Runs	Wkts
1932/33	1st	Sydney	1st innings	13	4	35	0
			2nd innings	4	1	15	0
	2nd	Melbourne	DID NOT PLAY				
	3rd	Adelaide	1st innings	16	7	31	0
			2nd innings	20	12	26	1
	4th	Brisbane	1st innings	27	12	39	0
			2nd innings	19	6	30	2
	5th	Sydney	1st innings	17	3	62	3
			2nd innings	19	9	33	5
			Summary:	135	54	271	11

Series: Bowling average 24.64
Second to Larwood in averages
Runs conceded per over 2.01 (6-ball overs)

Year	Test	Ground		Overs	Mdns	Runs	Wkts
1934	1st	Nottingham	1st innings	34	9	65	1
			2nd innings	17	8	48	1
	2nd	Lord's	1st innings	36	15	61	7
			2nd innings	22.3	8	43	8
	3rd	Manchester	1st innings	53	24	78	4
			2nd innings	5	4	2	0
	4th	Leeds	1st innings	46.5	15	113	3
			2nd innings	—	—	—	—
	5th	Oval	1st innings	43	7	123	0
			2nd innings	14	3	43	0
			Summary:	271.2	93	576	24

Series: Bowling average 24.00
Second to Farnes in averages
Runs conceded per over 2.12

Year	Test	Ground		Overs	Mdns	Runs	Wkts
1936/37	1st	Brisbane	1st innings	28	11	52	1
			2nd innings	DID NOT BOWL			
	2nd	Sydney	1st innings	3	0	17	2
			2nd innings	19	7	55	1
	3rd	Melbourne	1st innings	14	4	24	2
			2nd innings	37.7	9	79	3
	4th	Adelaide	1st innings	16	4	47	0
			2nd innings	37	17	54	0
	5th	Melbourne	1st innings	41	5	127	1
			2nd innings	—	—	—	—
			Summary:	195.7	57	455	10

Series: Bowling average 45.50
Fifth to Voce/Farnes/Hammond/Allen in averages
Runs conceded per over 2.32 (8-ball overs)

Year	Test	Ground		Overs	Mdns	Runs	Wkts
1938	1st	Nottingham	1st innings	7.3	0	36	1
			2nd innings	62	27	102	3
	2nd	Lord's	1st innings	35.4	9	103	4
			2nd innings	13	5	29	2
	3rd	Manchester	MATCH ABANDONED WITHOUT A BALL BEING BOWLED				
	4th	Leeds	1st innings	19	6	30	1
			2nd innings	5	2	24	1
	5th	Oval	1st innings	5	1	15	0
			2nd innings	7	3	15	2
			Summary:	154.1	53	354	14

Series: Bowling average 25.28
Second to Bowes in averages
Runs conceded per over 2.30

ALL TEST MATCHES V. AUSTRALIA

Overs	Mdns	Runs	Wkts	Average	Runs conceded per over
756	257	1656	59	28.07	2.01**

** in arriving at this figure, the eight-ball overs bowled in Australia have been converted to six-ball equivalents.

NEW ZEALAND

Year	Test	Ground		Overs	Mdns	Runs	Wkts
1931	1st	Lord's	DID NOT PLAY				
	2nd	Oval	1st innings	22.1	8	52	2
			2nd innings	12.3	4	33	2
	3rd	Manchester	MATCH RAIN-AFFECTED ENGLAND DID NOT BOWL				
			Summary:	34.4	12	85	4

Series: Bowling average 21.25
Third to Tate/Allen in averages
Runs conceded per over 2.45

Year	Test	Ground		Overs	Mdns	Runs	Wkts
1932/33	1st	Christchurch	1st innings	23	7	58	1
			2nd innings	3	1	6	0
	2nd	Auckland	DID NOT PLAY				
			Summary:	26	8	64	1

Series: Bowling average 64.00
Seventh to Bowes/Voce/Tate/Allen/Mitchell/Brown in averages
Runs conceded per over 2.46

Year	Test	Ground		Overs	Mdns	Runs	Wkts
1937	1st	Lord's	1st innings	25	13	48	1
			2nd innings	14	7	33	1
	2nd	Manchester	DID NOT PLAY				
	3rd	Oval	DID NOT PLAY				
			Summary:	39	20	81	2

Series: "Also bowled" in averages
Runs conceded per over 2.07

ALL TEST MATCHES V. NEW ZEALAND

Overs	Mdns	Runs	Wkts	Average	Runs conceded per over
99.4	40	230	7	32.85	2.30

SOUTH AFRICA

Year	Test	Ground		Overs	Mdns	Runs	Wkts
1935	1st	Nottingham	1st innings	41	18	52	3
			2nd innings	DID NOT BOWL			
	2nd	Lord's	1st innings	28	10	61	3
			2nd innings	38	16	56	3
	3rd	Leeds	1st innings	12	9	5	2
			2nd innings	13	11	4	0
	4th	Manchester	1st innings	20	4	48	1
			2nd innings	20	10	24	0
	5th	Oval	DID NOT PLAY				
			Summary:	172	78	250	12

Series: Bowling average 20.83
First in averages
Runs conceded per over 1.45

Year	Test	Ground		Overs	Mdns	Runs	Wkts
1938/39	1st	Johannesburg	1st innings	44.1	16	61	4
			2nd innings	16	8	17	0
	2nd	Cape Town	1st innings	36.6	13	70	5
			2nd innings	10	5	13	0
	3rd	Durban	1st innings	8	4	9	0
			2nd innings	35	10	71	3
	4th	Johannesburg	1st innings	37.5	10	127	3
			2nd innings	—	—	—	—
	5th	Durban	1st innings	55.6	14	97	2
			2nd innings	40	9	87	2
			Summary:	283.2	89	552	19

Series: Bowling average 29.05
First in averages
Runs conceded per over 1.95

ALL TEST MATCHES V. SOUTH AFRICA

Overs	Mdns	Runs	Wkts	Average	Runs conceded per over
455.2	167	802	31	25.87	1.46**

** in arriving at this figure, the eight-ball overs bowled in South Africa have been converted to six-ball equivalents.

INDIA

Year	Test	Ground		Overs	Mdns	Runs	Wkts
1933/34	1st	Bombay	1st innings	27	11	44	3
			2nd innings	20	9	50	1
	2nd	Calcutta	1st innings	23.4	13	64	4
			2nd innings	31	12	76	4
	3rd	Madras	1st innings	23.5	10	49	7
			2nd innings	27.2	6	104	4
			Summary:	152.5	61	387	23

Series: Bowling average 16.82
First in averages
Runs conceded per over 2.53

Year	Test	Ground		Overs	Mdns	Runs	Wkts
1936	1st	Lord's	1st innings	18	5	42	2
			2nd innings	16	8	17	4
	2nd	Manchester	1st innings	17	5	41	4
			2nd innings	22	8	66	1
	3rd	Oval	1st innings	25	12	30	3
			2nd innings	16	6	32	1
			Summary:	114	44	228	15

Series: Bowling average 15.20
First in averages
Runs conceded per over 2.00

ALL TEST MATCHES V. INDIA

Overs	Mdns	Runs	Wkts	Average	Runs conceded per over
266.5	105	615	38	16.18	2.30

WEST INDIES

Year	Test	Ground		Overs	Mdns	Runs	Wkts
1939	1st	Lord's	1st innings	16	3	34	0
			2nd innings	14	4	20	2
	2nd	Manchester	DID NOT				
	3rd	Oval	PLAY				
			Summary:	30	7	54	2

Series: Bowling average 27.00
"Also bowled" in averages
Runs conceded per over 1.80
(These were eight-ball overs; the equivalent for six-ball overs
would be 1.35)

BY COUNTY

	Best bowling in an innings
Derbyshire	6–12, 1933, Hull
Essex	9–44, 1933, Leyton
Glamorgan	9–60, 1930, Swansea
Gloucestershire	7–47, 1939, Bristol
Hampshire	7–26, 1930, Bournemouth
Kent	9–12, 1936, Sheffield
Lancashire	8–107, 1932, Bradford
Leicestershire	8–28, 1935, Leeds
Middlesex	6–49, 1933, Lord's
Northamptonshire	8–39, 1932, Northampton
Nottinghamshire	10–10, 1932, Leeds
Somerset	6–28, 1932, Bath
Surrey	6–11, 1931, Bradford
Sussex	8–80, 1937, Eastbourne
Warwickshire	10–36, 1931, Leeds
Worcestershire	8–40, 1936, Stourbridge

INDEX

(compiled by L.F. Hancock)

Alexander, H.H., 60, 61, 65
Ali, Mushtaq, 72, 111
Ali, Nazir, S., 71
Ali, Wazir, S., 71
Allen, G.O., 42, 49, 52, 53, 55, 56, 57, 59, 61, 99, 101–104, 110, 111, 146
Amar Singh, L., 72
Amarnath, L., 73, 110
Ames, L.E.G., 40, 53–57, 75, 76, 99, 108

Bakewell, A.H., 71
Balaskas, X.C., 112
Barber, A.T., 33
Barber, W., 15, 31, 44
Barling, T.H., 88
Barnett, C.J., 6, 33, 70, 71, 78, 79, 103–106, 128, 145
Bartlett, H.T., 41, 67, 114, 119
Bates, L.A., 39
Baxter, A., 131
Beckford, D.P., 92
Bedser, A.V., 107
Blythe, C., 90, 141
Booth, A., 31, 35
Bowes, W.E., 6, 30–36, 38, 42, 43, 44, 47, 51–56, 63, 67, 68, 76, 77, 79–92, 94–97, 106–109, 112, 121, 122, 138, 139, 144, 147, 148
Bradman, Sir Donald, 45, 46, 49, 52, 55, 56, 59, 60, 67, 69, 75–78, 101, 102, 104–109, 111, 112, 145
Brockway, Cpl J., 125
Bromley, E.H., 56, 59
Brown, F.R., 51, 53
Brown, W.A., 77, 78, 105

Cameron, H.B., 41, 112, 146
Cardus, Sir Neville, 29, 37, 75, 77, 78, 93, 95, 98, 102, 105, 106, 107, 143
Carew, Dudley, 118
Carr, A.W., 44
Chapman, A.P.F., 65
Chester, Frank, 88
Chipperfield, A.G., 79
Clark, E.W., 72
Close, D.B., 5
Coen, S.K., 131
Cook, T., 30
Cox, G., 117, 118, 119
Cranfield, L., 22
Crisp, R.J., 131
Croom, A.J., 38

Darling, L.S., 56, 60
Davis, S., 71, 145, 146
Dempsey, Lt. Gen. M., 130, 133
Dempster, C.S., 147
Dipper, A.E., 32
Donaghey, H., 125
D'Oliveira, B.L., 23
Douglas, S., 31
Duckworth, G., 108
Duleepsinhji, K.S., 42
Drake, A., 37

Edrich, W.J., 113
Emmett, T., 90

Fagg, A.E., 91
Farnes, K., 78, 106
Fender, P.G.H., 29, 74, 77, 78, 80, 81
Fingleton, J.H.W., 49, 52, 66, 102, 103

Fisher, H., 31, 92, 93
Fleetwood-Smith, L.O'B., 105
Fletcher, W., 18
Fry, C.B., 66, 88

Garlick, G., 98
Geary, G., 42, 77, 78
Gibb, P.A., 92
Gimblett, H., 111
Goddard, T.W.J., 90
Greenwood, F.E., 38
Gregory, J.M., 107
Grimmett, C.V., 79, 107
Gundill, J., 128
Gunn, G.V., 44

Hammond, W.R., 42, 49, 53, 56, 61, 65,
    75, 78, 102, 105, 106, 107, 111, 113, 142,
    145
Harris, C.B., 44
Hawke, Lord, 17, 35, 83, 85, 91
Headley, G.A., 91, 92
Hendren, E.H., 37
Henty, T.H., Cpl., 137, 138
Hesmondhalgh, L., 128, 132
Hindlekar, D.D., 111
Hirst, G.H., 6, 12, 15, 18, 20, 24, 25, 28,
    29, 33, 76, 85, 92, 93, 142
Hobbs, Sir John Berry, 7, 50, 56
Hodgson, I., 29
Holmes, A.J., 41
Holmes, P., 37, 38, 44, 45, 83, 89
Hopwood, J.L., 95, 96
Hovington, G.R., 125
Hutton, Sir Leonard, 6, 82, 85, 86, 87, 93,
    98, 100, 108, 113, 114, 118, 119, 120, 121,
    123, 140, 145

Iddon, J., 95, 96
Ironmonger, H., 55, 58, 65

Jackson, A.A., 19
Jardine, D.R., 47, 51, 53, 56, 57, 60–70,
    72, 73, 74, 76, 79, 80, 141, 142
Johnson, Lt. Col., 131
Johnston, Dr. J.M., 125

Kay, E. (Sen), 16, 24, 26
Kay, E. (Jnr), 24, 27, 68
Kay, J., 22–26, 28, 31, 37, 48, 87, 140
Keeton, W.W., 43, 44
Kelly, P., 125
Kilburn, J.M., 46, 83, 91, 96, 97, 99, 107,
    117, 118, 120

Kilner, N., 38, 39
Kilner, R., 32
King, P., 139

Lancaster, T., 17, 18, 19, 21
Langridge, James, 72, 73, 110, 111, 112,
    118, 119
Larwood, H., 36, 43, 44, 47, 52–60, 64, 65,
    66, 107, 145
Lee, P.K., 61
Leyland, E., 25
Leyland, M., 31, 32, 41, 47, 54, 85, 94, 95,
    103, 123
Lilley, B., 44
Lister, W.H.L., 96
Llewellyn, C.H., 19

Macaulay, G.G., 31, 37, 38, 39, 44, 45,
    82, 88, 89, 90, 94, 112
McCabe, S.J., 49, 52, 53, 58, 59, 105
McDonald, E.A., 107
McDougall, E., 23
McFarlane, A., 125
Marriott, C.S., 112
Mead, C.P., 34
Merchant, V.M., 72, 111
Mitchell, A., 15, 30, 34, 38, 39, 40, 43, 47,
    66, 67, 77, 84, 92, 93, 95, 97, 147, 148,
    149
Mitchell, T.B., 111
Moody, Pte T., 136, 137
Morgan, H., 125
Morgan, Lt. R., 125

Nagel, L.E., 53
Naoomal, J., 72
Nash, J., 26
Nayudu, C.K., 71, 72, 73, 110, 111
Nayudu, C.S., 71
Nissar, M., 71
Nourse, A.D., 104
Nutter, A., 96

O'Brien, L.P.J., 60, 107
Oldfield, N., 97
Oldfield, W.A.S., 60, 64, 65, 79
Oldroyd, E., 40
O'Reilly, W.J., 52, 53, 55, 58, 59, 61, 79,
    106

Paine, G., 39
Palliser, J.H., 4, 5
Parker, C.W.L., 32, 36

Parkin, C.H., 94
Parks, J.H., 117, 119
Parks, H.W., 118
Parsons, Rev. J.H., 39
Patiala, Yuvraj of, 72
Paynter, E., 41, 47, 54–59, 73, 93–97, 99, 113
Pearson, F., 24
Peate, E., 29, 63
Peebles, I.A.R., 66
Peel, R., 12, 17, 29, 47, 63, 93
Phillipson, W.E., 96
Pollard, R., 96, 98
Pollock, W., 70, 103
Ponsford, W.H., 56, 59
Pope, Major (K.O.Y.L.I.), 133
Pratt, S., 87
Prittie, T.C.F., 99, 145

Ramsden, Lt. Col. B.V., 122
Ranjitsinhji, K.S., 88
Rankin, J., 125, 128
Rennoldson, Pte T., 121, 134, 135, 136
Rhodes, W., 1, 7, 12, 16, 25, 29, 30, 32, 33, 34, 35, 47, 56, 63, 77, 84, 85, 91, 93, 98, 108, 142, 143, 149
Richardson, V.Y., 49, 59, 65
Ringrose, W., 120
Robertson-Glasgow, R.C., 66, 87, 99, 100, 116
Robins, R.W.V., 108, 110, 111
Robinson, Ellis, 82, 84, 92, 96, 118, 119, 146, 147, 148
Robinson, Emmott, 32, 34, 35, 36, 94, 108, 142
Roll, H.T., 25

Santall, S., 25
Schwarz, R.O., 112
Sellers, A.B., 43, 82, 83, 84, 87, 88, 89, 94–99, 117, 119, 120, 142, 148
Shaw, Lt. Col. A. (Green Howards), 72, 121, 130, 131, 132, 141
Shipston, F.W., 43, 44
Sibbles, F.M., 94
Sievers, M.V., 102
Sims, J.M., 111
Sinfield, R.A., 32
Smailes, T.F., 82, 91, 96, 99, 139
Sparks, H., 113
Squires, H.S., 88
Staples, A., 44
Staples, S., 44

Stott, W.B., 5
Surridge, W.S., 43
Sutcliffe, H., 38, 42, 44, 45, 47, 52, 53, 66, 75, 77, 79, 83, 89, 92, 94, 97, 99, 108, 117, 123, 142
Swain, Dr., 87
Swanton, E.W., 114
Synge, Capt. W.A., 134

Tate, M.W., 30, 53, 107
Thomson, A.A., 98, 143
Townsend, L.F., 73
Trumble, H., 102
Turner, C., 15, 84, 148
Tyldesley, G.E., 95
Tyldesley, R.K., 94
Tyson, F.H., 22

Valentine, B.H., 73
Verity, Amy (granddaughter), 3
Verity, David (grandfather), 2
Verity, Douglas (son), 3, 4, 23, 123
Verity, Edith (mother), 2, 4, 8, 14
Verity, Edith (sister), 1, 5, 11, 14
Verity, Elizabeth (aunt), 3
Verity, Grace (sister), 1, 4, 5, 6, 10, 13, 15, 40, 123, 129, 130, 141
Verity, Hedley (father), 1–16, 20, 21, 40, 43, 62
Verity, Hedley (grandson), 3
Verity, Jessie (aunt), 3
Verity, Mrs. Kathleen (Mrs. Verity), 39, 128, 129
Verity, Mary (aunt), 3
Verity, Wilfred (son), 3, 123
Vizianagram, Maharajah Sir Vijaya, 110
Voce, W., 43, 44, 53, 55, 57, 59, 60, 61, 66, 67, 103, 104

Waddington, A., 12, 140
Walker, Cpl H., 136
Walker, W., 44
Wall, T.W., 59, 79
Walsh (family), 126, 127
Walters, C.F., 71, 72
Warner, Sir Pelham, 42, 64, 76, 104, 106
Washbrook, C., 98
Whitaker, F., 9
White, J.C., 48
Wilson, Mrs. E., 128, 129
Winfield, Mary (niece), 140
Wood, A., 15, 40, 44, 84, 96, 123, 146, 148

Woodfull, W.M., 52, 59, 60, 61, 64, 65, 76, 77
Woolley, F.E., 40
Worsley, Sir William, 123
Wright, D.V.P., 105, 107, 111
Wyatt, R.E.S., 38, 52, 54, 56, 57, 61, 63, 64, 65, 76, 78, 80, 81, 90, 91, 99, 103,· 104, 111, 144
Yardley, N.W.D., 83, 87, 107, 113, 116, 118, 119, 120, 125, 128, 130, 131, 132, 133, 140, 141, 146